# Acclaim for
## *Emotional Branding*

"In *Emotional Branding*, Daryl Travis has aptly demonstrated that branding is not a program or activity you can buy off the shelf, but rather the hundreds of little things an entire organization does well all the time with every important audience. It embraces the same thinking that the Postal Service used to turn its culture into one focused on exceptional customer service. The book is a must for every CEO who is frustrated about how to capture the hearts and minds of his or her customers and associates."

—MARVIN RUNYON,
former U.S. Postmaster General

"This is a 'must-read' for any executive who cares about building and leveraging their brand. The brand is not part of the business; in many ways it *is* the business. And it's just too important to be left to anyone other than the CEO. Every CEO will want to become a passionate steward of their brand after they read this book."

—MARGUERITE SALLEE,
chairman and CEO, Frontline Group

"The idea that the brand drives a company is not a new one. But the reality that the world's most powerful business tool is the least understood may come as news to many. Every CEO will be enthralled by what's really behind brand value and success. Through his thoughtful and insightful *Emotional Branding*, Daryl Travis offers dozens of practical ideas that can be used to create extraordinary results for any business."

—PETER JABLOW, former executive
vice president and chief operating
officer, National Public Radio

# EMOTIONAL BRANDING

## How Successful Brands Gain the Irrational Edge

**Daryl Travis**
(with help from Harry)

CROWN
BUSINESS
NEW YORK

Published by Crown Business, New York, New York.
Member of the Crown Publishing Group, a division of Random House, Inc.
www.randomhouse.com

CROWN BUSINESS and colophon are trademarks of Random House, Inc.

Originally published by Prima Publishing, Roseville, California, in 2000.

Printed in the United States of America

**Library of Congress Cataloging-in-Publication Data**
Travis, Daryl.
    Emotional branding : how successful brands gain the irrational edge / Daryl Travis.
        p.    cm.
    1. Business names—Psychological aspects. I. Title.
HD69.B7 T69 2000
658.8'343—dc21

                                                                    00-057436

ISBN 0-7615-2911-X

10 9 8 7 6 5
First Edition

*To Donnita, Lacey, and Mary Carolyn . . .*
*the loves of my life.*

# CONTENTS

# FOREWORD

The idea that business is strictly a numbers affair has always struck me as preposterous.

For one thing, I've never been particularly good at numbers, but I think I've done a reasonable job with feelings. And I'm convinced that it is feelings—and feelings alone—that account for the success of the Virgin brand in all its myriad forms.

It is my conviction that what we call "shareholder value" is best defined by how strongly employees and customers feel about your brand. Nothing seems more obvious to me that a product or service only becomes a brand when it is imbued with profound values that translate into fact and feeling that employees can project and customers can embrace.

By profound, I mean simple. Everybody appreciates being treated decently. Everybody admires honesty. Everybody wants excellence and value. Everybody likes to have fun and to feel part of something bigger than himself.

These values shape my rather simple view of business, but they are (or should be) universal, which is why I find it astonishing that it has taken so long to capture such a view between the covers of a business book. This one does so, and does so very well.

Richard Branson

## ACKNOWLEDGMENTS

The solitary thing about a book is the reading of it. No one writes a book by himself and I certainly didn't write this one alone.

The ideas are those of many who I can't begin to recall. They've become mine over time and with this I'm staking a formal claim to them. Most of what is explored in these pages is, however, the result of daily interactions with a few very smart and talented people. It is these collaborations that make my work and my life at work more fun than I ever believed possible. It is what makes me stay late because I want to, not because I have to.

The insights and intuitions of Doug Grant, my partner and co-founder of Brandtrust, are woven through many of the thoughts and ideas presented. His passion for our work and this work are a mirror image of my own. It is very hard to tell where my ideas start and his end or the other way around.

Many of my associates, past and present, at Arian, Lowe & Travis and Brandtrust contributed to this book in so many ways with their constant seeking of ideas in their everyday comings and goings. Their always clever and creative solutions to demanding and ever changing client scenarios are the stuff of inspiration.

John Summers, a Senior Consultant on the Brandtrust team, guided the thinking and greatly influenced the chapter on evaluating brands. John is irascible and curmudgeonly among other things and he routinely challenges me to engage my left lobe more often. John read this book before anyone and caused it to practically be rewritten. I consented to include his thinking simply to appease him and shut him up. I must admit that it is now better than it was before. John's contribution is not forgotten nor forgiven.

Without the love and support of my wife, Donnita, I would not and could not have completed this book. Her Kellogg MBA and nearly 20 years in the advertising business came in handy, as well. I'm sure she isn't fully aware of how much her insights, her feedback and her straightforward critique contributed to the final work. In the end her objective and enthusiastic endorsement of the text convinced me we had a book that was readable and worth reading.

Patti Schuldenfrei was indefatigable in helping prepare the original book proposal and get the final manuscript into a form fit for submission. Her part in this endeavor certainly wasn't glamorous but she did it like the star she is. She also deserves full credit for the subtitle "How Successful Brands Gain the Irrational Edge."

Harry's Monique tirelessly proofed and nurtured the final galleys. Her savoir-faire in these manners is matchless and I am very thankful for her finishing touches.

And then there is Harry. A lot of people think I made him up, but I always explain to them that he made himself up. Imaginary or not, one thing is sure, I can throw him an old dry bone of an idea and he'll toss me back a lamb chop with mint jelly. He's my favorite writer, raconteur, and boulevardier. Without him this book would be . . . well let's just say you would never have gotten to this part.

# INTRODUCTION:
## WHAT YOU'RE IN FOR

John Kenneth Galbraith once said that an ordinary person, wheeling a shopping cart through the aisles of a supermarket, is in touch with her deepest emotions.

Strange as it may seem, business people are just awakening to this idea—that the business of business is to be found in a very simple question about the product or service they have to offer: How does it make you feel?

The simplicity of this question frightens some business people, who think business is about numbers and transactions and the price-performance ratio. But once they get the idea that the business of business is to create lasting relationships, they find powerful new ways to prosper with the use of the "F" word—F-E-E-L-I-N-G-S.

This book is about the wisdom of brands. It's about their ability to create emotional connections with customers. It's the story of a brand's ability to build customer loyalty. It explores both brand mystique and the brand experience. It shows how brands build bigger profits. It tells by example how to be a leading brand, as well as a leader of brands. It talks about what to do and what to avoid in brand creation and brand maintenance. It gives examples of exemplary brands, both big and small, with insights on how they got to be where they are.

*Emotional Branding* isn't a textbook. It's a think book. It adheres to the belief that serious thought is best provoked and made more palatable with the use of humor. While I have strived for depth, I have also strived for what is commonly called "an easy read." As *Megatrends* author John Naisbitt once said, "In the '90s, communication and information are entertainment, and if you don't understand that, you're not going to communicate."

# FEELINGS, BRANDS . . .

# AND PROFITS

## CHAPTER 1

# Understanding Feelings in Business

It was a watershed event in my life, a defining moment in my career. A prospective client, a Harvard MBA and a very intelligent man who had built a tremendously successful company, told me something I thought I might never hear.

Admittedly, he is left-brain dominant, which means he relies on the logical, left side of his brain more than the intuitive right side. After all, his company is a leader in information technology, and it thrives in a world where it's rather foreign to consider the mumbo jumbo of advertising and marketing relevant, much less necessary. He had given thoughtful consideration to the whole concept of branding and the role of the irrational in marketing, and concluded in a strictly linear fashion that there was something to it. To my surprise, he confessed less than full comprehension of what it's all about.

Now, this is a man recognized by his peers and associates as smart, just plain smart. He's one of those guys that you can marvel at in actually seeing his brainframe processing. He knows a lot. Including what he doesn't know. So he said, "I don't get it, and that's why I need you. Explain it to me."

This is a request I love and hate. It means I get to share my passion and the wisdom of over twenty-five years at this work. But it means I'll actually have to explain something that's soft, emotion-ridden, and out of context in many business discussions. I actually have to use the word "feelings" and explain how they arise in the right brains of human beings. And I'll have to explain another, often

more compelling P-to-E ratio—the one that means not price to earnings, but promises to emotions.

## PARITY RULES AND ACCEPTABLE PERFORMANCE

I described to my client how today's marketplace is so crowded that very few people have the time or the inclination to search through claims of product superiority. By now, they've seen it all. Parity rules and acceptable performance is the price of entry. And this is increasingly true in technology markets. Buying decisions are made on promises that transcend products, and promises are rooted in human emotions. It's all about feelings, not figures, and it's all about things that happen in the right brain. It's about vision and creativity in managing the brand and in building trust by keeping your promises. It's looking outward toward your customers, not inwardly toward your engineers. It's trying to find a meaningful difference that will set your brand apart within its category. It's thinking less about what you can make in your factory and more about what your customers want. It's about the lovely fact that people—you and I—rarely behave rationally in our life's choices.

As I went on describing our process for discovering the essence of a brand, he stopped me and joked, "I'm convinced that the cells in my right brain no longer function. On that side, I'm brain-dead. I believe what you're saying, but it's so far from my reality." I quipped back, "No, you're not brain-dead; you're brand dead."

> Buying decisions are made on promises that transcend products, and promises are rooted in human emotions

I actually got it for the first time. After years of helping companies build their brands, I'm still baffled by the reason why smart business people still don't understand the concept. It's the first time I realized that the one thing that has dramatic impact on the success or failure of a company is also the least understood.

You would think the world's most powerful business tool would be on everyone's lips; that every corporate manager would know more about branding.

disciplines than any other issue. But they don't. Most simply don't understand it. Brand building isn't a skill mastered in business school; in fact, it isn't even taught in most business schools. It's not as black-and-white, empirical, or cold-blooded as most want to think about business. Sadly, for many companies, being brand dead is a natural state.

## Your Brand *Is* Your Business

A lot of CEOs think branding is hiring a company to design a logo and a set of standards for using it. It's like they're saying, "Okay, the logo looks the same at the bottom of the ad and on the side of the truck, so we've got a brand. Now we can get on with the real business of the business, which is making stuff, counting the beans, and sticking it to the competition."

Well, of course. You need a consistent use of your name and logo so that you always present the same face to the world. But a name is not a brand and neither is a logo. It's what these symbols mean and the feelings they engender that makes the value of the brand.

I also hear the argument that brands and their equity are the business of the marketing department. But as business writer Harry Beckwith says, "Marketing is not a department. Everyone in your company is responsible for marketing your company" (Beckwith, 1997). Your brand is not *part* of your business. It *is* your business. This is so important that I'll say it again. *Your brand is not part of your business. It is your business.*

Going a step further, your product isn't always your brand, but your entire company and what it stands for is. If Coca-Cola fired all its employees, sold all its real estate, fired its ad agencies, and canceled all its contracts with bottlers, it would still have the equity of the brand. Coke's fixed assets are worth something like $7 billion, but according to one consulting firm, its brand value is worth $84 billion.

How's that for an intangible!

Herbert Baum, president of Campbell's Soup, sums up intangible value when he says, "When you look at our balance sheet, you sight through the cash, accounts receivable, plants and equipment on the asset side, to our brands. Our brands are the real assets we own. Without them we have nothing" (Fombrun, 1996).

## EMOTIONAL EQUITY

Thinking about the value of a brand in terms of its emotional equity—how it makes your customers feel—requires the use of intuition, which makes some execs feel like a fearful fish out of water. It's a lot easier to deal with how many widgets you sell in Kalamazoo than how your worthy Kalamazoo customers feel about you and your widgets. From day to day, it may seem more important to solve something like a pesky production problem than to deal with issues that are, as one grizzled CEO saw it, "touchy-feely horse pies!" When you say to harried execs that, "A brand is like a bridge between you and your customers," they might look at you as though you were a sixties refugee from Haight-Ashbury, wearing a flower in your hair. It's like when George Bush talked about "the vision thing," as though having a vision for America were something sophomoric. If you're faced with persuading such a boss on the wisdom of branding, make sure he first understands that you're not talking about branching out into cow punching. Or on second thought, you can use cow punching as an analogy. Branding your animals sets them apart from all the other animals on the range. Branding your products sets them apart from all the other products in their category.

> **I**t's a lot easier to deal with how many widgets you sell in Kalamazoo than how your worthy Kalamazoo customers feel about you and your widgets.

Middle management is also leery of reinvention, re-engineering, and magic-bullet management schemes, and they might think a sudden, new interest in branding is one of them. I heard recently that *The Economist* summed up the average worker's attitude toward faddish management schemes-of-the-month with the acronym BOHICA: bend over, here it comes again. But branding isn't a scheme; it's your company's life's blood. Nurturing your brand is no more of a fad than nurturing the relationship you have with your customers. It's no more of a fad than deciding to be the best that you can be in delivering a serious promise and creating the trust that has been the foundation of all business since the flood.

Pressure on the people in the middle of the company pecking order to deliver short-term results is often a gun to the head. Wanting to look good in the eyes of the boss this quarter is a powerful stimulus, and short-term thinking is the biggest enemy of brand building. It's not that the results of brand building take a long time to show. They don't have to. But it does take a great deal of thought and work and investment in what might be unfamiliar territory to a lot of traditionally trained managers, including post graduates with prestigious Ivy League MBAs.

## UNDERSTANDING BRANDING

As I have said, brand creation is most comfortable in the largely intuitive side of business that isn't taught in business school. There is no course called Brand Building 101. Northwestern University is often named the best business school in the country. It has taught marketing for 45 years. But it initiated its first-ever brand course in 1997. Branding can't be learned like double-entry bookkeeping, and you can only copy what another company does to a certain extent. Maybe that's why many examples of successful brand building come from passionate maverick leaders, like Phil Knight of Nike, who started 30 years ago by selling waffle-soled shoes to runners out of the trunk of his car when he was still moonlighting as an accounting teacher. As a recent *New York Times Magazine* article said, "He spoke to them in a language understood only by people who could run a mile in less than five minutes. Now his company slogans are uttered by presidents and schoolchildren the world over. By Nike's own research, the swoosh brand is recognized by 90 percent of Americans, and every man, woman and child in the United States spends an average of $20 a year on the company's products." Another journalist says in the *Financial Post,* "Disturbing though it may be to contemplate, it's also a testament to the marketing savvy of Nike founder and chairman Phil Knight that a running shoe brand, through its slogans and visual imagery, has fundamentally changed the way North Americans and others around the world think about sport." Even as the company's fortunes appear to be changing, this remains a formidable accomplishment.

While there are a lot of execs who just plain don't get it, there are clearly a few who can teach us all a thing or two about branding. Some are truly inspired; for example, not too many marketing directors have the lyric ability to say things like, "A great brand is a story that's never completely told. A brand is a metaphorical story that's evolving all the time. This connects with something very deep—a fundamental human appreciation of mythology. People have always needed to make sense of things at a higher level. We all want to think that we are part of something bigger than ourselves. Companies that manifest that sensibility in their employees and consumers invoke something very powerful."

These are the words of Scott Bedbury in *Fast Company* magazine. He worked at Nike and Starbucks before becoming a consultant. He shows that a highly successful businessman involved with dynamic, growing, profitable brands can express himself—dare I say it?—with the voice of a philosopher. Business is not cut and dried to people like Scott Bedbury and Phil Knight. It isn't all logic and no emotion. They know the intangibles of a business are actually more important and more valuable than buildings and machinery. They would tell you so in no uncertain terms. And I bet if you asked them, they would say creating and nurturing a brand is as much fun as you can have in business with your clothes on.

While few CEOs are as comfortable with the irrational side of marketing as Scott Bedbury, more and more of them do see the value of building customer loyalty; in fact, a U.S. Conference Board survey of 656 international CEOs pegs "customer loyalty retention" as the issue that is second only to "downward pressure on prices" as a management concern.

Now the important idea that has to attach itself to these concerns is that the customers in whom our CEOs so fervently want to promote loyalty live more by their feelings than their reason. It's simply human, and in that respect, we're all somebody's customer.

## CHAPTER 2

# Portrait of a Brand Lover

My friend Harry is vain. When he looks in the mirror to shave every morning, he blows his reflection a kiss and says, "Thank you, God!" He put off getting reading glasses for years because he thought they would spoil his image. They signified middle age and the end of his sex appeal. But squinting began to deepen the crow's feet around his eyes. He finally consented to an exam from an eye doctor with all the enthusiasm of a visit to his proctologist.

Then a funny thing happened on the way to the optometrist's display case.

He discovered something that changed the way he felt about wearing glasses. He discovered the magic of a brand—a brand called Giorgio Armani.

When he first tried on Armani's elegant spectacle frames, he decided that, far from being a handicap, they added a certain *je ne sais quoi* to his noble profile. Wearing them was like playing dress-up with his face. He could see that in a certain light, it wasn't stretching the truth too far to say his Armani's made him look like Gregory Peck in the classic movie *To Kill A Mockingbird*.

## FEELING A BRAND

The Armani's did the opposite of making him feel like a four-eyed geek. While he decided they gave him the *look* of a Gregory Peck, they made him *feel* like the debonair Marcello Mastroiani, nonchalantly accepting a steamy encounter with the young and nubile Sophia Loren. They might be the most expensive frames in the display case, but out of the dozens of options for sale, he could see no other choice than the Giorgio Armani's. He plunked down his Amex card and ordered four pairs—one for reading at the office, one for reading at home, one for distance and watching TV, and one tinted for driving. Well over a thousand dollars later and with his Armani's carefully ensconced in their handsome brown, hard-cover cases, Harry was a happy man. The store where he bought the glasses was in a mall, but the Armani brand made him feel as though he had made his purchase at Armani's head establishment at 6 place Vendôme in the 1st arrondissement of Paris, where, with his enhanced sophistication, he could saunter across the street for a glass of something very French at the bar of the Ritz.

If you think this is an exaggeration, you don't know either Harry's imagination or the power of a brand. Harry illustrates how you can use a four-letter word that starts with F to advance your career, create bigger and better profits for your company, and be the hero that makes your business prosper.

That word is *feel,* and how your customers feel about your brand isn't a casual question. It is the crucial question. It isn't simply important to the marketing and sales department. Chief executives and their financial counterparts have a vital interest in feelings. It's everybody's job to court people like Harry with feelings that turn him into a loyal convert for your brand. That's why the most important answer you might ever seek is the answer to the question, "But how does it make you feel?"

> How your customers feel about your brand isn't a casual question. It is the crucial question.

The fact is, we develop a deeper emotional response to the brands in our lives than our rational minds can fathom.

Harry's glasses are, in fact, a few bits of ground glass and plastic, held together with small screws. They probably cost not much more to make than the cheapest glasses in the display case. They don't work any better than any others to improve Harry's vision, and he could have chosen frames that were a fourth of the cost. It's highly possible that Giorgio Armani doesn't even manufacture them. But none of that matters in the bright light of Harry's perception.

There's an ugly kind of logic that would say Harry is a sucker for going for a bunch of fashion hype. As is often the case, logic would miss the point, and we can only thank God that not everything we do is logical.

The value of the new glasses exists in Harry's head and heart. The value to Harry is in how they make him *feel*. The power of any brand is, simply, how your association with it makes you *feel*. You might say you have rational reasons for choosing one brand over another, but even these reasons translate into emotional preference. They simply help us rationalize emotional choices to others and ourselves. We often hate to admit it, but emotions rule the roost we call the mind.

## EMOTION FOR THE BRAND

If you scoff at this idea, think about the car you drive. Is it simply a means to get you from A to B? Is there no emotion in your feeling for the brand? And how would you feel switching to an inferior product? Why does the water you pay for taste better? And why on earth would we pay more for a bottle of Evian water than we pay for a bottle of beer? Tell the guy sporting a Harley-Davidson tattoo that Honda makes a more macho bike. If you know somebody who owns a Rolex, suggest that he would be just as happy with a Timex. If a banana could decide its destiny, would it rather be a plain banana or a proud Chiquita? Ask yourself why a gift that comes in a Tiffany's blue box shows such a special appreciation for the recipient. If these aren't emotional questions with emotional answers, I don't know what are.

## WHEN IS SALT NOT MORTON'S?

On a totally mundane level, ask why a huge majority of people prefers Morton Salt. Even after it's explained that salt is salt; that no difference exists between brands; that you can't make premium salt; that no matter how you slice it, one molecule of sodium combines with one molecule of chlorine to make sodium chloride. That's the whole story. Salt is pretty much the definition of a commodity. But amazingly, Morton's is overwhelmingly preferred even after it is explained that Morton produces the salt that goes into the packages of less expensive brands. The truth is that when you buy Morton's you buy a healthy pinch of trust along with your sodium chloride—

trust that the product is clean; uncontaminated; a fair measure; and is the same product your mother, aunts, and grandmothers used for generations of successful cooking. Good old Morton Salt is full of emotions you simply do not find in other salt brands. It's a wonder that any others continue to exist.

## IN YOUR HEAD AND YOUR HEART

Going back to luxury, it's plain to see that Giorgio Armani designs beautifully simple glasses, but it's Giorgio Armani's name and its link with expensive, exquisite taste that imparts the magic that nearly has Harry going around talking in a romantic Italian accent. It shows that a product is made in a factory but a brand is made in your head and heart. Products might leave your factory by the thousands a day, but brands are sold one at a time, and they are sold by F-E-E-L-I-N-G-S.

What can happen next is that Harry's enthusiasm will act as a missionary for the Armani brand. Everybody he knows is going to be treated to the sight of him in his new specs. His friends will be invited to try them on. He doesn't call them glasses. He calls them "my Armani's," and he's talking about buying a couple of Armani suits and maybe some Armani shoes and cologne to go with them. In a few years, when he needs a brand new lens prescription filled, it's likely that he will at least want to try on the newest Armani frames ahead of all the other fashion marques. The loyalty he feels now for the brand could be worth many thousands of dollars in years to come. You could say that Harry has become a walking pyramid scheme for the Armani brand. But if Armani lets Harry's fervent brand loyalty fall through the cracks through negligence or oversight (and so far, his response from the brand has been limited to this single transaction), Harry is likely to lose his passion. Along the road, he could be tempted by another brand and an opportunity to cross-sell will have been lost, perhaps forever.

> **P**roducts might leave your factory by the thousands a day, but brands are sold one at a time, and they are sold by F-E-E-L-I-N-G-S.

The potential of a powerful brand to generate sales at higher prices is awesome. It doesn't matter what product you make or service you offer. It doesn't matter if it is old or new, big or small. Your customer might be the end consumer. Maybe you sell business-to-business. You may be a hospital or a steel company, a scrap iron yard or a dairy farmer, a corner candy store or a mail order catalog, a software IPO or a package goods giant; whatever. You have every right to the security of the higher profit a brand can generate. Branding doesn't discriminate. Brands don't have any sense of the difference between consumers and business-to-business customers. A brand is an equal opportunity employer. And this book will show you how you can have a brand that stands out from the crowd with as much ability to create passion in your users as Giorgio Armani does in Harry.

That's a promise.

Incidentally, as much as I love Harry, I sometimes get a perverse pleasure in cooling his jets. When he came fishing for compliments about his new Armani's, I looked him over for a minute before I said, "Very nice, Harry. They make you look like Alan Greenspan."

# PART TWO

# WHAT BRANDS ARE AND

# WHY THEY MATTER

# 3

# What a Brand Is, Isn't, and Can Be

The other day I went to the drug store to buy some Band-Aids. You would think it would be a simple process, but as I stood before the display, I realized that Band-Aids has become a category name, like Kleenex. It struck me that I couldn't remember what band-aids were called before there was a brand called Band-Aids. I went through an internal dialogue for a minute (as I made the momentous decision about which box to take from the shelf), something like this: "Geez, I didn't know there were so many kinds of Band-Aids. And should I get cloth or plastic? I thought Elastoplast just made really big-bandage stuff, like to cover a whole knee or maybe a head or something. What kind of a brand is Option? Is it the house brand? It's probably just as good as the others, but, hey, you can't go wrong with good, old Band-Aids. 'I'm stuck on Band-Aids and Band-Aid's stuck on me.' I can hear the jingle and see the commercial. They all seem to be pretty much the same price. If I had any guts, I'd get the cute ones they make for little kids. There's nothing like a Fred Flintstone Band-Aid to make a boo-boo feel all better. Hey, get a life, Travis. Get the 50-box plastic Band-Aids and *gedoudaheah*."

This internal chatter shows the difference between brands as they exist—not in fact, but in pure perception—molded by memory, awareness, and a cowardly preference for the familiar. It also illustrates what brand-builder Scott Bedbury means when he says, "In an age of accelerating product proliferation, enormous customer choice, and growing clutter and clamor in the marketplace, a great brand is a necessity, not a luxury" (*Fast Company*, 1997).

But a brand is a slippery little devil that defies easy definition. It's almost easier to say what it isn't than what it is.

## WHAT *IS* A BRAND?

A brand is not a factory, machinery, inventory, technology, patent, founder, copyright, logo, or slogan. Not even your product is your brand (as said earlier, a product is made in a factory; a brand is made in your mind).

Your mind may see BMW as a flashy extravagance and Mercedes-Benz as a rich snob. But it might also see BMW as a thrill on wheels and Mercedes as a paragon of technology and prestige. Just as it does with people, your mind has likes and dislikes that go from weak to violent. Some are highly conscious and others linger in the background until triggered by some kind of stimulus.

A brand—at least, every brand worthy of a proper noun—has a specific identity, and identity is something for which we all strive and probably cannot live without. You garner identity in all sorts of ways—from your background, your job, your financial status, the way you look and dress, the way you speak and listen, plus other external and internal guides that help the rest of us keep score. You also get it from your choice of brands.

A brand can be like a badge that lends you a certain identity. You might say you drive a BMW because you demand high performance, even when you drive two blocks to the convenience store for a quart of milk. But it's hard to believe that getting admiring glances at the traffic light along the way doesn't play a role in your choice of fine German wheels. Your BMW says you've 'made it'; that you are a success; that you have money; that you appreciate the better things in life; that you are an automotive connoisseur and a bit of a sport.

> A brand can be like a badge that lends you a certain identity.

Most people resist admitting the need for external status symbols, but let's face it—the BMW brand creates very loyal followers.

The Beemer fanatic would probably feel psychologically uncomfortable having to switch to a Buick Regal. You can almost see him slinking down behind the wheel, white with fear that somebody might see him in it when he stops for a traffic light. The idea that we wear brands like identity badges sometimes gets a bit far-fetched, but it's hardly news that we do use external trappings to show other people a thing or two about who we are. Psychological value (how a brand makes you feel when you possess it) surely accounts for the success of every luxury brand on the planet, just as much as any rational value. We even like being associated with the prestige stores that sell the prestige goods. Walking around New York with a Bloomingdale's shopping bag carries more prestige than one from Wal-Mart. Carrying it, you become a willing accomplice in the branding process.

## BEATING FEELINGS OFF WITH A STICK

For years, General Motors seemed not to care an awful lot about the sincerity of its handshake. David A. Aaker writes, "In many situations it is difficult to get rid of a customer—to get them to move to a competitor. You literally have to work at it. For perhaps two decades, General Motors had, by many objective measures, inferior cars. Logically, its share of the U.S. market should have fallen to zero—yet it remained in the 33% range. The fact is that customers do not like to change; you almost have to beat some of them off with a baseball bat" (Aaker, 1991).

### CLEVER BRANDING

Harry sent me a newspaper clipping that claims brands serve a tribal function. It says, "Alexis de Tocqueville predicted in the 1830s that new demarcations of social identity would be required in the absence of class distinctions. Today clever branding has become nothing more than an exercise in loading a product with the social values consumers want. Brand affiliation, or rejection, tells the world who you are and who you want to be. Even what you want to believe." It goes on to illustrate the point with how brand names can be used in personal ads, as in "Land's End type looking for a Martha Stewart" (*National Post*, 2000).

## SAVING TIME

Another reason to turn to a brand is because it saves you time. You don't have to worry about whether it's legitimate. It promises a predictable experience. When you think about the shrinking of time that has befallen our lives, this can be significant. You just know Goodyear makes a tire that's unlikely to fall apart as you go whizzing down the highway. If the tire store is out of stock on the size of the Goodyears you need for your wheels, you feel fine with the substitution of Dunlop or Pirelli or some other familiar name. You haven't a clue what these people put in their tires. You simply trust them. But you might not have the same degree of confidence in Yokahama Mamas that you're hearing about for the first time in a retail ad featuring tires at half-price. You would certainly want the immediate confidence you feel for a brand if you were an aircraft manufacturer buying engines from Rolls Royce rather than Joe's Discount Jet Parts. That's why a brand is more than a symbol. A brand, hopefully your brand, behaves like a guarantee.

> A brand is more than a symbol. A brand, hopefully your brand, behaves like a guarantee.

Perception is just about everything. If you feel that a Hyundai isn't put together as well as a Toyota, it's true; whether it's factual or not. A few years ago, there was a joke going around that if you're buying a new Jaguar, you should buy two—the first one to drive and the second one as a spare while the first one is in the garage being fixed. Only recently has the Jag started to overcome the stigma of shoddy workmanship, which for a while reflected on British workmanship, in general. Was it fact or fiction? When damage is being done, it hardly matters. On the reverse side of the coin, a perception of quality is hard to overturn. You don't expect a Lexus to come off the showroom floor with any defects. If it does, you're likely to put it down to a fluke. A defect becomes just a peccadillo.

## REPUTATIONS AND PERCEPTIONS

Just like people, every brand has a certain character and reputation, whether they like it or not. You can't not have an identity. If your character and reputation are the sort that will get you into heaven, you can handily build on them. If they are of the variety that practically guarantees you a place in the hothouse down below, you have a harder row to hoe. You can change the identity of a brand more easily than the identity of a person, but it's by no means a cinch. Perceptions are stubborn. They cling like Saran Wrap over our most fervent protestations.

Just look at President William Jefferson Clinton. Consider him for a moment as a brand. Despite a very good performance record, his reputation as a "Slick Willy" appears to be written on a slate that he can never wipe clean. It started in the primaries and continued to dog him even before he came a cropper with his second-term indiscretions. Shooting yourself in the foot is usually the result of an

## WHO THE REAL MARKETING EXPERTS ARE MIGHT SURPRISE YOU

The feelings you try to "put into" a brand aren't nearly as important as the feelings your customers take out all on their own. Brand consultant Mark E. Smith will tell you that "consumers position brands, not marketers . . . When a brand is first being introduced, there is a short period of time when marketers can influence its positioning. But after that, consumers decide what it means, and once they've decided, they don't like to change it. Thus, the role of the marketer of an established brand is to be the caretaker of the brand's meaning and positioning" (*Financial Post*, 1999).

accident. In Mr. Clinton's case, it would appear that he actually took careful aim on his big toe. Mr. Clinton survives, but if you were asked to manage Mr. Clinton as a brand, I'm sorry to say you might have to request that he spend the rest of his life in a monastery. (I don't take any pleasure in Mr. Clinton's troubled presidency, but it always brings to mind the words of Stella Campbell. Mrs. Campbell was an English aristocrat of the Edwardian era and an observer of her generation's sexual scandals, of which she said in 1910, "My dear, I don't care what they do, so long as they don't do it in the street and frighten the horses.")

## PEOPLE-BRANDS

People sometimes become brands. Oprah is an admirable brand with a net worth of $675 million. She's a brand that gets $37 million a year for starring in a TV talk show alone. When she recommends a book on her show, its sales are likely to increase tenfold. She's a brand with 150 employees and her own production studio called Harpo (which is Oprah spelled backward). Martha Stewart is another person-brand, and it's not just the name. The brand Martha Stewart and the physical Martha Stewart are inseparable. She is a successful magazine that reaches 2.3 million people. She is books. She is bed and bath linens for K-Mart. She is her TV and radio shows. She is a Web site that gets millions of visitors a week. It all folds into a brand that makes $200 million a year and a person who is worth over a billion dollars after a stunning IPO in October of 1999. It would appear that America's very busy *grande dame* of good taste runs a tight little empire as flawless as her famous face. But trust Harry of the Armani's to find his idea of a fault. He asks, "How could such a smart, major babe see Bill Gates as a role model?"

A brand can also just about be destroyed when a serious flaw becomes headline news. You no doubt remember how Audi sales plunged after a CBS "Sixty Minutes" report that suggested mysterious and dangerous engine surges. It took years to overcome, even after the surges were put in serious doubt. The name Perrier used to be synonymous with bottled water until 1990, when traces of benzene were found to tarnish its fabled purity. The discovery forced a worldwide product recall that practically put the brand out of business. Its proud 50-percent share of the bottled water market has never been regained.

## MAKING MISTAKES

These examples show how a break in the trust level of a brand can work with just as much hazard as a break in the trust of a person. It can dramatically change the way you feel. But by the same token, you're often willing to forgive a brand in much the same way that you might forgive a friend. If a brand makes a boo-boo, which is inevitable, you're willing to kiss and make up because it's the human thing to do. Like people, no brand is perfect, but a strong brand can be a blunder buster. It can weather the slings and arrows of outrageous fortune. It can survive the mistakes you make with it, as well as accidents that befall it. A brand can be your rainy-day insurance, your ace in the hole that can be put on the table when badly needed. The proof is that Audi sales are bright again. Perrier still has 20 percent of the bottled-water market. And look at how, twenty years ago, the stalwart and powerful brand Tylenol survived product tampering and a self-imposed massive recall off the shelves. Few people even recall the headline scare. If you do remember it, you're also likely to recall the kudos Tylenol won for its forthright honesty and swift, no-holds-barred action to get the product out of the consumer's reach. It shows how a potential disaster can be a potential positive. The product tampering was serious, but it wasn't Tylenol's fault and was never seen as such. Promptness of action and forthright admission increased the perception of Tylenol's integrity as a brand.

> A break in the trust level of a brand can work with just as much hazard as a break in the trust of a person.

## A BRAND'S RESPONSIBILITIES

The fact is a brand carries an awesome responsibility. A brand bears both the burden and the strength of a serious promise in the mind of all its customers, a promise that is enveloped by the following definitions:

- **A brand is an unwritten contract of intrinsic value.**
- **A brand is an expectation of performance.**

- **A brand is a covenant of goodness with its users.**
- **A brand is predictable.**
- **A brand is an unwritten warrantee.**
- **A brand is a mark of integrity.**
- **A brand is a presentation of credentials.**
- **A brand is a mark of trust and reduced risk.**
- **A brand is a reputation.**
- **A brand is a collection of memories.**
- **A brand can be—*must be*—more than the sum of all these parts.**

The best news is that the sum of these definitions adds up to intrinsic worth that translates into sustainable customer loyalty at a higher price. The sum is the reason your brand can have a space in someone's life and a space in everyone's marketplace (Advertisers, 1996).

## EMOTIONAL RESPONSE, TANGIBLE BENEFIT

But, of course, a brand isn't just a vague emotion. The emotional response to a good brand is also tempered by the offer of a tangible benefit that helps us rationalize our purchases to others and ourselves. Harry sees the benefit of his Armani's as the ultimate chic (emotional benefit) in well-designed spectacles (rational benefit). Coveting a BMW, he would describe the benefit as the ultimate mobile status symbol (emotional) with meticulously fabled engineering (rational). It takes both sides of a benefit to help us separate one brand from another in our minds. The rational gives the emotional permission to believe. They work together to give a brand the ability to carve its own, singular imprint into the brain of its prospects— one that other brands have a hard time dislodging. A brand's firmly occupied territory in the mind creates a seesaw between emotion and reason as to why we choose one brand over another. It's why I say about branding that we make decisions with our heads and commitments with our hearts.

Perhaps the simplest way to think of a brand is to use the metaphor of the handshake. A brand represents the handshake that has been used by generation after generation of ordinary people as the sign of a deal well done. Your handshake is your word and your bond. It is the symbol that signifies the possibility of mutual satisfaction between you and your customer. It is the seal on your reputation. It tells us why a brand may indeed be the world's oldest business tool.

## CHAPTER 4

# A Little History, a Little Context

There's nothing terribly new about brands. They've been around since some ancient Egyptian put his name on bricks being sent to pave the floor of pyramid tombs. Logos and brand names have been important since before the industrial revolution—from old signs that showed you were a member of a guild to new fads (such as Beanie Babies) that come along to assault parents' pockets. If you stole a trademark back in the sixteenth century, you stood a good chance of being nailed by your ears to a public pillory. This may be why Shakespeare wrote, "He who filches my good name robs me of that which not enriches him, and makes me poor indeed."

Thieves still know the value of a brand when they see one. The theft of quality brand names goes on all the time with counterfeit Rolexes, phony Vuitton luggage, fake Calloway Big Berthas, and ripped-off software. This occurs more frequently since brands became international symbols of excellence and prestige. Now, in even the most remote parts of the world, everybody from nine to ninety knows about ubiquitous brands like Coca-Cola and Levi's. A genuine Bedouin would probably walk a mile for a Camel, and a Hero of Stalingrad would probably swear off Lenin for a shot of Absolut. When counterfeiting products was less widespread several years ago, Harry impressed a lot of girlfriends by giving them "Cartier" watches he bought from a street vendor in Bangkok for ten dollars each.

A few years ago, even brands went into decline. As former Starbucks Marketing Vice President Scott Bedbury said, "In the 1980s and 1990s, a lot of companies sold out their brands. They stopped building them and started harvesting them. They focused on short-term economic returns, dressed up their bottom line, and diminished their investment in longer-term, brand-building programs. As a result there were a lot of products with very little differentiation. All the consumer saw was who had the lowest price—which is not a profitable place to be" (*Fast Company*, 1997).

> Branding is becoming more and more important across all product and service categories.

About the same time, there was a lot of talk about name brands giving up their place in the shopping basket to generic and store-labeled products. But this was another trend that never happened. As Harry Beckwith (not the same as Harry of the Armani's) says in his brilliant little book, *Selling the Invisible*, " . . . store and generic brands own 7 percent of the market; name brands own the remaining 93 percent. Considering the much lower cost of generics and store brands, the heavy publicity about the high quality of many store brands, and the number of savvy consumers who realize that many store brands are simply name brands in store packaging, the fact that these store and generic brands still own only 7 percent of the market seems amazing—until you recognize the enormous power of a brand" (Beckwith, 1997).

## BRAND BUILDING

Business is coming to its senses with the recognition that brand building is business building. Branding is becoming more and more important across all product and service categories. This is helped by new knowledge of what makes a brand powerful. We've gained critical new insights that redefine the meaning of the brand. We know more about the role of the brand in creating profit and loss. We know more about how a brand can court and keep its best, most profitable customers for an immediately healthier bottom line. We know how it can reduce marketing costs and increase perceptions of quality. And we know more about creating (or reviving) positive customer response to a brand for long-term vigor.

In a white paper on branding called *Focused Branding for Specific Consumer Decisions*, Rob Docters and Sheldon Lieth provide a simple, compelling case for branding with a study of public pay phones. Brand-name pay phones in the same airport locations as independent pay phones attract over 250 percent more traffic. This whopping advantage holds true even though the brand-name pay phones were identical, or even less modern, than the independent pay phones. Docters and Lieth's thesis is that the less consumers understand about a product category, the more likely they are to make up their minds on the basis of perceived brand value (Financial Post, 1999).

Branding becomes truly important when we realize supermarkets will see the introduction of about 3,000 new products in the next year. That's right: 3,000. You (and your bank manager) will have a choice of 750 car names from which to choose. Women will be able to drive men mad with 150 brands of lipstick. Cat lovers will have 93 brands of food to feed their beloved felines. It goes on and on and on, with more and more competition for the mind of the consumer and the channels of distribution (Aaker, 1991).

And, of course, you will continue to be attacked by thousands upon thousands of advertising messages, extolling the virtues of old and new products and services—some of which you may even need. You will see them not only on your TV (to the tune of personally eyeballing over 40,000 commercials a year); you will also hear them on the radio, and they will fill your mailbox. They will invade via your telephone at dinnertime and be readily available on the worldwide Web. The ultimate purpose of the advertising barrage will be to get into your pocket. But something has to happen before your pocket becomes available: The advertising has to get into your head. If it's very good, it will also get into your heart, which gives the product or service a shot at becoming a brand, and therefore, part of your life. A brand isn't a brand *to* you until it develops an emotional connection *with* you.

## WINNERS AND LOSERS

Getting through the proliferation of new stuff and the cacophony of the marketplace to make such a connection has never been tougher. Failure isn't difficult. Even a guy with the clout and confidence of Bill Gates has been known to say that Microsoft is always two years away from failure. He knows that a kid in a dorm room can invent a technology that will make him shiver, like when Mark Andressen of the University of Illinois created the Web browser that ultimately became Netscape Communications (Petzinger, 1999).

> The overall crash rate of new products and services fills a list a mile high. *New Product News* estimates that almost 90 percent of over 15,000 products introduced this year will fail.

Adding to predicted failure in the grocery aisle, the overall crash rate of new products and services fills a list a mile high. *New Product News* estimates that almost 90 percent of over 15,000 products introduced this year will fail (*Forbes*, 1999). Many deserve to fail, but it's still scary stuff. It's a very good idea to make sure you and what you have to sell are not listed among the losers. As long as you fulfill some kind of fundamental consumer need with your product or service, you can avoid a flop—the way you avoid foot odor—if you learn how to create the magic of a brand. As this book shows, a great brand is a force that finds renewable energy in the conviction of its promise, the vision of its caretakers, and the willing power of its customer loyalty.

## CHAPTER 5

# The Beautiful Bottom Line of Brand Building

Harry and his intuitive right brain would agree with Woody Allen, who said, "The mind does all the thinking but the body has all the fun." On Wall Street, however, it's the logical left-brained mind that splits a gut laughing all the way to the bank when it comes to the subject of brands. That's because all the hue and cry about building brand equity has a central purpose: To create a stream of brand-loyal customers that turns into a never-ending torrent of higher profit. We used to think of brand equity as a strategic tool, but when you realize that the point of building brand equity is to create customer loyalty, you start a fresh page in your ledger book. You learn that creating customer loyalty is neither strategy nor tactic; rather, it is the ultimate objective and meaning of brand equity. Brand loyalty *is* brand equity. Brand loyalty is the base of your business simply because it's the most profitable way to get the most from your sales. And it introduces the idea that a high sales volume doesn't necessarily mean high profit.

Larry Light, a well-known brand thinker, crowns the process of building brand loyalty with the title Brand Loyalty Marketing. He says, "While marketers have long viewed brands as assets, the real asset is brand loyalty. A brand is not an asset. Brand loyalty is the asset" (Light, 1994).

Creating customer loyalty is neither strategy nor tactic; rather, it is the ultimate objective and meaning of brand equity.

## BRAND EQUITY

When I said earlier that the Coca-Cola brand is worth $84 billion "all by itself," I was really talking about the loyalty of the brand being worth $84 billion. Putting it another way, Light says, "Brand equity is the financial value of brand loyalty."

This is a lot more than opinion. In his work with the Coalition for Brand Equity, Light has amassed fact after fact from over 30 years of research to prove that creating, keeping, and rewarding customer loyalty is the means to true brand profitability.

He cites many studies that prove it costs four-to-six times more to convert a customer than it does to retain one; keeping a customer costs only about one-fifth as much as attracting a new one; and companies can "boost profits up to 100 percent by retaining just 5 percent more of their customers."

Light's revelation of the mind-blowing facts of customer loyalty could stir the souls of CFOs with something akin to poetry. Quoting from a book written in 1993 (and therefore quoting 1993 dollars), he says " . . . in the automobile industry a lifetime loyal customer is worth an average revenue of $140,000. In appliance manufacturing, a lifetime loyal customer is worth more than $2,800. The local supermarket gains around $4,400 each year from loyal customers." He calls Brand Loyalty Marketing a genuine revolution of how marketers manage their brands. It follows mass marketing, target marketing, and now global marketing with a new way to get and gauge profitability. He quotes researcher Joel Robinson as saying brand loyalty is "the DNA of marketing."

Light talks about the necessity of attracting not just loyal customers, but the *right* loyal customers—the loyal heavy users. He quotes part of a proprietary study done by The Campbell Soup Company, which segmented its buyers into four consumer groups: *most profitable, profitable, borderline,* and *avoid.* The *most profitable* group delivered three times the profit of the break-even *bor-*

*derline* group. All of one brand's profits came from a mere 10 percent of its customer base.

## THE 80/20 PRINCIPLE

Management is hearing more about the old 80/20 principle. It suggests that a minority of causes or inputs lead to a majority of results, as in 20 percent of your customers generate 80 percent of your profits.

A strong brand like Maytag provides a close example: Its share of the appliance market is 15 percent, but its share of the loyal high end is 30 percent (*Financial Post*, 1999).

Obviously, how a brand grows depends on how long it has been around. New, young brands have to induce trial through publicity and/or advertising aimed at new prospects. The more unique the story, the more likely you can get free publicity. But Light has turned up a huge body of research that shows enormous bias for how the advertising budget of a mature brand should be spent to promote loyalty, even at the expense of trials. Measuring the efficiency of marketing expenditure, Campbell Soup exec Kathleen MacDonnel said, "The research into one specific brand showed that during the past two years, 60 percent of our marketing dollars were wasted. So were 63 percent of trade promotion spending and 95 percent of advertising and media spending. That meant that out of a $33 million marketing budget, over $20 million would have been better off unspent."

If that isn't enough to put a frost on the bloom of conventional marketing thinking—that marketing dollars should be primarily spent to attract new customers with advertising and discount promotions—MacDonnel brightens the picture by saying, " . . . the *most profitable* group tends to pay more for your product, buys less frequently on deal, and is very favorably disposed toward your brand."

## PRICE ISN'T EVERYTHING

As is often the case, one kind of insight turns up another that in hindsight seems almost too obvious to state—that more sales don't necessarily translate into more profit. If you run a hotel and sell all your rooms at 75 percent off the regular price, you could keep a 100 percent occupancy rate and go broke. Selling on price is never as valuable as selling on the promise of quality and service that begets loyalty that begets repeat purchase that begets wonderful word of mouth, all of which begets higher profit—*much* higher profit.

Researcher Josh McQueen of the Leo Burnett Advertising Agency has done studies to show that mature brands with a market penetration higher than 30 percent should direct no more than 30 percent of all advertising to expanding market penetration. "A full 70 percent should work to move an existing buyer up the ladder of loyalty. No marketer should rest until all of its customers can be counted as *brand allies and brand advocates*." (Light and Mullen, 1996).

> **M**ore sales don't necessarily translate into more profit.

Says Light, "Knowing, serving and indulging one's best customers no longer conflicts with widening profitable growth as the goal. Frequent-flyer, frequent-visitor, frequent-buyer programs are a regular fact of BLM life. Brand Loyalty Marketers know that it is better to reward brand loyalty than to exploit brand loyalty while diverting resources in trying to attract the indifferent. Knowing, serving and indulging one's loyal customers is the best way to serve consumers and it is the best way to serve shareholders."

The message seems to be taking hold. More and more companies are shifting their focus from attracting new customers to retaining their more profitable ones. An Anderson Consulting survey of 200 senior executives in North America, Europe, and Asia shows that the number of businesses aiming for customer retention as a critically important measure in the next five years has jumped to nearly 60 percent. Nearly 50 percent say also that customer profitability will be a critical measure by 2002—up from 26 percent today (*INSIDE 1to1*, 1998). In another survey conducted by the U.S. Conference Board, 656 international CEOs peg "customer loyalty or retention" as the issue that is second only to "downward pressure on prices" as a management concern.

> **M**ore and more companies are shifting their focus from attracting new customers to retaining their more profitable ones.

If that strikes you as common sense, you wonder why vigorous programs for customer retention aren't more commonly practiced. It may be because common sense isn't at all common. As our own indomitable Harry said to me recently, "All my life I carried huge suitcases for miles around different airports. Then I got one with little wheels and a handle on it so I could drag it. I can't believe such a dumb invention took longer than the atomic bomb. Any schmuck could think of putting wheels on a suitcase. Even me."

## BEYOND LOYAL CUSTOMERS

Courting loyal customers isn't the only way to influence your stock price. There are many other groups that a brand must impress for the sake of fidelity. Look at this excerpt from *Driving Brand Value*:

"The benefits of having a multiple stakeholder focus have been proved by Kotter and Hesket. They found the companies that emphasized three groups—customers, employees, and shareholders—significantly outperformed those that only focused on one or two of these groups. Looking at an 11-year period, they found that companies that focused on all three groups had revenue increases of 682% versus 166% for groups with a more limited stakeholder focus. In addition, the multi-stakeholder-focused companies saw their stock appreciate 901 percent versus only 91 percent for the other companies. An internal analysis of the multi-focused companies found a value system that communicated the importance of all three stakeholder groups integrated into their total operations. Employees in these companies described it as corporate integrity and 'doing the right thing'" (Duncan and Moriarty, 1997).

## CEO—CUSTOMERS, EMPLOYEES, AND OWNERS

Keeping an eye on all your audiences makes more sense than concentrating solely on customers. Certainly, employees and shareholders have enormous influence on the success of your company and its brands. As business writer and pundit Peter Drucker says, "You have to triangulate among the demands of the workers, the suppliers of capital, and the customers. Customers dictate the purpose only because they have the ultimate power of veto" (*National Post*, 1999). Is it any wonder that enlightened CEOs think CEO means customers, employees, and owners as well as chief executive officer!

The final word on the importance of brands goes to Larry Light. When he was asked for his perspective on marketing three decades into the future, he said: "The marketing battle will be the battle of brands, a competition for brand dominance. Businesses and investors will recognize brands as the company's most valuable assets. This is a critical concept. It is a vision about how to develop, strengthen, defend, and manage a business. . . . It will be more important to own markets than to own factories. The only way to own markets is to own market-dominant brands" (Aaker, 1991).

# Three

# BRAND BUILDING:

# FOUNDATIONS

# Right Brain, Left Brain, and No Brain at All

Brands work with a combination of emotional and rational appeal to eventually create emotional links with customers. To understand how this behavior works, we have to take a look inside the brain.

Dr. Charles Kenny of Kenny & Associates (also known as *The Right Brain People*), says that behavior takes its cue from information that comes from both sides of the brain. The left side provides logic, language, intelligence, and reasoning. The right side is where you find intuition, feelings, emotion, humor, creativity, and motivation for decision making. The left brain acts as a balance to control and explain actions that begin in the right brain. Understanding the differences between the two hemispheres helps us more clearly understand the question, "But how does it make you feel?"

## RIGHT OR LEFT?

The playful part of you in the right side might decide to roller-blade to work. The left side will make sure you get there safely and by a good route. The right side is where you find such things as music, art, poetry, and magic. It's where an actor might find the motivation for a certain reading of his lines, but the left is where he finds the means to memorize them.

## A LITTLE BIT OF BOTH

Nobody is right-brained or left-brained. Everybody is a bit of each. But one side is likely to dominate to one degree or another. If you majored in English and write country songs for a hobby, you're probably more right-brained than somebody who studies economics and loves statistical analysis, but has never had a guitar in his hands. If you pride yourself on being a logical person with a lot of practical common sense, you lean left. If you live more by the way you feel, you lean right. A left-leaning mind buying a stereo will do extensive research before making a purchase decision. A right-leaning mind will go to the store and rely on how the system sounds on the spot. The manager in you takes inspiration from the left, the leader in you from the right. One isn't better than the other, and you can't get along with just one or the other. We're simply all a product of both. Because a brand is in large part a product of intuition and feelings, the right side is terribly important, but a brand also needs the guiding hand of the left to keep it on course. For example, a brand taps the deep well of emotion and long-term memory that resides in the right, but the cool hand of reason makes sure that the emotions are preserved with consistency.

## LATERAL THOUGHT

The right is also the source of leaps in lateral thinking. Edward de Bono wrote several books on how to integrate lateral thinking into education. As a right-brain activity, he says lateral thinking involves humor, insight, and creativity. Left-brained, vertical thinking involves reason and logic. He says, "Vertical thinking moves forward by sequential steps, each of which has to be justified . . . In lateral thinking one may have to be wrong at some stage in order to achieve a right solution; in vertical thinking (logic or math, for example) this would be impossible."

We've all heard the story of a truck getting stuck as it tries to pass under a bridge. A large group of motorists stands around with everybody scratching their heads, trying to figure out how to get the truck out of its predicament. One person surveying the scene goes to each wheel

> A left-leaning mind buying a stereo will do extensive research before making a purchase decision. A right-leaning mind will go to the store and rely on how the system sounds on the spot.

and simply lowers the height of the truck by letting half the air out of the tires. That's lateral thinking.

De Bono says lateral thinking is the provocation of new thought patterns, looking in a different way at things that have always been looked at in the same way. When Harry was assigned the job of writing a TV commercial for a waterproof boot, he first thought the ordinary—of showing somebody walking in deep puddles to suggest that water can't get in. But that was standard thinking. Instead, he showed water being poured into the boot to show that it can't get out. The latter is infinitely more engaging. It needs no words. It involves the viewer visually. And it surprises us by looking at a common situation with new eyes. You might say that the right brain is like a big inner eye because it relies so much on visual thinking.

## VISUAL THOUGHT

People with dyslexia are highly right brained. While they visually flip letters of the alphabet (they mix up *d*s and *b*s and *p*s, for example), they're often very good chess players because they can flip the board around in their imagination, which allows them to see the game from the opponent's point of view. This ability to flip images is also important for activities like sculpture, warfare, building, and games like LEGO. There is evidence that visual thought is 400 times as fast as verbal thought because so much can be packed into a picture (*National Post*, 1999).

Here are two of my favorite examples of what de Bono would call "provocation of new thought patterns" that are also highly visual:

A client calls a meeting with its ad agency to discuss how usage of Drano can be expanded. There's talk of current research to discover bigger and better motivation of the consumer. Also raised is the expansion of the sales force, an increase in distribution channels, increased spending for media advertising, and a price promotion— all of which requires a ton of work and a huge jump in the marketing budget. Somewhere in the middle of what could have been a long meeting, the copywriter, who is doodling on a pad and saying nothing, suddenly mumbles, "Why don't you just make the holes in the can bigger?"

You've probably had the experience of a small pickle falling out of a sandwich into your lap. It's maybe why only 3 percent of the 35 billion sandwiches made in American homes every year contain sliced pickles. Researchers at Vlasic came up with a fabulously simple solution—the kind that makes you want to commit suicide because you never thought of it before. They came up with the idea of slicing the pickles lengthwise rather than crosswise. That way you can put the slice in a sandwich and it won't fall out. This brilliant "duh" idea (called Sandwich Stackers) was a hit. Sales reached $60 million the first year. Same pickle, different slice. One great idea begets another as Vlasic went on to develop a strain of giant cucumbers that can be sliced crosswise. They cover an entire burger. They don't end up in your lap, either, the way little pickles do.

## IDEA OR PRODUCT?

One of our past projects was to brand an idea rather than a product or service, which proves you can brand just about anything. The problem was secondhand tobacco smoke, and if you've wondered how it became such an issue in America, blame our proprietary process and ourselves. As it happened, 98 percent of adults understand the dangers of secondhand smoke but fewer than 4 percent were willing to take any action against it. When the CDC asked us to work with them to turn the situation around, our investigative process and collaborative analysis showed the way. Conventional wisdom might have been to attack smokers, to portray them as monsters who harm nonsmokers. But the lateral thinking of our process showed this up as a red-flag direction. Instead, we turned the nation's nonsmokers into a huge lobby group motivated to attack the smoking environment rather than the smoker. Most of America's public places are smoke-free today, thanks to the integrated marketing campaign, which inspired both the government and nonsmokers to take action.

## NO BRAIN AT ALL

An experience I had shows how *not* to think laterally (or any other way for that matter). As a young account executive working on the American Standard account, I attended a meeting to discuss a critical problem facing the brand. It had been discovered that awareness for the brand was much higher among men than women. It was also discovered that the discrepancy could be attributed to the different use of the toilet between the sexes. Men go with the seat and lid up, thereby exposing the brand name. Women go with the seat down, thereby obscuring it. What to do was a major problem, and I was puzzled because nobody seemed to leap to the obvious solution of simply moving the brand name to where it would be seen by either boys or girls when nature calls. The group met several times over the next few months and even commissioned expensive research to prove their intuition about the upness or downness of the seat's effect on brand recognition. The problem was never solved while I worked on the account. For all I know, the gents who run American Standard are still meeting to discuss it.

> There's always conflict between the two sides of human nature. The need to reason and measure is a fight with the need to be free for useless flights of fancy you can never tabulate.

### HARRY'S THEORY

Harry sees the right/left-brain dichotomy a little differently from the established facts, but that just means he loves being contrary. He thinks that the left and the right brains simply allow us to have many propensities and talents, including orientations toward either moralism or libertarianism. He says, "Left-brain people prefer rules, including the one that intelligence rules *über alles*. Right brainers like a little chaos, including the messy business of being a card-carrying member of a fallible human race that can never remember where it left its keys." He believes the difference might have a cultural bias, as in the Swiss like to make watches and the Italians like to make love. He says, "There's always conflict between the two sides of human nature. The need to reason and measure is a fight with the need to be free for useless flights of fancy you can never tabulate. My doctor, for example, is appalled that I can easily tuck away a right-brained bottle of wine a day. He says from his left brain, 'Harry, why don't you drink half a bottle and save some for the rest of us?'"

*Praise be* that I don't always have to agree with Harry and his original but off-kilter views. I think his left brain fled in horror at his birth.

## CHAPTER 7

# "But How Does It Make You Feel?"

Scotland's favorite poet Robert Burns wrote, "I wish to God the gift he'd gi'e us, to see ourselves as others see us."

This could be the patron prayer of brand building because how your customers see you and feel about you doesn't always jibe with how you see and feel about yourself. It's easy to fool yourself otherwise, which is why you must build a dialogue with your customers to set and keep the record straight. How you see your brand doesn't matter. How your prospective and current customers see it is the real rub. They may even know your brand better than you do. And if this is true, all you've got to do is listen.

Look at the gaffe Coca-Cola made in the mid-1980s when it tried to go with a new, sweeter taste. Consumers hated it. They wanted nothing to do with it. They reminded Coke in no uncertain terms that Coke represents heritage. You might wonder how such a successful company that lives or dies on the feelings people have for the brand could make such a mistake, but it's scary how even the most popular brands can have a very weak grasp of what their brands mean to consumers. Coke heard what it wanted to hear rather than what was said. It made the mistake of thinking people drink the brand for the taste. Coke had to rediscover that the strongest reason to drink the brand is because it feels familiar and comfortable and—perhaps most important—authentic.

The fact is that all successful brands have their own singular, little sweet spot in the brain of their prospects and, hopefully, a warm

> Coke had to rediscover that the strongest reason to drink the brand is because it feels familiar and comfortable and—perhaps most important—authentic.

spot in their hearts. This sweet spot holds both the facts and feelings of what makes you different from your competitors. If your brand doesn't start out with a big difference, perhaps your customers can help you find it. As Yogi Berra said, "You can observe a lot just by watching." I add that you can hear a lot just by listening.

## CONNECTING TO THE CUSTOMER

Dialogue with your customers is as integral to brand building as whales to water. You never stop trying to find out where your brand resides in the mind of the customer and how its perception can be improved. Every infantry regiment has an Intelligence and Reconnaissance squad in its headquarters company. These I&R guys probe the terrain to scout opportunities. In the battle for hearts and minds that we call marketing, it makes plain sense to do the same. Just make sure you don't end up as Theodore Roszak noted, "Data, data everywhere and not a thought to think."

## YOUR CUSTOMER'S NEEDS

Scott Bedbury, of Nike and Starbucks fame, will tell you that to determine the emotional or experiential connection of a brand with consumers, marketers need to reshape their thinking about the processes they utilize to learn about the consumer's needs (*Delaney Report*, 1999). Bedbury says, "Every product category at some point has the opportunity to define a higher emotional ground. To resonate with the consumer on a deeper level. But that doesn't mean you go out and do a lot of quantitative or qualitative research. You have to become sensitive to the consumer in different ways. You need to spend 'real time' with consumers. See the world through their eyes. Get to know what they care deeply about . . . But you have to show genuine sympathy. You have to be careful not to pander to them or in any way demonstrate that you are in it just for the buck. You have to remember who you are with and respect them."

## LISTEN, LISTEN, LISTEN

One of my favorite examples of brand research by "spending time with customers" comes from business guru Peter Drucker (*Harvard Business Review*, 1989). He tells the story of Willowcreek Community Church in South Barrington, Illinois. He says it "has become the nation's largest church—some 13,000 parishioners. Yet it is barely 15 years old. Bill Hybels, in his early twenties when he founded the church, chose the community because it had few churchgoers, though the population was growing fast and churches were plentiful. He went from door to door, asking, 'Why don't you go to church?' Then, he designed a church to answer the potential customers' needs; for instance, it offers full services on Wednesday evenings because many working parents need Sunday to spend with their children. Moreover, Hybels continues to listen and react. The pastor's sermon is taped while it is being delivered and instantly reproduced so that parishioners can pick up a tape when they leave the building because he was told again and again, 'I need to listen when I drive home so that I can build the message into my life.' But he was also told: 'The sermon always tells me to change my life but never how to do it.' So now, every one of Hybel's sermons ends with specific action recommendations."

> Being a great listener who can hear between the lines is the secret to finding the great little sweet spots in customer wants and needs.

## THE TRUE ART OF LISTENING

This lovely example proves my point that research is nothing more than the art of listening. But it is a skill that isn't easy to acquire. Whenever a client concedes that we need to talk to some customers, I urge them to consider that we really need to listen, and not to talk to them at all. Being a great listener who can hear between the lines is the secret to finding the great little sweet spots in customer wants and needs.

Fortunately, I had this imprinted on me early. I managed one of the agency teams that helped FedEx launch their Overnight Box and Tube. It's an experience that has shaped my entire career, and I urge you to remind yourself of this story every time you have the privilege to meet with your customers.

Focus groups conducted all over the country taught us some valuable things. We knew which graphic scheme for the boxes was preferred, and even how the boxes should be constructed for ease of use and storage. We knew that FedEx customers thought the Box and Tube were good ideas and that they were likely to use them. If you were in the workplace in those seemingly distant times, you'll recall the scramble that invariably took place when it came time to ship something late in the day. There never seemed to be a box to put things in so that they could be shipped. You had to find wrapping paper, tape, twine, the scissors that always managed to hide themselves, anything you could use to get your package out the door.

We weren't surprised at the need for shipping material since we had all watched every imaginable package configuration move through the FedEx hub in Memphis. We once saw parts of a mannequin wrapped round in paper tapes, eerily looking like dismembered mummies. Our pleasant surprise was the universally positive consumer response to the idea that packaging materials would now be readily available.

### SOMETIMES, THE BEST-LAID PLANS . . .

Our team and the talented marketing folks had determined all the conventional marketing stuff and confirmed things we had mostly anticipated. But the thing that really made the difference was that the customers expected the boxes to be free. You can imagine the cost and the risks involved, not to mention the waste. FedEx people cringe every time they see one of their precious purple-and-orange packages delivered by a UPS courier. The idea that the boxes would be free was difficult to digest. We seriously considered charging for them. But the FedEx promise is "Absolutely, positively overnight." Could you expect anything else from a company that conveys and believes this brand promise?

The decision was made to give the boxes away. As I recall, it was such a big issue that it ultimately required board approval. The rest of the story is history. The products were a huge, immediate success, and the airfreight industry was forever changed—nearly overnight—and these products have been a major contributor to Federal's revenue stream ever since. It's all because FedEx made it part of their brand DNA to listen to and respond to their customers. It's a lesson I never forgot.

## ETHNOGRAPHY

Maytag takes listening to customers to new extremes (*Financial Post*, 1999). President Bill Beer describes how Maytag researchers go into the homes of real people to "sit in the corner like a little mouse." It's part of a developing science called "ethnography." Maytag researchers observe people using appliances in real time and look for an "unarticulated" need. "What we're trying to do is find the need that hasn't yet been expressed, and meet that need so that when people see our product, they go: 'Why hasn't anybody ever thought of that before?'" A new product of this intense listening is a kitchen stove called the Gemini. It gets rid of the drawer you find at the bottom of a conventional stove and offers two ovens instead. It answers the discovery that different foods need different cooking temperatures and times. If this seems like an obvious innovation, ask yourself why you didn't think of it the last time you wanted to cook a roast beef and an apple pie at the same time.

## BRAND PERSONALITIES

Other kinds of out-of-the-box research can help a brand figure out and refine the specific identity every brand has. It's a little like each brand has a psyche. They project a personality that emanates from an intrinsic character. Even a new brand has one, possibly as a reflection of its category. You want to explore what characterizes your brand in relation to its competition. Is it David Bowie or Pavarotti? Is it Meryl Streep or Madonna? Is it Tom Hanks or Hulk Hogan? Is it a lion or a pussycat? A duck or an eagle? A paper cup or a crystal goblet? Warm as mom and apple pie, or as technical as a stainless steel refrigerator?

## BACK TO THE FIELD

Scott Bedbury (*Fast Company*, 1997) says, "Anyone who wants to build a great brand first has to understand who they are. You don't do this by getting a bunch of executive schmucks in a room, so they can reach some consensus on what they think the brand means. Because whatever they come up with is probably going to be inconsistent with the way most consumers perceive the brand. The real starting point is to go out to consumers and find out what they like or dislike about the brand and what they associate as the very core of the brand concept."

He adds that you have to avoid the risk of this fairly conventional formula leading you to a too-narrowly focused brand. "To keep a brand alive over the long haul, to keep it vital, you've got to do something new, something unexpected. It has to be related to the brand's core position. But every once in a while you have to strike out in a new direction, surprise the consumer, add a new dimension to the brand, and re-energize it."

> Focus groups give you the *rationalizations* people use for what they buy, but these can lead you down a wrong path, simply because as human beings we often say one thing and do another, particularly when we are in company.

## FOCUS GROUPS

One thing to look out for is the limited value of focus groups. They can tell you what people do, but they cannot tell you why they do it. They can provide valid information based on group dynamics, but when was the last time you made a buying decision in a group? They give you the *rationalizations* people use for what they buy, but these can lead you down a wrong path, simply because as human beings we often say one thing and do another, particularly when we are in company.

Focus groups are often misused. Certainly beware of using a focus group as a planning committee. As Harry Beckwith says, ". . . consider the major innovations in service marketing: automated teller machines, negotiable certificates of deposit, storefront tax services, legal clinics, predictive dialing systems, junk bonds, frequent flyer and other loyalty marketing programs, credit cards, money market mutual funds, extended service contracts, home equity lines of credit, alternate dispute resolution services, drive-in and drive-up services, home delivery, database marketing, home shopping, and dozens of others.

"*Did* focus groups generate any of those ideas? *Could* focus groups have generated any of those ideas? Could a focus group inspire the personal computer, personal copier, cellular telephone, electronic digital assistant, fax machine—or anything like them? . . . Consider three recent innovations, skinless Kentucky Fried Chicken, McLean (lower-calorie McDonald hamburgers), and low-fat Pizza Hut pizzas. Focus groups *loved* these ideas. Real people, unfortunately, did not, and KFC, McDonald's, and Pizza Hut abandoned all three products."

As Beckwith says, maybe focus groups can brainstorm for you, but you should never bet on it. I say further that focus groups are fatally flawed. Do you seriously think you could be invited to a strange place with a dozen strangers and reveal your deepest emotions?

## STEREOTYPES

I recommend also that you avoid using research that relies on stereotypes. Researchers used to love big consumer classifications. Dealing with individual customers was considered a waste of time. How much easier to break society up into huge groups (like DINKS—double income, no kids), and have them all think and act and talk alike. It made life easier in the age of mass marketing. But as Regis McKenna says in his wonderful book *Real Time*, this approach "is unlikely to survive the reign of the new consumer."

## HE HAS MORE THAN THOSE BLUE BEDROOM EYES

Speaking of looking out for research excess, I love the story of the actor Paul Newman and his Newman's Own food company. A research outfit wanted $400,000 to do a taste test of one his new products. He decided he could do just as well by inviting a dozen friends over to his house and letting them test the taste. I suppose he figured that the entire brand started as a bit of a lark, and he'd like it to stay that way. Fifteen years ago, he and his friend and partner A. E. Hotchner bottled a salad dressing to give to a few friends at Christmas, and it went on from there to become a food empire that has earned over $700 million in gross sales from dozens of products. He and Hotchner give every cent of the earnings to children's charities, including their Hole In The Wall Gang Camp, of which there are now five set up for kids who have cancer and other life-threatening diseases. Astonishingly, it's all done with no advertising and a lot of good humor, which is reflected in the company motto, "Shameless exploitation for the common good." Not only do the brands taste good, but buying them makes you feel as though you're doing good. That's the definition of a very fine bargain.

## GOING BEYOND THE NORM

At Brandtrust, we believe there is great value in research that goes beyond the norms. We like to ask what a good psychologist would make of a brand problem. Or how a documentary filmmaker might approach it. Or an investigative journalist. These aren't techniques; rather, they help us to look and see with other, fresh eyes as we search for basic, actionable, human truths.

## THE ZMET TECHNIQUE

There are some remarkable new ways of getting inside your customer's psyche to get the real skinny on how they see your product or service. Jerry Zaitman of the Harvard Business School uses techniques that get at hidden knowledge, that get at "what people don't know they know." Part of the success of these new techniques is that they speak the right language. Cognitive scientists know that we think in images, not words, but most research is what Zaitman calls "verbocentric." It relies on words, not images. A *Fast Company* article on Zaitman (1998) says, "Poets and psychiatrists understand that metaphor—viewing one thing in terms of another—is central to thought and crucial to uncovering latent needs and emotions. But marketers are so caught up in the literal that they neglect the metaphoric." In the same article, Zaitman says, "People can give us only what we give them an opportunity to provide. To the extent that we structure the stimulus—whether it's a discussion guide in a focus group or a question in a survey—all people can do is respond. And there's value in that. But I see those as strip-mining techniques." He suggests that using metaphor will take you much deeper, where the really valuable stuff resides. Of that really valuable stuff, he says, "Our native tongue is powerless to call it out of hiding; a second,

## LOOK, MA. NO RESEARCH!

Sometimes, you come across a stroke of intuitive difference that makes your heart sing without the benefit of consumer research. This newspaper story, titled "Wife's gloves inspire innovative dog muzzle," did it for me (*National Post*, 1998):

Paul and Sandy Paglericcio had a choice—stop their nine German shepherds from barking or get rid of the dogs.

Their desperation gave birth to the Husher—a muzzle that allows a dog to breathe, but puts an end to barking . . .

The Paglericcio's problems began . . . when new neighbors complained about the barking in the kennel. The dispute ended up in court.

A few days before the court date, Mr. Paglericcio and his daughter were sitting on the front porch. And the idea hit.

He said, "Geez, go in the house and get mom's spandex gloves."

He snipped off the fingers, attached a few strings, and tied the contraption to the dog's head. The spandex is elastic enough to allow the dog to open its mouth to drink and pant, but not to bark.

The Paglericcios won an award for product innovation and have sold more than 125,000 Hushers at $24.95 apiece.

The article did not say what the dogs think of the Husher.

more obscure language is needed. But few who speak to us in the marketplace even know this language exists—let alone how to speak it." His insights led Zaitman to patent ZMET—"a technique for eliciting interconnected constructs that influence thought and behavior."

Starting with conventional research, DuPont found out that women hate pantyhose because they're hot, uncomfortable, and prone to run at the worst possible moment. But Zaitman's ZMET marketing-by-metaphor used visual stimulation to turn up a deeper response—that women actually have a "like-hate" relationship with their nylons. The "like" end of the spectrum gave DuPont and its fiber customers new directions for communication. They could proceed with the new knowledge that, despite the negatives, pantyhose also makes a woman feel thin and tall. They made the women's legs feel longer and therefore sexier to men.

Nestle's Crunch used Zaitman's techniques to go beyond the expected response that the candy bar was a small indulgence in a busy world and a source of quick energy that tasted good. ZMET revealed that, "The Nestle Crunch bar turns out to be a very powerful icon of time . . . it was less a workday pick-me-up than a time machine back to childhood." This and dozens of other examples show that you can indeed go deeper than a conventional peep-show focus group to get answers you might never think to even ask. You can indeed get the real answer to "But how does it make you feel?"

## THE RAPAILLE METHOD

Chrysler uses the Rapaille method to get at feelings (*Wall Street Journal*, 1999). G. Clotaire Rapaille is a French-born medical anthropologist who literally helped Chrysler design its new PT Cruiser. Rapaille got people into a deeply relaxed state, and then asked them to write stories about the prototype. The result is what Chrysler feels is a sure-fire "segment buster." The unusual design looks a little like a 1930s gangster car masquerading as a London taxi. Chrysler says it's got the room of a minivan, the flair of a sport-utility, and the practicality of a small car. Rapaille's methods get much of the credit for refining the design.

## IN-SIGHT

At Brandtrust, we work with Dr. Charles Kenny, who uses one-on-one, deep relaxation research techniques to give us an astonishingly clear picture of consumer (and often employee) behavior and feelings. Called IN-SIGHT, the technique explains the "why" of behavior and its underlying emotions. The idea behind it is simple: If you know which feelings really motivate people, you gain an enormous advantage for every aspect of your brand.

Dr. Kenny and IN-SIGHT pointed the way for the marketing of GM's Saturn division that made shopping for a car a delight instead of a horror. It showed the way to a very different *experience* of car buying that includes no-hassle pricing, no-pressure salespeople, salaried salespeople, and a market-area approach that, for example, has you shopping at Saturn of Minneapolis rather than Joe's Chevrolet. Stores were designed to emphasize service, including a large window from the showroom into the service bay, so customers could see their cars being worked on. It's a brand solution that welcomes the question "But how does it make you feel?"

> **I**f you know which feelings really motivate people, you gain an enormous advantage for every aspect of your brand.

## HATE THOSE BUGS!

Some of Dr. Kenny's findings seem terribly obvious in hindsight. For example, Terminex is a company that gets rid of bugs and other pests in the home. As a form of drive-around advertising, Terminex vehicles used to have a huge bug mounted on their roofs. I say 'used to' because as Dr. Kenny found out, women hated having those vehicles parked in their driveways. It said to the neighbors that the woman's house had bugs, bugs mean a dirty house, and a dirty house means a dirty person. This kind of insight not only got rid of the threatening vehicle-top bugs, it shows (among other things) what the vehicles ought to look like; in fact, it speaks volumes for the direction of the brand in its dealing with customers.

## REALITY AND REALISTIC

One of my favorite IN-SIGHT stories involved a group of funeral homes. It literally shows funeral directors how to help their buyers deal more effectively with grief. Dr. Kenny says, "The critical insight showed that people want a funeral home to help them deny death rather than accept it. People who attend a funeral want everything to be 'realistic'—as if the person is just asleep, not really dead." You can imagine what these findings do to traditional views within the industry. The study led to a 180-degree change in how the funeral directors saw their role. It affected how and where caskets were placed in the funeral homes, how to present the bodies, the colors of the funeral vehicles, how to advertise, staff training, and selling pre-arranged funerals.

Similarly, Dr. Kenny will tell you from his right-brain research with insurance brands not to position life insurance against appeals of security. He says, "There's no way life insurance can add to security, since you have to die to collect it; rather, the brand approach should emphasize immortality and the need for control. The quest for immortality is very strong, and what better way is there to extend and lengthen your life than through the family that you leave behind to perpetuate you for generations to come?"

## A LITTLE WEIRDER THAN WE WANT

Harry gets excited about the power of this kind of insight. He says, "Armed with that kind of knowledge, you could change the entire death experience, which on the scale of things, has to be a lot less fun than birth. You could promote ideas like 'Fun Funerals' and 'Enjoying Death.' You could have staged rehearsals, as in 'Dead For A Day.' You could lay the dear departed out for viewing in the casket wearing Mickey Mouse ears so that their final act was to make the mourners laugh instead of cry."

As usual, Harry goes way too far, but his daft musings do show how research that digs deep into the emotional side of the brain can turn up deft strategic action. Finding the emotional key to your customer's feelings unlocks the power of your brand in ways you can never come up with by talking to each other around the boardroom table.

## CHAPTER 8

# Brands Think Relationships, Not Transactions

Harry once went away to a cabin in the woods to figure out his philosophy of life. He cut himself off from civilization to think deep thoughts for a weekend, from which he expected to emerge with the mind of Bertrand Russell and the insight of the Dalai Lama. But he gave up before his weekend of monkhood was over. He reported with considerable consternation, "I really tried, but I couldn't think of anything to think about. My deepest thought was, 'what's for lunch?'"

The moral is that you can't manufacture brand thinking. You can't order it up like a BLT in a deli. If Harry had started with a smaller, more realistic question rather than one intended to plumb the meaning of life between barbecues over the weekend, his trip to the woods might have been more profitable. (Harry's approach to real metaphysical pondering reminds me of the Woody Allen character who said he didn't approve of reality but had to admit it was the only place to get a good steak.)

## BRAND THINKING

Start your brand thinking at the beginning. Start by exploring the very basic things a company needs in order to be successful, and think dumb. Ask yourself, "What does it take to create a successful brand?" The most obvious answer you will get from nine out of ten people is that a brand measures success by profit at the bottom line.

When Jim Barksdale, president and CEO of Netscape Communications, stands before 50 newly recruited employees in an orientation session, the first question he asks is, "What's the purpose of this business?"

"To make money," replies one new employee.

"Wrong!" says Barksdale. "Our purpose is to get and keep customers. Somehow each of you has to be part of that process" (*Fast Company*, 1988).

Barksdale reflects what we can all learn from Peter Drucker (1999), who, through management seminars forty years ago, got the Japanese "to accept what they originally thought was a very strange doctrine. They have come to accept my position that the end of business is not 'to make money.' Making money is a necessity of survival. It is also a result of performance and a measurement thereof. But in itself, it is not a performance . . . the purpose of a business is to create a customer and to satisfy a customer. That is performance and that is what business is being paid for. The job and function of management as the leader, decision maker, and value setter of the organization, and indeed, the purpose and rationale of an organization altogether, is to make human beings productive so that the skills, expectations, and beliefs of the individual lead to achievement in joint performance."

> The purpose of a business is to create a customer and to satisfy a customer.

There used to be a saying going around ad agencies that advertising would be a lot more fun if we didn't have to think about clients. Well, there appears to be a lot of companies that behave as though business would be a lot more fun if we didn't have to create customers.

## START AT THE BEGINNING

While I believe the most important thing a brand can offer is a strongly focused promise, I sometimes surprise a client when I start a brand-building discussion by talking about the quality of their employees and their attitudes toward customers. I think they expect me to start by talking about product differentiation and how to advertise it with a snappy slogan. But advertising often isn't the most important part of brand building. Starbucks spends very little on advertising. Newman's Own Foods has never indulged in the art. The Virgin Group of companies gets along quite well without much of the expense. And your brand could have quite good advertising that attracts customers, only to have them turned off by the reception they get from your employees.

There's a famous story about the British Rail Service's search for a new ad agency. When they went to the offices of Allen Brady & Marsh in London, they were met by a rude receptionist, and were told to wait. Finally, an ill-kempt person arrived to show them into the conference room, which was dirty and cluttered with plates of stale food. They waited some more. A few agency people arrived one at a time in a lackadaisical manner, showing very little interest in what the BRS execs had to say. Just as the railway people were about to walk out in disgust, one of the agency people piped up, saying something like, "Gentlemen, your treatment at AB&M isn't typical. We behave the way we do to point out what it is like to be a customer of British Rail. The real problem at British Rail isn't your advertising. It's your people. We suggest we help you fix your employee attitude before we attempt to fix your advertising." The agency got the account.

Of course, as Peter Drucker reminds us, "Achievement in business is not a happy workforce, however desirable it may be; it is a satisfied customer who reorders the product."

## A TRANSACTION OR A RELATIONSHIP?

But I'm sure the eminent thinker would agree that if we are to get into the habit of cultivating loyalty in our customers, motivated employees must play a central role. The first three ingredients for building a brand are customers, customers, and customers. The golden rule for building the equity of a brand is to stop thinking about what you can do for your cash register; start thinking about what you and your employees can do for your customer that the other guy isn't. In other words, *stop thinking transactions and start thinking relationships.*

You need a lot of other ingredients to build the equity of your brand, but if you start with an unfailing commitment to building a relationship with every customer—including the stunningly obvious option of appreciating them—you've made a most important first step. The idea is to stop seeing dollar signs (a transaction) when a customer comes a-calling, and start seeing a person (a relationship).

A transaction is like a one-night stand, and it's never going to be as satisfying or rewarding as falling in love. A transaction makes the cash register ring once. A relationship makes it ring again and again. And selling takes on a new dimension when you put it in the context of a relationship. Selling is often talking *to*. A relationship is usually talking *with*. Transaction implies a selling monologue, such as when a home-heating salesman calls you at home, and you know he's reading from a prepared script. Relationship implies dialogue, such as when you interrupt the home-heating sales pitch with a question, and the guy doesn't get flustered and lose his place. You sell to a client. You have a relationship with a person. You add up transactions in *cost per thousand*. You add up relationships in *cost per one*.

> A transaction makes the cash register ring once. A relationship makes it ring again and again.

## CHEERS

It's disconcerting when you walk into your favorite tavern, and there's a new person behind the bar. She doesn't know you. All of a sudden the familiar becomes strange. You feel a sudden loss of identity. The former barmaid used to have your favorite brew and a cheery greeting on deck before you could get up on the stool. Because she doesn't know you, the new one treats you like a customer rather than a friend. In a place you think of as close to home, you're suddenly a stranger buying a beer in a transaction, rather than you stopping in for a beer and a chat with somebody who is interested in you. Of course, it doesn't take long to get over the confusion. The new barmaid soon becomes a buddy, but it illustrates the security you find in a relationship rather than a transaction. The situation comedy "Cheers" comes to mind with its theme song, "You want to be where everybody knows your name." How would Norm, the erstwhile accountant, and Cliff, the postal worker, feel if there was no Sam Malone to pull their personal pints while all are at the mercy of waitress Carla's caustic wit?

It doesn't have to be that personal. Harry told me just the other day about going into a Staples subsidiary to shop for a fax/telephone/answering machine. After fifteen minutes of looking on his own, he had to ask for help. When it arrived, it was totally off-hand. The one machine my friend had found by himself was out of stock. He was offered the floor model at ten percent off, but it came without a box and no manual. The salesman made no effort to offer advice on the merits of one machine versus another; in other words, the salesman made no effort to establish a relationship. He wasn't rude, but he appeared not to care. My friend left the store feeling confused and undervalued. The store lost a sale of about $500 (plus any future sales).

Just down the road was a store called Future Shop, where Harry's experience was entirely different. The salesperson's name was (funnily enough) Carla. She was a pleasant young woman who appeared promptly. She clearly knew her business. She asked what Harry's needs were and steered him to a machine in the middle of the price range she thought would do the job. My friend bought the machine and a three-year service contract. Carla gave him the phone number of the brand's tech service, plus she gave him her business number in case the tech service didn't work out. Then, she carried the boxed machine out to his car. But rather than drive straight off, Harry went back into the store and asked to speak to the manager. He told the manager how well Carla had treated him in comparison with the competition next door. He also said he would be back to buy a big-screen TV set within the next couple of months.

This was a win-win victory for both sides of the counter. It shows how two nearby stores selling the same products can produce a customer response as different as the north and south poles. But the real moral of the story is that acceptable service looks like great service in comparison with bad service. By simply doing her job, the Future Shop salesperson made her company look heroic. She treated Harry like a person who needed a bit of help. She simply asked what his needs were and found a pleasant way to fulfill them. She didn't try to sell him the most expensive machine; rather, she recommended the one that best met his needs. By simply behaving normally in a customer/vendor relationship, she scored big points for the brand called Future Shop. The fact that I'm writing about it speaks marvels for the potential power of word-of-mouth advertising, as it goes from my friend to me to you in a book that will hopefully have a big audience.

## TEACHING EMPLOYEES TO FOCUS ON CUSTOMERS

Ukrop Food Stores is an independent grocery chain of 23 stores in Virginia that intuitively understands the importance of the employee in attracting and keeping customers (Duncan and Moriarty, 1997). Cashiers are obviously one of the most critical points of customer contact. A little research showed that the behavior of Ukrop's people could use improvement. There was no budget set aside for meaningful training, but it was a critical-enough issue that the company decided to take an unusual step. It moved money from advertising into a customer-focused training program. The results have been phenomenal. *Driving Brand Value* reports that Ukrop has a 34 percent share of its market, with per-store volume 50 percent higher than its nearest competitor. This is despite the fact that competitors spend more in advertising, stay open longer, and often have lower prices. Ukrop also doesn't sell alcohol or state lottery tickets, and it closes on Sunday so that employees can spend time with their families.

Amazon.com founder Jeff Bezos says that if he had to write a book about starting, managing, and making a business grow, he would focus on customers, customers, customers (*Business 2.0,* 1999). He says, "I think everything falls out of that. It's especially true online, because the balance of power shifts away from the company and toward the customer. Customers have a bigger voice online. If we make a customer unhappy, they can tell thousands of people. Likewise, if you make a customer happy, they can also tell thousands of people. With that kind of megaphone in the hands of every individual customer, you had better be a customer-centric company."

## WHAT ARE COMPANIES THINKING?

We've all had the experience of rude or sub-par service in retail stores and from service companies and civil servants. It makes you wonder how the purveyors of bad service live. If you were to go to their house for dinner, would they snarl at you when you rang the doorbell? Would they greet you with indifference? Would they leave you alone in the living room with your coat on for an hour? When you speak to them, would they look down their nose at you as though they just encountered pond scum? Would they go out of their way to turn you off by constantly answering the cell phone during dinner? Would they snap gum in your face or defiantly chew their peas with their mouths open? Would they serve you a warm martini with a hair in it?

The mind truly boggles.

Why would anybody run a business on the basis of being rude to the people who provide them with a living? Why would anybody go to work in a service business, only to despise the people they serve? Maybe there's a strange breed of folk who thinks annoying people is a good time. Not only is it no way to run a business—it's no way to run a life. While you may wonder how they survive, I bet you can recall dozens of examples when you've shrugged off a lack of courtesy from people you've favored with your business. But just as readily, you can probably recall times when you have decided never again to do business with a bad-mannered merchant. A lot of these people might believe their jobs are menial. But there are no menial jobs— only menial attitudes.

> **W**hy would anybody run a business on the basis of being rude to the people who provide them with a living?

## LOOKING DEEPER

If rule one for building brand equity is to start thinking relationships rather than transactions, you might think you've made a first step with a bit of staff training and weeding out the bad apples. But as much as I hate to say it, perhaps you should look at yourself and your fellow managers before your staff. Perhaps the cancer of bad-mannered service starts at home. Managers who treat their employees like so much fodder are likely to create an atmosphere that fosters pandemic rudeness. Staff training from such managers is also likely to produce cliché responses to customers. Telling a departing customer to "Have a nice day" is better than telling him to get lost, but it's not as valuable as treating him properly from the moment he enters the store with the kind of genuine, personal response that can only come from interaction of the most human kind. The fact is that good employees and loyal customers are like the chicken and the egg. You never know which comes first.

---

## TAILOR-MADE SERVICE

One of my favorite service stories is this example of the art from Hans Willimann, who runs the Four Seasons Hotel in Chicago (*Fast Company*, 1998): In 1989, the hotel was hosting a fund-raising dinner for a local hospital. Nancy Reagan was to attend, and just before her appearance at a small pre-dinner gathering, one of the men in the room was alarmed to discover that he was the only guest in the room without a tuxedo. Willimann could see that the guest was distressed, so he summoned the maître d'hôtel and said, "This man needs a tuxedo."

The unflappable maître d' disappeared and returned minutes later with a tux—the one off his own back, freshly pressed. When the man put it on, says Willimann, "It was a little too big, so we had the pants tightened by the hotel seamstress. The man went to the party and enjoyed himself."

Willimann's fast service tip is, "It's not hard to treat people with dignity. And that applies to employees as it does to guests. The only difference is the guests have more money. If an employee needs to be bailed out of jail, okay. If a guest needs a filet mignon at one in the morning, we do it."

---

### DOES IT FEEL LIKE FAMILY OR A HORROR SHOW?

In a restaurant I go to regularly, some of the female staff actually greet me with a kiss on the cheek. This makes me feel like family rather than like a customer. Their reaction is genuine rather than forced. Nobody has to tell them to engage customers. I notice that the atmosphere of the place is created by owners who work in the business and treat the staff as one big family. You can't tell who is an owner and who is an employee.

Contrast this charming example of customer care with the horror show of my experience with Northwest Airlines.

I travel a lot and find that I become oblivious to much of the everyday inconvenience of weather and air traffic control. I've developed a kind of (can you believe this?) tolerance to the setbacks in my best-laid plans. But at the hands of Northwest Airlines, I recently had the worst travel experience of my life.

It wasn't so much that mechanics were canceling flights to call attention to union problems. It wasn't even that I was forced to repeatedly change my plans. It was the way the debacle was handled that caused the experience to be so horrific for myself and several hundred others.

I was in Detroit, and several flights to Chicago had been canceled over a period of a few hours. There was no problem with the weather, but the Northwest people never bothered to explain what was wrong. At every announcement, you could hear a collective groan reverberate in the terminal. But fortune finally smiled as my fellow flyers and I got on board the next-to-last flight, and the plane taxied out to the runway. The smile froze, however, as we sat motionless on the ramp for a very long time and were told several different stories about the delay. One hour goes by. Then another. After citing several mechanical problems, the reason was eventually given that the flight was to be canceled because of a thunderstorm in Chicago. You couldn't help but wonder how long Northwest thought a thunderstorm was likely to last.

The plane returned to the gate, and we were told we would have to return to the main terminal ticket counter to get some disposition on our alternatives. If you've ever been in the Detroit airport, you realize this is not pleasant news. It's a long, miserable trek. And I see that departure time for the last flight is drawing near—not that it matters much because I also know that four other canceled planeloads are trying to get a seat on that last flight.

After schlepping back to the main ticket counter, I actually witness a Northwest customer service agent *yelling* at an elderly lady for asking a simple question. Really: I heard the question. But by now, it's obvious that I'm not going to get a flight out. It's nearly 11 P.M., and there are no other options from other carriers. But I remain cool and calm in the sure knowledge that stuff happens. The problem was, I didn't realize then that the stuff was far from over.

My plan was to simply retrieve my bag, stay the night, and get on another carrier in the morning. I say another carrier because I calmly resolved never to fly Northwest again. Ever. Which is when the real fun began.

The baggage handling crew had left for the day. Bags from several canceled flights were simply not available. At all. I have medication and contact lens paraphernalia in my bag, and I can't have it. I suddenly lose my pleasant demeanor and demand my bag, explaining in a loud voice that they must give me my bag since I never intend to fly Northwest ever again. I know they can't send my bag on a plane without me. But apparently Northwest can and will.

The airline offered nothing. Not to me. Not to anyone. No hotel. No transportation. Nothing. Nada. Not even an apology. In fact, I believe the customer service people must be specially trained to behave like attack dogs because human beings are not naturally that evil to one another. And they won't give me my bag.

I had to rent a car, find a drug store, buy necessities, and rent a hotel room, for which I had to pay double. You might think it couldn't get worse, but it did. After I arrived back in Chicago via another carrier, I began trying to find my bag. For more than *ten* hours, my assistant and I tried to reach someone on Northwest's baggage line. Busy. Busy. Busy. Finally, around 7 P.M., someone answered the phone. I explain the problem, and the guy tells me my bag is in Chicago. Good news. He'll be happy to get it for me when I come to the airport. That is at least an hour and a half drive, and an extremely inconvenient proposition in Chicago. He informs me that he will put it in a cab and send it to me, but I will have to pay for the cab. That's 35 bucks.

Now, I'm willing to accept that such incredible inconveniences can happen. But I cannot grasp why Northwest would ever treat customers with such contempt. My incredulity explains why the experience continues to upset me, and I continue to tell anyone and everyone who will listen. In fact, I will actually go out of my way to tell people how bad this horror show was—out of my way to make sure it is included in this book to show you firsthand how you must be aware of word-of-reverse-mouth, to point out the value of treating customers the way you would want to be treated. Otherwise, you might not know how the airline got its other, more infamous, name.

Using customer interaction with staff members to promote a brand at every point of contact may be the most important and effective ingredient in brand building simply because it makes all the other ingredients ring real and true. You might *say* how much you value your staff as an important stakeholder, that your most important asset crosses your threshold every morning—but their behavior will say more about how much you value them than any of your words. At the advertising agency that bears my name (Arian, Lowe & Travis), one of the most important employees is our receptionist/telephone operator. She's usually the first point of customer contact, day in and day out. She never tires of courtesy or good cheer. Even when she takes a break and a substitute fills in for her, you will be greeted by genuine cheerfulness, intelligence, resourcefulness, and desire to help. A friend who recently came to visit me at the office paid us a wonderful compliment. He said, "You get the feeling here that the people love coming to work in the morning."

> Using customer interaction with staff members to promote a brand at every point of contact may be the most important and effective ingredient in brand building.

## EMPLOYEES AS INVESTORS

Too many employers say "our people are our most important asset" without meaning a word of it. They really think labor is a cost, like furniture or paper clips. The president of Global Learning Resources, Kevin Wheeler, suggests that you should think of your employees as investors. They invest in your business with their time, talent, skill, and energy, instead of dollars. They have every right to expect a decent return on their investment, just as financial investors do (*Montreal Gazette*, May 1999). This refreshing point of view could change the way you think about compensation and incentives. For example, should paying a bonus be viewed in the same light as your company paying a dividend?

Rick Born has made Born Information Services into a business with $92 million in revenues—first and foremost with his people (*Inc.*, 1999). He literally believes his success is based on the way his employees feel. He says that in the technology-consulting industry,

## Reward for value. Value for reward.

Keeping good employees sometimes requires grand gestures. As *Fast Company* (December 1998) notes, you have to "wow" people with opportunities for growth, for freedom, and for impact. But money doesn't hurt, either. The magazine quotes John Sullivan, the Michael Jordan of hiring, who says, "I recently worked with a big semiconductor company that was worried about losing one of its most gifted engineers. The company asked me to come in and talk about a retention strategy. I learned how important the chip that this guy was working on was—and how important he was to the chip. Then I asked . . . 'How would losing this engineer affect time-to-market for the next generation of that chip? How badly would his leaving disrupt the team? What if he left and went to your main competitor?'

"I did a few calculations and then took my final figure to a top executive at the company. This one engineer, I estimated, was worth $29 million to this company. So you know what that executive did? He wrote the engineer a check for $1 million. That was exactly the right reaction. Most people don't appreciate how valuable they really are. If they did, then lots more of them would be getting million-dollar bonuses."

*Where do I sign up?*

customers are not the problem. It's employee turnover that can kill you, which is why he set out to differentiate his brand by "being the very best company to work for." This involves much more than the usual array of benefits and financial perks. It means also turning down lucrative contracts he feels his employees would find dull. Work on Y2K fell into that category. The company accepts only those challenges that offer its people an opportunity to work on leading-edge projects. Born also endorses the revolutionary HR idea that because of the disruption to home life, no employee is required to travel. Instead, the company incurs the expense of opening its own regional branches, seeded with people from existing offices. Going further, Born opens offices only in cities where people want to move. This automatically rules out profitable places like New York, Chicago, and Los Angeles, in favor of Milwaukee, Denver, Dallas, and Atlanta. These and many other initiatives result in high employee satisfaction and very low turnover. Born credits this "employee-first" policy with obtaining three appearances on the *Inc.* 500 ranking of the country's fastest-growing private companies. The icing on the cake is that Born turned down a buy-out offer that would have paid him 85.5 percent of $30 million because employees asked him, "How could you sell *our* company?" Born proves that "people first, strategy second" is a great strategy all on its own.

## DIFFERENT ROUTE, SAME RESULT

A luxury, all-inclusive resort on the island of St. Lucia called LeSPORT takes a slightly different route to accommodate a brand that caters to human comfort. Management works with employees to cover all its points of guest contact. The aim is to build a high standard of mutual guest/employee involvement. With this in mind, founder and CEO Craig Barnard proves that a small, family-owned company can do a strong branding job with a clear mission and a product difference to set itself apart.

The resort provides all the fun and sport of a beach vacation and then goes one better by including a unique program of rejuvenating spa treatments and life-style enhancements. With a hundred rooms, LeSPORT can only hold 200 people at most, and customer satisfaction on all fronts is over 90 percent, with many guests coming back again and again. Occupancy rates go to 100 percent during the prime season; they even stay high during the normally dead summer months, with a slightly discounted price when many other resorts in the area practically close down.

Hotel employees are considered an integral part of the vacation experience rather than servile step-and-fetchers. Manager Michael Bryant recognizes that his local staff of about 200 have the capacity to make or break the customers' precious holiday time; going further, he sees the staff—all of the staff—as ambassadors, and he trains them accordingly. He says, "Few businesses have an opportunity to interact with each customer every day for at least a week of very close proximity. It means that every employee point of contact has to exhibit maximum performance morning, noon, and night, and it's performance of a very human variety. That's why training to higher and higher levels never stops. The training is also linked to a unique incentive system that keeps the performance and loyalty at a peak level and promotes a friendly competitiveness for good guest evaluation between different departments."

Integrating all of its branding efforts with training, and on-going product and property improvements, has made LeSPORT (also known as The Body Holiday) one of the most successful, top-dollar resorts in the Caribbean. As Craig Barnard says, "Our fabled care of guests and their interests can never take a vacation!"

## NOT ALL CUSTOMERS ARE EQUAL

It would hardly seem necessary to talk about the importance of being nice to customers, but it's sadly true that you will also get the occasional customer who isn't worth keeping. Some people go out of their way to find fault. Others love to complain for little or no reason. If you get one who is constantly abusive to your staff, who undermines them at every turn, who ruins the company morale you work so hard to build, and who infects the satisfaction of other customers, you have to have the guts to ask him or her to ever-so-politely take a hike, to please blow-your-pop-stand, to head for a happier horizon. It's rare, but when Craig Barnard feels forced to turf the guest from Hades, he does it with in-depth investigation and the very gentle nudge of a complete refund. This might even make them feel too sheepish to falsely bad-mouth LeSPORT when they get home.

## GOOD SERVICE IS REAL

Good service isn't servile service. Boot licking is offensive. Fawning is phony. Groveling is a turn-off. In fact, the best service is like a collaboration between you and your customer. It's a genuine partnership between the two of you for attaining the customer's best route to satisfaction. In Transactional Analysis, it's known as an "I'm Okay-You're Okay" situation. There are always two winners. You win from knowing you're doing a job as well as it can be done. The customer wins by never having to do a bad imitation of Mick Jagger singing, "I can't get no satisfaction."

> Good service isn't servile service. Fawning is phony. Groveling is a turn-off. In fact, the best service is like a collaboration between you and your customer.

## JAPANESE GRINNING LESSONS

Training Japanese employees to smile when greeting a customer is serious business (*Montreal Gazette*, March 30, 1999). Their culture teaches suppression of emotions. Smiling is frowned upon. One must not move the face or body too much. Excessive smiling can even be a symptom of a tendency toward suicide. If you're ever called upon to make a speech in Japan, don't bother starting off with a joke. It's likely to be met with stony silence. Retailers and service businesses have resorted to sending workers to smile schools.

The least they could do is wear happy-face buttons!

## TECHNOLOGY AND SERVICE

In *Real Time* (1997), Regis McKenna writes in his elegant fashion about the benefits of technology. He says, "Service is not an event; it is the process of creating a customer environment of information, assurance, and comfort. Technology has made it possible to establish such an environment with unprecedented finesse." He gives an example: "Intel discusses plans for future microchip models with designer-engineers at customer companies. As Dave House, a former senior vice president of Intel, explained to me, by blending marketing and engineering, the company has been able to achieve a faster return on investment in new products. Working closely with key customers on specifications—balancing prototype products' technical capabilities against customers' receptivity to new features and requirements—Intel has developed a remarkable relationship with those customers, who are then primed to use the products they helped design."

McKenna goes on, "This sort of intimate dialogue between a company and its customers creates a brand loyalty immeasurably deeper than catchy jingles riding on advertising blitzes ever could. It creates a quasi-symbiotic tie. The new interactive technologies collapse the space between the consumer and the producer. The extraordinary attentiveness to customers' desires by companies using these tools leads their customers to expect a similar response from other companies.

Of course, even the most dedicated service providers can get up on the wrong side of the bed once in a while, which means service may never be perfect. There are also customers who never get the bees out of their bonnets and are rarely satisfied. But because service may be the arena in which you win or lose with your competitors, you simply want to avoid the axiom old soldiers have been known to quote. They say that wars aren't won by the most competent army; they're won by the least incompetent.

By the way, when I told Harry I was going to use his little story about going away for the weekend to contemplate his navel, he said, "It's not quite true that I had no thoughts. At least after the weekend, I decided I wanted to be remembered for more than a prodigious ability to grow ear hair."

# Different Is Better. Better Is Different.

Focusing on your customers rather than just your machinery is a fundamental fact of building a brand. But customers have to come from somewhere. Unless you offer something as totally unique as a guaranteed cure for baldness, they will have to come from an expanding market and/or the guy up the street. A problem-solving brand like Viagra doesn't come along every day, but it's a striking example of what Monty Python means when they want your attention and say, ". . . and now for something completely different." It's as old as the hills, but the best way to attract customers is by offering something different within the product or service category in which your brand has to fight for attention.

I don't mean to suggest that being better doesn't count. Obviously, quality matters. An assurance of quality is part of the covenant a brand takes on with its customers. Quality is part of the deal, something a customer likes to think can be taken for granted. That's why it's difficult to get away with a shoddy product more than once, and a service that doesn't deliver on its promise is eventually (and hopefully) doomed. But the fact is that if being better were more important than being different, you would buy only the products that make the grade in *Consumer Reports*.

## A TANGIBLE DIFFERENCE OR A VAGUE PROMISE?

It's simply easier for customers to grasp a tangible difference than a vague promise of quality. A naive advertiser might want his ad agency to say a product is "high quality" or that it's "where quality

> The fact is that if being better were more important than being different, you would buy only the products that make the grade in *Consumer Reports*.

and value meet," and he doesn't understand why the agency resists. Quality by itself is too vaguely intangible. And anyone who knows anything about the communication process knows that offering a tangible difference is the key to opening up emotional preference.

Consumers don't question the quality of established brands. They simply want to feel that somehow they're doing the right thing when they choose what a brand has to offer. Paradoxically, perhaps the most successful brands are the ones we think about the least. Like Morton Salt, they have simply found a place in our lives. Like a pair of old slippers, they provide us with a comfort level we find no reason to challenge. Marketers get excited about brand loyalty, but it's funny to think that in many cases, brand loyalty might best be sustained by simply letting sleeping dogs lie!

## REINFORCING LOYALTY

While preservation of the *status quo* is a desirable notion for loyalty, you can't afford to take even a loyal customer's business for granted. Even Morton Salt runs the occasional ad. Loyalty must be reinforced.

The fact that there are two scoops of raisins in a package of Kellogg's Raisin Bran (rational difference) translates easily into the feeling of better taste and smart choice. It's a case of the left side of the brain leading the right side. The "two scoops" are the stimulus that leads us to a response of yumminess and shopping wisdom. In fact, if Kellogg's Raisin Bran has become just another part of your morning routine (and that's what Kellogg's wants), it's a warm familiarity (feeling) with the two scoops (fact) that will keep it there.

You might think the two scoops make Kellogg's Raisin Bran better than Post's version of the same cereal. But being better than the other guy is often moot.

## WHAT DO YOU THINK?

It would be difficult to gauge whether a Mercedes-Benz is better than a Volvo. But we do feel that a Benz is different from a Volvo. You hear the name Volvo, and you're likely to think about safety. You hear the name Mercedes, and you probably think about fastidious prestige. It's not that you think the Mercedes is unsafe, or that the Volvo is a slop box. It's that well-known brands occupy a specific spot in our minds, and we don't like changing it. Often, we use the facts of a brand to rationalize to others and ourselves all the emotional reasons for buying it. A few years ago, Harry bought a Prince tennis racquet. He said it was because the oversized Prince would improve his game—an impossible task for any racquet. But I happen to know the real reason he bought it was because all the chic people he knew had one, and he thought it made him look "with it" when he carried it around in its loudly labeled case.

## TANGIBLE DIFFERENCES

Innovation of tangible differences puts new emotional life back into old products and product categories time after time. At $1,100, Maytag's Neptune washing machine costs twice as much as a conventional washer, but ecology-minded consumers are snapping it up because it saves about $100 in power and 7,000 gallons of water in a year. They like looking green, and the cost is worth it.

Gillette absorbed more than $1 billion in R&D and $300 million in advertising to launch its Mach 3—the first triple-blade razor. It costs 50 percent more than the Sensor Excel, launched a few years ago. After a year, Mach 3 became number one in every national market where it was introduced. Apparently Gillette users like to be on the cutting edge! (OUCH!)

## PRODUCT INNOVATION

Product innovation is often the ante you need simply to get into the game. I heard a beautiful example on CNBC the other day. Mike Wood, a lawyer, was playing with his young son. They were using alphabet blocks, and Mike was trying to get his son to sound out the letters as a precursor to reading. Mike sounded out the letters "keh," "ah," and "te," to get the word 'cat.' But his son wasn't getting it,

## A DIFFERENT IDEA AND THE ACCIDENTAL BILLIONAIRE.

It's hard to figure how an innocuous hobby could make you a multi-billionaire in two years. This is the story of 31-year-old Pierre Omidyar, who founded a very different kind of brand called eBay Inc. His fiancée, Pamela Wesley, collects Pez candy dispensers, but she couldn't find an easy way to buy or sell them on the Internet. In 1995, Omidyar suggested they start a different kind of auction Web page that would allow people to list items for sale and take bids over several days. As reported in the *New York Times* (November 15, 1998), the service was free until "the page grew so big that it outgrew Mr. Omidyar's personal Internet account and had to be moved to a much more expensive business account. So early in 1996[,] he started charging a few dollars to list an item and collected a small commission if it was sold. It took just a few months before he quit his day job."

Mr. Omidyar didn't set out to create a huge business, but more than a million people have registered for the service, and 70,000 new items are put up for sale on eBay every day. While Mr. Omidyar's stake is worth about $2 billion, what he's most proud of is how he has helped eBay customers turn their collection hobbies into careers. He says, "They became accidental entrepreneurs and found they could quit their jobs." To Mr. Omidyar, this must sound like an awfully familiar scenario.

which is when Mike had a brilliant idea. He remembered the greeting cards that say or sing a message when you open them. He thought, What if you could squeeze building blocks and out would come the sound of the letter being squeezed? It would teach kids to sound out the letters without any apparent teaching going on. To shorten the story considerably, Mike Wood no longer practices law. He did some market research to check out customer approval and lined up solid financing to found a brand called Leapfrog Toys.

Leapfrog was serendipitous in that it might never have happened if a man hadn't stopped working long enough to play with his son. It's a great example of how play and "fooling around" can turn up something the other guy couldn't possibly imagine. Play releases the ability to think laterally because it allows you to sneak up on a problem rather than confront it. Play appeals to the right side of the brain where creativity lives. It allows for happy accidents and serendipitous thoughts. All work can include a healthy dose of it with highly creative results (the funniest thing about fun is how profitable it can be, which might be the origin of the expression "laughing all the way to the bank").

> **P**lay releases the ability to think laterally because it allows you to sneak up on a problem rather than confront it.

## PRODUCT LONGEVITY

As much as good brands value them, however, tangible differences are often difficult to maintain. It's a little like being the fastest gun in the west: It may not be today, and it may not be tomorrow, but some day somebody's going to ride into town willing to prove she's faster on the draw than you are.

Club Med invented the all-inclusive vacation and had a hammerlock on it for over 20 years. It was a unique experience in its day. For the price you paid your travel agent, you got your flight, your room, your food, a plethora of land and water sports with instruction, and your entertainment—all in an active, gregarious, village-like atmosphere. Social coordinators called *"gentil organisateurs"* (gentle organizers) mingled with the guests and made sure you met other people. It was a fabulous formula that nobody had ever had the imagination to copy—until Hedonism was launched in

## THE MOST DIFFERENT, NEW PRODUCT OF THE PAST 2,000 YEARS.

An online magazine called *Feed* (www.feedmag.com) asked some scientists and philosophers to choose the most important invention of the past 2,000 years. Some good but safe candidates were put forth—such as the telescope, movable type, and Darwin's theory of evolution by natural selection. But the one that startled me was hay.

Freemon Dyson, professor of physics at the Institute of Advanced Study in Princeton, New Jersey, says, "The most important invention of the last 2,000 years was hay. Without horses, you could not have urban civilization. Some time during the so-called Dark Ages, some unknown genius invented hay, forests were turned into meadows, hay was reaped and stored, and civilization moved north over the Alps. So hay gave birth to Vienna and Paris and London and Berlin, and later to Moscow and New York" (*Financial Post*, January 15, 1999).

I asked Harry what he thought was the best invention of the past thousand years. He said, "I think you would have to go a long way to find something as useful as the rolling lint remover."

Jamaica. At the time (the late seventies), there were only two Club Meds in the Caribbean. They were always so full that it was hard to get a booking. Hedonism was launched on the premise that it would try to outdo Club Med at every turn, including the adoption of a staff attitude that was trained to be more relaxed and friendly than Club Med's chic, but sometimes haughty, French one.

Except for complimentary wine with lunch and dinner, Club Med sells plastic beads that are used to buy drinks at the bar. At Hedonism, even the drinks are included. The brainchild of our Harry, Alan Murphy, and George Whitfield, it quickly became one of the most successful resorts in the Caribbean and remains so to this day. Of course, success is a spur to the copycat. It wasn't long before Club Med and Hedonism were copied by Couples (also designed by Harry and friends), which was copied by Sandals, which has been copied with variations by dozens of others all over the sunny side of the world.

## TECHNOLOGY CREATES NEW DIRECTIONS

There's not much novelty in the funeral casket business, but there's a new way to sell them: online. Joseph White, vice-president of Catskill Casket, says his sales from his online retail outlet have doubled every year for the past three years, now bringing in about $200,000 annually (*Business 2.0*, 1999). Harry wonders what people do with a casket. Do they buy it and keep it in the basement until they need it? Do they set it up as a coffee table? If they buy it for an expired relative, do they keep him in the basement until the casket arrives? And do they pray that there won't be a UPS strike while an odorous body lies in state?

Technology often stimulates a brand to go in a new direction with new and improved benefits. Mixed with a healthy dose of imagination, it allows Progressive Insurance to turn itself inside out with revolutionary ways to help you deal with car insurance. Chances are, if you get in an accident, a Progressive claims adjuster will be on the scene before the police. The adjuster is authorized to assess the damage, write up a claim form on her trusty laptop, and cut you a check right on the spot! Because you don't know when an accident will happen, the service is available round the clock and on weekends. Can you imagine an insurance company that treats an emergency like an emergency and settles a claim in minutes instead of months?

> Technology often stimulates a brand to go in a new direction with new and improved benefits.

CEO Peter Lewis drives this sea change with the philosophy that anything the company does has to be good for the customer or they won't do it. He calls one of his innovations "information transparency." It's a policy of sharing with their customers information on prices, costs, and services—including what Progressive's competitors are offering, even when the competitor's rates are cheaper. It's a case of honesty pays and speed sells because it saves money, helps customer and employee morale, improves on-the-spot accuracy, and lowers prices. Is it any wonder that Progressive is taking on the big boys and growing at a rate that is six times the industry average? Just writing about it gets me excited. You can call 1-800-AUTO-PRO, or visit Progressive on the Web for a quote. It's one of the first companies to sell car insurance over the Web in 15 states (*Fast Company*, 1996).

## SHOP 'TIL YOU DROP

Internet shopping for the consumer is almost sure to provide very different ways to buy all the ordinary things that you need every day. It provides a great opportunity for a whole new category of brands created to emulate the carriage trade of a hundred years ago. I find it fascinating that a company called Streamline Inc. delivers groceries, dry cleaning, and photo processing to the homes of over 2,000 online shoppers near Boston. You need a garage so that the deliveryman can access a specially installed refrigerator when you're not home, but for $30 a month, you can forgo fighting the hordes at the supermarket. What's most telling is that Streamline has a 90 percent retention rate among customers, who order on average 47 out of 52 weeks of the year. By building a productive database on its customers' wants and needs, Streamline can customize and add to its delivery repertoire as a way to build customer loyalty.

A company called Peapod has a similar service in the Chicago area, and others are starting up across the country. There will always be people who like pushing a cart around the supermarket rather than spending another precious weekend hour in bed. They like the sociability of rubbing shoulders. It's a form of entertainment. Harry swears grocery shopping is a great way to meet women, and there's also the squeeze factor (you can't squeeze the plums on the Internet). But my bet is that online shopping for ordinary products will become as normal as picking up the phone and ordering a pepperoni pizza.

## TECHNOLOGY AND DISCLOSURE

Winning customers through complete disclosure is another new point of difference that finds its origins in technology. Discount broker Schwab aims to use the Internet to be the utopian integrator of all your personal financial planning and execution. Citicorp and Bank of America are available online with good investment products, but rather than go to a source that tells you only what it wants you to know, you can now go to Schwab and get the information you need to choose from a multitude of financial products and services that cover retirement, investing, mortgages, taxes, and insurance. Schwab's Co-CEO David Potruck believes the Internet makes vendor-specific products a liability. Online, the competitor's product is just a mouse click away. He says, "Companies don't own the customer anymore. So trying to build walls around the customer isn't going to work" (*Fortune*, 1988).

## SUSTAINED DIFFERENTIATION

The Schwab example proves another point: A tangible, demonstrative product difference will always be manna from heaven, but it is indeed tough to maintain, and it may be as Tom Duncan and Sandra Moriarty say in *Driving Brand Value* (1997): "Sustained differentiation must now come from the softer side of the business—superior customer service, useful information, and a commitment to shared values." In other words, differentiation doesn't have to come from a physical fact like two scoops of raisins. An emotional difference can be just as compelling. "It's the real thing" is the rallying call of Coca-Cola's authenticity and could provide the company with a lot more than a slogan for its advertising. It so pervades the world's psyche that it could give Coca-Cola an opportunity to be "real" in all its dealings—not just with customers, but with its bottlers, employees, local communities where it has plants, government, Wall Street, and all the others in its potential constituency. "It's the real thing" is (or could be) a declaration of character and the yardstick by which Coke measures the strength and projection of its reputation. It's not a slogan. It's a philosophy. Customers love the intimacy of knowing

> A tangible, demonstrative product difference will always be manna from heaven, but it is indeed tough to maintain.

what a company stands for. I will never understand why Coke doesn't simply go with this great brand idea.

Soft-side differentiation is becoming the heart and soul of the new brand and the building of customer loyalty. It's just as real as any benefit we think of as tangible. Example: Harry went to his local dry cleaner to pick up what had been a badly stained linen jacket. He gave the owner, Dominique, the receipt and the exact amount of money. The dry cleaner handed back a dollar. Harry thought it was a mistake, but Dominique said, "I used less cleaning fluid than I first thought I would, so I'm not going to charge you what I first thought it would cost." Harry says, "Don't you think Dominique is going to get every gravy stain I will ever have the pleasure of creating?"

The soft side is exciting because it puts the emphasis on tangible feelings, as well as tangible things. Dell Computer offers a huge price advantage with its direct-sales business model, but there's also nothing vague about Michael Dell's vision of service. He says, "From the start, our entire business—from design to manufacturing to sales—was oriented around listening to the customer, responding to the customer, and delivering what the customer wanted. Our direct relationship—first through telephone calls, then through face-to-face interactions, and now through the Internet—has enabled us to benefit from real-time input from real customers regarding product and service requirements, products on the market, and future products they would like to see developed" (Dell, 1999).

Nothing could be softer than that, but it's difficult to imagine anything adding more to Dell's differentiation in the marketplace. Could it be a big part of the reason why Dell is now worth $18 billion and gets stunning Internet sales of $12 million a day?

Home Depot helps build its hardware empire with soft information that says to the customer, "We're with you all the way." The brand gives you free courses on common construction projects, such as laying tile, building fences, and all kinds of other useful stuff. You can get instant, expert project advice from just about any member of its floor staff, which is the way the old village hardware store used to do business. A small contractor can get a slew of valuable services that are quite unique.

Home Depot also allows you to return any product for any reason with a refreshing absence of bureaucracy. If you take back a curtain rod because the end part is missing, chances are the security person at the store entrance will simply take back the old rod and let you go into the store to get a new one on your own. You don't have to go through the hassle of going to a return-merchandise desk to prove you have a receipt. That kind of trust is totally refreshing. One story I heard about Home Depot is that they took back a set of tires they don't even sell.

## THE SOFTER SIDE OF . . .

Speaking of hardware, it's difficult to see the words "soft side" without thinking of Sears and the admonition to "Come see the softer side of Sears." I would like to think that this wonderfully alliterative thought is a lot more than a slogan; that it refers to more than the suggestion of Sears as a purveyor of merchandise that goes beyond its traditional association with hardware. The "softer side" could be a forecast of the gentle treatment you will get when you deal with Sears—not in lip service, but in fact. It could characterize the good manners Sears wishes to demonstrate in all its brand relationships. It could be a promise of outstanding behavior, not just of outstanding advertising.

## HE MADE MY DAY

Sometimes soft-side differentiation comes through in little more than a different attitude. FedEx people are notoriously efficient and good mannered, but they occasionally outdo themselves. I was in Toronto on business recently and had to send an early morning FedEx package. I called the FedEx office at 7 A.M. and said I had to send a rush package to Chicago. The FedEx person on the other end of the line said, "Oh, goodie, goodie! We *love* doing that kind of stuff!" It was as if I were maybe the third person who had ever called on FedEx to deliver a package. That young man's simple utterance made my day.

By all means: be better; but above all: be different. And remember that being truly human is the biggest and best of all differences.

## CHAPTER 10

# The Experiential Brand

We truly feel brands. Imitating Bill Clinton, we even feel their pain. When Levi's ran into difficulty in 1999, it was like an old friend had gotten himself into trouble and we should rush in to help. It made us feel sad. There was a genuine hue and cry of anguish across the land. Stories full of analysis and advice appeared in newspapers for over a week. The influential *New York Times Magazine* ran a feature article.

There used to be a saying, "What's good for General Motors is good for the country." For a while, it seemed as though what was bad for Levi's was bad for the country.

It's astonishing how an inexpensive pair of trousers can become a totem for a nation. It's the same with a sticky-sweet, brown liquid that I don't even have to name to have you know it. Step right up and down one, and you feel a lot more than slaked thirst when that great sip goes down. One good swig and you can hear the stirring music of the Star Spangled Banner played by the Marine Corps band. You might feel like placing your hand over heart, as you imagine the ascent of the Stars and Stripes up the flagpole in your head. If it weren't so true, it would be ludicrous.

## POWERFUL EMOTIONS SELL BRANDS

I thought of calling this book The Brand Experience because I think the most powerful brands engender powerful emotions. They all go way beyond the confines of their product dimensions. They create their own mind space. They give you not just a physical product or service, but an experience that engages your imagination. It's often hard to describe the feeling some brands give you when you use them because much of it lives in the shallows of your consciousness. When you strap on your Rolex in the morning, do you really feel like a business titan going off to do battle on the corporate seas? Yeah, I suppose, but who will admit it even if they think it? When you get behind the wheel of that BMW to go to the corner store, do you really feel like you're charging down the autobahn like a virtual king of the road? Yeah, maybe, but it sounds silly when you say it. It's like Harry and his Armani spectacles. Wearing them is a real trip somewhere in that deep, dark place that is the background of his mind.

## THE EXPERIENCE OF BRANDS

While all brands engender feelings, some are designed to give you more of an experience in the true sense of the word than others. The most powerful of them go beyond the conventional to steal your heart away. The most famous example is the Disney brand, which gives all ages engrossing entertainment that becomes a temporarily transforming experience in its theme parks. Adults might set out for Disneyland for the sake of their children, but they're soon won over by Mickey and his fellow comic stars to become ardent Disneyphiles, just like the kids. Walt Disney Attractions exec Tony Altobelli says of the brand, "We sell happiness. It is the best product in the world" (*National Post Business*, 1999). General Foods and P&G (to say nothing of the corner coffee shop) could easily have thought beyond coffee as a commodity. But it took Starbucks to turn a cup of java from its gleaming, hissing, and gurgling machines into a deeply satisfying coffee experience. They took on the role of the protagonist for everything that is good about coffee. They made the brand a status symbol with a flavor, not only of rich coffee, but also of European chic. You go into Starbucks to order your

> Adults might set out for Disneyland for the sake of their children, but they're soon won over by Mickey and his fellow comic stars to become ardent Disneyphiles, just like the kids.

double espresso, and you feel like a coffee connoisseur somewhere in France or Italy. It's easy to rationalize three or four bucks a cup for the rich brew because it *feels* so good. And we don't mind that Starbucks' margins are five times the industry average because the *experience* is worth it. Giving us such an intense experience is why Starbucks became a $700 million global brand in relatively short order.

The *Harvard Business Review* talks about creating this new kind of "market space" in its January/February 1999 issue. "What Starbucks did for coffee, Swatch did for budget watches," say writers W. Chan Kim and Renee Mauborgne. Citizen and Seiko were serving us well enough with watches that gave us accurate time from quartz technology, but you bought one watch and it lasted a long time. Swatch turned budget watches into fun fashion statements. The article says, "In Italy the average person owns six Swatches to fit their different moods and looks." Once more, one brand gives you a certain experiential advantage with an emotional component you simply don't get from any other. The brand becomes nothing more than an artifact that points the way to an experience.

Barnes & Noble and Borders opened book superstores that give a very different experience in a new kind of market space. As the article notes, they hire people with an intelligent love of books to help you find them. They encourage browsing and provide comfortable chairs and quiet corners to do it in. They stay open late. Some have coffee shops where you can sip a sophisticated *latte* with your purchase. You actually feel smarter in their stores than in an ordinary mall bookstore. They "transformed the product from the book itself into the pleasure of reading and intellectual exploration. In less than six years, Borders and B&N have emerged as the two largest bookstore chains in the United States, with a total of more than 650 superstores between them."

Vacation resorts used to think the only thing they had to give you was a clean room, a key, and a beach. France's Club Méditerranée changed all that with a total vacation experience. I won't repeat the story told in a previous chapter, but if you've ever been to a Club Med and seen the assembled, scantily-clad vacationers singing a rousing chorus of the club song ("Hands up, baby, hands up, baby, give me your heart, give me, give me, your heart, give me, give me, . . ., etc.), you realize that a brand can be a little like a contagion. As already discussed, other brands came along to copy the Club Med model (Hedonism, Couples, Sandals, etc.), but it was Club Med that changed the conventional vacation paradigm and consequently changed the sandy coasts of several Caribbean countries with a vast proliferation of all-inclusive resorts.

Lexus gave us a new definition of a luxury experience that was perhaps more approachable (or less intimidating) than Mercedes, BMW, or Jaguar. As Kim and Mauborgne say, "Creating a new market space is critical[,] not just for start-ups but also for the prosperity and survival of even the world's largest companies. Take Toyota as an example. Within three years of its launch in 1989, the Lexus accounted for nearly one-third of Toyota's operating profit while representing only 2 percent of its volume. Moreover, the Lexus boosted Toyota's brand image across its entire range of cars."

Going back to Swatch, they report of parent company SMH, "Its collection of watch companies ranges from Blancpain, whose watches retail for over $200,000, to Omega, the watch of astronauts, to midrange classics such as Hamilton and Tissot and the sporty watches of Longines and Rado. Yet it was the creation of Swatch and the market of fun, fashionable watches that revitalized the entire Swiss watch industry and made SMH the darling of investors and customers the world over."

## WHAT'S FOR DINNER?

Even such a seemingly plebeian experience like grocery shopping can be full of fun and feeling. And why not? An activity as charged with fundamental energy as food gathering should touch the deepest wellsprings of the human psyche. *Fast Company* magazine (April 1999) writes about Central Market in Austin, Texas, where the shopping experience is so intense that it has become a tourist attraction. It goes beyond the sheer abundance of choice that includes 17 varieties of apples, 30 kinds of handmade sausage, 18 blends of citrus juice, 200 varieties of olive oil and 500 cheeses. Central Market Vice-President John

> Even such a seemingly plebeian experience like grocery shopping can be full of fun and feeling.

Campbell says, "It's about the shopping experience, not about selection. We want people to feel uplifted when they walk out of here."

Kids receive helium-filled balloons. Customers can take a cooking course from the resident chef. Employees are called partners. A person with the title of "Foodie" walks around all day talking to customers as a food consultant. She has a free hand to rip open any package and let customers taste the product.

Conventional supermarket wisdom puts all the merchandise on shelves arranged in aisles to make it easy for customers to shop as quickly as possible and head for the cash registers. Central Market has no aisles; rather, merchandise runs along a single path that winds through the 63,000 square-foot building—a layout that allows for 20 percent more shelf space and makes sure customers get an eyeful of the market's lavish and inviting presentation style.

A couple who met in the store while shopping in the cheese section actually asked to get married there. Store staffers built a cheddar wedding arch, beneath which the couple exchanged vows.

The Central Market experience goes on and on. *Fast Company* states of the store, "Last year, it began bringing in a million dollars a week on a regular basis. The store, which cost $10 million to $15 million to launch, needed two years to reach profitability." Another Central Market was recently opened just a few miles down the road. If you can't get to Austin, you can visit the market at www.central-market.com.

## AN INTERNATIONAL FLAVOR

John Summers, who works with us at Brandtrust but makes Toronto home, tells me that the Loblaws chain is racking up huge success with supermarkets that give the customer the feeling of shopping in an enormous, international gourmet deli. He says he "feels" the food experience because it goes so far beyond just filling a cart with what's on the grocery list. It's a colorful celebration of delectables—an overflowing cornucopia of delicious things to eat and drink from all around the world. The store's superb private-label brand (called President's Choice) is actually being sold in some U.S. grocery stores as a regular brand.

You have to wonder why more supermarkets don't catch on to the idea that shopping for food can be made almost as exciting as Zsa Zsa Gabor shopping for exotic jewelry. My friend raves about President's Choice Decadent Chocolate Chip cookies. He says he would testify in a court of law that they are indeed decadence to die for. He says they also took 30 percent of the Canadian cookie market in a matter of months and are now Canada's best selling cookie brand.

Loblaws has a cooking school also, and you get the feeling that its employees are food experts, not clerks. The brand lives up to the ad line under its logo, which says, "A Passion For Food."

## YOU MUST DELIVER THE GOODS

Planet Hollywood was supposed to give you a theme-inspired restaurant experience, but the concept is in trouble, to the point of bankruptcy. Its stock has gone from a high of $25 to around a buck in the spring of 1999. One blinding glimpse of the obvious might be that the restaurants get poor food reviews, and the food is expensive for what it is. As *Marketing* magazine (October 16, 1999) reports, "A bread-and-circuses approach to dining only works if the 'bread' is palatable." Another reason might be that Sylvester, Arnold, Bruce, and Demi might be losing both their interest in the restaurants and their ability to draw the younger crowd that would be attracted to such an experience.

As Emily Dickenson wrote:

**Fame is a bee.**
**It has a song —**
**It has sting—**
**Ah, too, it has a wing.**

As a brand concept, Planet Hollywood always struck me as transparent plastic hype, but that could be because I'm outside the demographic profile. I know we go to restaurants for entertainment, as much as food, but I find it hard to associate the principal stars with even a vaguely tasty dining experience. They may represent beefcake, but what have they got to do with relevant gourmet noshing? And does anyone honestly expect to rub shoulders with a roomful of movie stars when they go to Planet Hollywood? As one reporter said, it could be a long time before you find a Sly in your soup.

## HITTING THE ROAD

Anyone who loves motorcycles is likely to acquire an ear-to-ear grin upon hearing the name Indian. Indian motorcycles first adorned the road in 1901. The company ran into difficulty and went kaput in 1953, but it's a tribute to the brand's cachet that enthusiasts manage to keep about 50,000 of them on the go. Now The Indian Motorcycle Company is about to bring the legendary brand back to life in many guises for a total life experience.

Working with the newly merged California Motorcycle Company, Indian President and CEO Murray Smith wants to make and sell $200 million worth of Indian machines in 1999. Five years from now, he expects Indian to be a billion-dollar brand, producing 40,000 motorcycles for sale in twelve countries. The major word here is *brand*. The image Smith wants to evoke is that of a comfortable, casual, classic lifestyle, populated by people with an appreciation for what he calls "vintage quality."

He intends to extend the reach of the motorcycle brand to include Indian Motorcycle Cafe & Lounge operations in twelve North American cities. He calls them "brand shrines." There is also a line of modern, casual, Gap-like clothing expected to grow beyond current sales of $6 million a year. He says, "Age doesn't matter—if you've got that appreciation, we've got the product for you, whether it be a motorcycle, our children's wear line, the bicycle line we're coming out with, going to the cafe for dinner or billiards or an evening of jazz, or just to look at the bikes."

He will also license the Indian name to other companies that make things like sunglasses, cigars, and video games. Says Smith, "The bike is the launch pad. The Indian-brand promise must always relate to that casual, comfortable, vintage, quality theme. If it does, we'll be a success" (*The Financial Post Magazine*, 1999).

## Study Demographic Trends

Excuse the pun, but it sounds as though the Indian brand intends to be an experience that will get you revved through many of your life's passages. But I would caution Mr. Smith to keep an eye on North American demographic trends.

If the Indian follows the Harley-Davidson example, its riders won't have to be young to appreciate the experience. But we do have an aging population and very few geezers ride motorcycles.

Boomers are now buying record numbers of motorcycles, but by 2010, most of the Boomer cohort will have passed fifty, and its leading edge will be well into its sixties. Younger people won't go away, but we'll have a lot fewer of them.

The number of aging Boomers guaranteed to be in our future will create an aged population unprecedented in human history. Their goal will be to preserve their bodies, not risk them by whizzing around on two skinny wheels. If they don't ride the brand, they may also not want to wear it or eat it. Quality goods based on vintage nostalgia work for something like Ralph Lauren's Polo brand, but wearing one of his blazers doesn't threaten to break brittle old bones!

For now, however, the rebirth of Indian motorcycles ties in nicely to a global demand for heavyweight bikes; a demand that amounted to $3.2 billion in 1999. But it poses no threat to Harley-Davidson. Harley is an example of what is probably *the* experiential brand of all time. The company nearly went under 25 years ago. It's funny to think that AMF could hardly give this brand away when it was sold to 13 Harley executives in 1981. Now a $2 billion brand, it can't make enough of the machines that are "a little special, a little mysterious, a little bad." Owning a "hog" literally represents a lifestyle and a source of identity; like Coke and Levi's, it presents a very American experience with a worldwide following.

> Owning a "hog" literally represents a lifestyle and a source of identity; like Coke and Levi's, it presents a very American experience with a worldwide following.

## THEY ARE SERIOUS ABOUT THEIR HOGS

There are quite a few brands that you can "wear" as a badge that signals who you are, but none compare with "wearing" a Harley. In fact, the most popular tattoo in the United States is the Harley-Davidson logo. David Aaker (1996) writes of Harley owners, "Over 250,000 of them belong to one of roughly 800 chapters of the Harley Owners Group (H.O.G.). The H.O.G. members receive a bimonthly newsletter and attend weekly or monthly meetings, as well as motorcycle outings sponsored by dealerships. A 'Ladies of

Harley' subgroup caters to the 10 percent of Harley owners who are women. Approximately forty-two state rallies are held each year in addition to a series of major national club rallies that include a Spring Bike Week in Daytona Beach and a summer gathering in Sturgis, South Dakota, that draws tens of thousands. In June 1993, more than 20,000 H.O.G. members (plus another 80,000 Harley-Davidson enthusiasts of all kinds) went to Milwaukee to celebrate the firm's ninetieth anniversary." Company personnel and dealers are all intimately involved with their customers. They are part of the rally and club action, which gives them close contact and important two-way communication opportunities with customers.

## A DIFFERENT PERSPECTIVE

The people who buy Japanese motorcycles are apparently very different, and the difference is yet another fascinating fact of the power of brand mythology. David Aaker notes, "Owners of Japanese motorcycles generally have a very different perspective toward life and their bikes. They tend to talk about the features of the bike rather than the riding experience. In fact, Japanese bikes are engineering marvels. They are quiet, smooth, capable of higher speeds than Harleys, and full of such features as digital instruments, rear speakers, reverse gear, fans, and even air conditioners. Their owners tend to look down their noses at the anachronistic design and noisy, throaty roar of Harleys. To a Harley-Davidson owner, however, the sound, feel, and look of his or her bike is part of the experience. Even the infamous Harley vibrations are treasured by aficionados. The owner of a Japanese motorcycle focuses on functional benefits, whereas the Harley-Davidson owner is much more concerned with emotional and self-expressive benefits."

## MOVING BEYOND JUST SELLING

In *The Experience Economy: Work Is Theater and Every Business a Stage,* B. Joseph Pine II and James H. Gilmore put forth the idea that the economy has moved to a new phase that revolves around the staging of experiences rather than simply selling products and services. "When a person buys a service," they say, "he purchases a set of intangible activities carried out on his behalf. But when he buys an experience, he pays to spend time enjoying a series of memorable events that a company stages—as in a theatrical play—to engage him in a personal way."

They believe "the experience sector will gobble up the service sector just as surely as the service sector has reduced the size and influence of the manufacturing sector." Going further, they believe that you should be able to charge for a really good service experience. People go into a store, such as the Sharper Image, and stroll around, playing with all the gizmos on display. They enjoy the shopping experience, but often walk out empty-handed. Pine and Gilmore apparently believe that if an even better experience could be staged, customers would be prepared to pay an entrance fee. The same for an intensified experience performed by a store such as Nike Town (like a one-on-one basketball experience with an NBA player) (*Fast Company*, 1999).

This concept is interesting speculation, and if nothing else, when anybody writes a book about a subject, it shows that the idea is getting thought and attention. This is particularly true of Joe Pine, who wrote the book *Mass Customization* (Harvard Business School Press, 1992).

## FIND THE ESSENCE OF YOUR CUSTOMER'S EXPERIENCE

Harry sees the merit of experiential brands, but he doesn't personally like experiential restaurants. He says they remind him of a Hungarian joint he used to go to years ago: "The place was decorated to simulate folksy Budapest. While you were eating dinner, a couple of very old guys dressed as gypsies would stroll around, playing deep-schmaltz rhapsodies on their violins. They would come up to your table and play for you and your date with big, maniacal smiles to go along with their very dramatic style of playing. Of course, you felt compelled to pretend you were listening very intently and with great pleasure. You could do nothing but sit there, nodding phony approval as your chicken paprika got cold. After what seemed like a lifetime, you were desperately wishing they would move on so you could get back to trying to impress your date. The only way to get rid of them was to slip them each a fin. You then took great pleasure in the discomfort they were causing at the next table on their rounds."

Harry's opinion notwithstanding, you have the opportunity to find the essence of the customer's experience with your product or service, and incorporate it into your branding effort. This is golden advice for a new brand, but please remember that an old dog can indeed learn all manner of new tricks. They simply have to be discovered, or, as is often the case, rediscovered.

A good place to start is with the kind of right-brain research described earlier. For many brands, there may be prophecy in Shakespeare's words from *As You Like It*: "All the world's a stage, And all the men and women merely players."

# PART Four

# BUILDING BRANDS

# WITH MEANING

# 11

# What Your Brand Stands For: The Principles of Principals

Mark Twain said, "Always do right. This will gratify some people and astonish the rest."

He could have been describing the behavior of so many of today's leaders who build brands by "doing right." They know that a product might exist in a social vacuum, but in today's transparent business atmosphere, a brand can't. Leading by and with an exhibition of values is a practical and philosophical imperative because it builds the trust that builds the relationships that build brand loyalty.

Much like Thomas Jefferson, these new leaders start with some basic truths and hold them to be self-evident. Values plainly spell out character. They form your brand's identity for all of the world to see.

A former top man at Coca-Cola, Robert Goizueta, said, "A CEO is ultimately responsible for the growth of a company as evidenced by its financial performance, its capacity for self renewal, and its character. The only way you can measure character is by reputation" (Fombrun, 1996). I add that the only way you can measure reputation is by how closely you observe self-imposed values.

Values aren't sucky. They give a company something to hold on to beyond an enviably fat bottom line, but even profit plays a role in values. As Peter Drucker says, " . . . the *first* social responsibility of a business is to produce an adequate surplus. Without a surplus, it steals the commonwealth and deprives society and the economy of the capital needed to provide jobs for tomorrow."

Self-interest makes the bottom line a matter of everybody's concern, but in dealings with each other and with the people over them, standing on a solid ground of shared values is surely what can sustain and guide employees day to day. Just as surely, they show up in our attitudes toward a brand's customers and its other vital stakeholders.

Shared values simply contribute to *l'esprit de corps* in immeasurable ways that affect a brand's overall competence. Think of the United States Marine Corps and its belief in the tradition generated by the motto *Semper Fidelis* (always faithful). Then think of how a CEO can build faith in his entire community, as he leads his brand into the business version of daily adversity and harm's way.

> Standing on a solid ground of shared values is surely what can sustain and guide employees day to day.

## THE HUMAN SOCIAL CONTRACT

Values for good or bad always find their source with the guys at the top, and we see that fostering beliefs and actions from well-conceived values isn't a pointless exercise in navel gazing; rather, it's very much of this earth. It's muscular ethics. It's brawny basics. It's practical purity. It's the vision thing mixed with no-nonsense common sense. It doesn't deny a tough, competitive spirit, but it sees that all things come around, so you might as well start at the right spot on the moral compass—a spot (that seems to me) inextricably linked with the simple ethic of making our dealings with each other more humane.

Somewhere along the line, we got the idea that business is about being as brutish and uncaring as a company of thugs. We even use terms like "cut-throat business tactics." But this notion cannot be anything but false. The foundation of business is now—and always has been—about relationships and the trust that exists in the human social contract. The contract may be sometimes broken, and sometimes *often* broken, but that indicates to me that it is indeed nothing more than human. And being more and more humane in business is something we're getting better at doing.

In *The New Pioneers* (1999), Thomas Petzinger Jr. writes about this phenomenon with brilliant clarity and elegance. He writes,

> But while the old order persists, the new order is rising alongside it—haltingly in some places, unevenly in others, but inexorably in every corner of the economy. How can I be so sure of this? Two reasons.
>
> First, the marketplace leaves companies with little choice. In an era when change arrives without warning and threatens to eradicate the foundations of entire companies and entire industries overnight, organizations can survive only by becoming more human. Businesses that fail to engage the eyes, ears, minds and emotions of every individual in the organization will find themselves overrun by obsolescence or crushed by competition.
>
> Second, the new, more enlightened way of business will persist because it hews more closely to what we are as humans. One of the many economic paradoxes . . . is that the advancing ethos of business is returning to what business has sometimes been in the past, and what it was meant to be.

> "**B**usinesses that fail to engage the eyes, ears, minds and emotions of every individual in the organization will find themselves overrun by obsolescence or crushed by competition."

## WHAT BRANDS TRULY MEAN

When it comes to brands, these "new pioneers" are likely to see them not as things, but as living entities with both rational and emotional content. We're beginning to see brands and what they truly mean in a bright, human light. Winning hearts is as important as winning minds for a brand's success. Brand loyalty is won with the facts of product performance, coupled with its broader mythology.

John Costello, president of Republic Industries in Fort Lauderdale says, "The essence of a brand is the sum total of the customer's experience. It's not just the latest advertising campaign or what (consumers) hear or read about a brand. It's what they experience in using your brand."

Promus Hotel Corp.'s Tom Storey adds, "The definition of your brand is broader than the actual product benefits and features. You have to look at the brand's total 'takeaway' and how it fits into the consumer's reference. At what makes people feel differently about your brand . . . People make decisions about brands for many reasons they don't tell you about. They rationalize about a decision they actually make on deeper emotional levels" (Delaney, 1999).

## DOING RIGHT

It's as though really successful brands develop a higher sensitivity—a sort of consciousness they can use to create both new opportunity and self-defense. This is why the concept of "doing right" isn't a branding frill. It's a conscious necessity for reaching out to all of a brand's stakeholders—customers, employees, shareholders, and governments. But since customers provide the critical pivot for success, it usually focuses on them. If you want to be crass about it, there's a lot of logic in the idea that a high moral sensibility makes hardheaded business sense.

If you think mooring a brand to moral accountability is softheaded nonsense, take a look at a highly successful company like Intuit. Intuit made its highly successful mark by pioneering financial software. With such a left-brain focus, it would seem like a highly unlikely candidate for anything as soft-sided as values. But cofounder Scott Cook will tell you that the company was indeed built on a set of core values that have contributed enormously to its success.

Cook says he has witnessed huge change at Intuit in the past few years, but if you ask him what stays the same, he will say, "Values." He will add, "The best companies stand for something. In our case, it is to do right by the customer."

*Fast Company* magazine (1998, October) reports that, "In 1993 Intuit identified a set of values that describes how it operates and what makes it different."

## VALUE OR PRINCIPLE?

Stephen Covey (1990) would say that Cook confuses the word "value" with the word "principle." He says the Nazis had values, but they violated basic principles. Values are maps. Principles are the compass. Maps can change. The compass always points true north. "An accurate map is a good management tool, but a compass is a leadership and empowerment tool."

I would add that a principle is like an objective, and values are the strategies for reaching it. Whatever classification the following are, I'm not about to split Scott Cook's hairs for him.

As *Fast Company* reports, "Lots of companies have value statements, of course. But few are as plain-spoken or as heartfelt as Intuit's."

Here are excerpts from Intuit's ten core values:

1. **Integrity Without Compromise. Having integrity means more to us than simply the absence of deception. It means we are completely forthright in all our dealings. We say what needs to be said, not simply what people want to hear.**
2. **Do Right by All Our Customers. Doing right means acting with the best interests of the other party in mind. An important word in this phrase is "all"—it includes every relationship at Intuit. We treat each other, our business partners, and our shareholders with the same care and respect with which we treat our customers.**
3. **It's The People. We have great people who want to do well, who are capable of doing great things, and who come to work fired up to achieve them. Great people flourish in an environment that liberates and amplifies their energy.**
4. **Seek The Best. We seek the best in two ways: We cast wide nets to find the best people to hire and the best ideas to adopt, and we base decisions regarding them on facts.**
5. **Continually Improve Processes. How do we know if a process needs improving? The answer is: it always does. We can always get better. We strive continually to improve our processes, to help people do their jobs better, and to produce higher quality at lower cost.**
6. **Speak, Listen, and Respond. Managers at Intuit have a responsibility to create an environment that encourages**

people to speak openly, knowing they will be listened to when they do. Listening, however, is only a first step. It's also key to *respond*—if not through direct action, then through acknowledgement or feedback.

7. Teamwork. Teamwork means focusing on the team's success, realizing that ultimately the team's success is your success. It also means that you succeed by helping other members of the team to succeed. The result? Decisions that are not "mine" or "yours"—but rather *better* solutions.

8. Customers Define Quality. Part of adapting to changing customer needs and desires is knowing what our customers want. Intuit has triumphed in part because we actively solicit input from our customers.

9. Think Fast, Move Fast. Customers want to benefit from our great ideas sooner—not later. So do we. Moving fast enables us to learn and to make better decisions over time. That's because the best learning comes from trying out more things in the real world.

10. We Care and Give Back. We believe that with our success comes the responsibility to give back to our community. We seek to contribute to our community in ways that reflect broadly held values, have meaningful impact, draw on our unique strengths as a corporation, and, whenever possible, reinforce our business objectives.

These aren't bad lessons for a company to live by, and "live" is the operative word. You might say them. You might write them down as Intuit has done. But they must not become motherhood. Unless you share them as values to live by with those around you, unless everybody takes them to heart to practice rather than preach, they're just expired air. From what I know of Scott Cook and Intuit, they are practiced as much as preached. It reminds those of us who run companies to ask ourselves, what are our principles and the values that emanate from them? And have we taken the time and trouble to write them down in plain and simple language so that they can be shared and adopted?

One way to think about principle-centered leadership is to consider the alternative. Can you be more successful if you don't value

> One way to think about principle-centered leadership is to consider the alternative. Can you be more successful if you don't value your employees?

your employees? What about ignoring integrity? Or purposely cutting corners? And not caring what customers think of you and what you have to offer? What about adopting a policy of taking advantage of your suppliers and cheating your employees every chance you get? These toxic alternatives are, of course, ridiculous. They make as much sense as shooting your toes off, so you never have to cut your toenails. But while a company would never publicly adopt such values, some of them give the appearance of doing just that. They may even give it a purpose under the misnomer of "shareholder value."

### MINDSPRING'S FOURTEEN DEADLY SINS

Another principle-based company that comes to mind is Mind-Spring, the Atlanta-based Internet service provider. Launched only five years ago, MindSpring Enterprises Inc. has 600 employees and a market cap of $1.5 billion. It has 600,000 customers around the country and annual revenues exceeding $100 million. Founder and CEO Scott Brewer reflects the company's "down-home" values. As journalist Gina Imperata writes, "Its 'chief operating Rottweiler' is a three-legged dog named Louie. There's beat-up furniture in the waiting room, and there are plastic lawn chairs in the chief executive's office." She quotes founder and CEO Charles Brewer: "Some companies can succeed with a high-spending style. That's not us."

Brewer attributes much of MindSpring's rising success to what he calls going back to basics, one of which is honesty and an apparent penchant for understatement. He says candidly, "A year after we started we were the leading ISP in Atlanta. Our service wasn't perfect. But we made customers happier than the competition did. We told the truth. When there were problems, we did our best to make things right. And customers felt that we were basically competent people. If you do that, people will give you a break."

President and COO Michael McQuary says, "The most important thing about this company is its culture," much of which is defined by nine core values and beliefs. One of those core values and beliefs states, "We make commitments with care, and then live up to them." Another notes, "Work is an important part of life, and it should be fun. Being a good business person does not mean being stuffy and boring."

The company also has "'The 14 Deadly Sins of MindSpring (or ways we can be just like everybody else). Sin #3: 'Make internal procedures easy on us, even if it means negatively affecting or inconveniencing the customer.' Sin #8: 'Show up at a demo, sales call, trade show, or meeting unprepared.'"

## FOLK WISDOM AND STREET SMARTS

Mixed with this kind of folk wisdom is a street-smart approach to gaining new subscribers. Customers who spread the word and provide referrals get credits against their bill. Last October, the company sent out 18,000 surveys to check up on service quality. The response was a whopping 60 percent.

Executive Vice President of Sales and Marketing Lance Weatherby says, "We get some great feedback. It's amazing. Our customers really want us to do well."

And no wonder. As Ms. Imperata's article says, "MindSpring's customer service centers handle more than 150,000 calls a month, with an average hold time of 3 minutes and 19 seconds—a stellar performance by Net standards."

Thomas Petzinger Jr. (1999) says of them, "While AOL and Microsoft often said 'don't blame us' for busy signals when local phone companies were to blame, an upstart outfit in Atlanta called MindSpring Corporation worked actively with local telcos to identify capacity problems in *their* networks—and refused to take on new customers in cities where the phone companies were slow to respond."

> Infectious enthusiasm is a mark of good leadership. If you can't be a builder of morale and confidence, who in your company can?

You get the feeling that MindSpring's executives take enormous pleasure in their business. Their infectious enthusiasm is a mark of good leadership. If you can't be a builder of morale and confidence, who in your company can? You also get the feeling that the whole company is going in the same direction.

If you've ever snorkeled and floated blissfully over a big school of fish in water as clear as vodka, you see how the entire school can change course on a dime at the slightest hint of danger or change in the environment. When you imbue your company with basic principles, you empower every member with the ability to act on everybody else's behalf, including yours. It forms a true gestalt, which means that the sum of the parts is much greater than the whole. And building with trustworthy principles means that every member of your organization—from the boy in the mail room to the chief operating rottweiler—can be effectively trusted to represent your brand. It's a wonderful way for the boss to get a good night's sleep.

Looking to our old friends, the left (logical) and right (intuitive) sides of the brain, it's easy to see that leading from a foundation of values is connected with feelings, and therefore, begins in the right side.

## LEADERSHIP AND MANAGEMENT

Stephen Covey helps illuminate our understanding by saying that leadership focuses on the top line, and management focuses on the bottom. Leadership deals with direction, while management deals with speed. Leadership deals with vision, effectiveness, and results. Management deals with the structure and systems that get the results. If you are both the manager and the leader of your brand, Covey suggests that you attempt to lead with the right brain and manage with the left.

When leading with the right, be aware of your own innate prejudice and conditioning. Call up the highest vision you can muster— one that will stir your group and you to go beyond transactional behavior. Covey says, "Every great leader has a high level of proactive energy and vision—a sense that 'I am not a product of my culture, my conditioning, and the conditions of my life; rather, I am a product of my value systems, attitudes, and behavior—and those things I control.'"

In other words, when it comes to principles and values, you can steer the brand with the conviction of classic, self-evident truths. You can center them on what you admire, what you think of as an ideal, and what you believe will inspire your staff, your suppliers, your shareholders, your customers, and, last but not least—yourself. It's as simple as knowing that all your stakeholders want to deal with a company of people they can trust and admire.

Harry says, "I can't think of anything more obvious than basing your values on the biblical thing about doing unto others as you would have them do unto you. It's advice that's been around for 2,000 years, and it comes from a guy who knew a thing or two about leading with values."

The climate for management-by-values has never been more promising. In his brilliant book *The Roaring 2000s* (1998), Harry S. Dent says, "Be sure of this: The baby boom generation will become the most moral generation in our history. Precisely because they experimented to such an extreme degree, they have learned the benefits of new approaches to life and the consequences of violating values that should endure. The next 30 years will see the baby boomers establish a new direction for cultural and moral values that will demand conscious intelligence and responsibility. It will be Generation X and the next civic-minded, millennial generation that will shape and refine these values and structures for many decades to follow."

> The climate for management-by-values has never been more promising.

## IT'S NOT PERFECT YET

Does all this mean that I believe we've seen the end of wrongdoing? That branding will ride to our moral rescue with all the noisy haste of the U.S. Cavalry? Or that all mankind has suddenly turned over a virtuous new leaf? Of course not. We will continue to see our fair share of charlatans, book cookers, swindlers, thieves, demagogues, power merchants, pirates, pilferers, crackpots, mountebanks, maniacs, bull-merchants, bullies, and Machiavellian jerks. And even when we are not operating at our worst, we have the legacy of our genetic endowment to contend with. Corporate hierarchies, for example, may indeed lose their baboon-like structural ground to horizontal organizations that work more efficiently and humanely, and principle-centered management will hopefully prevail. But there are nagging doubts that must be acknowledged along the way: We are still primates with a penchant for creating societies made up of alphas and the rest of us. We will still form exclusionary tribes and clans. We will elect leaders who demand—and get—our fixed attention with their royal jelly. Power will continue to confer sexual advantage. We will still build fences and suspect strangers. And perversions of the human spirit will continue to shock us to our very boots.

One of nature's great mysteries is why we have such poor insight into our innate behavior. We have the intelligence and imagination to invent electricity and immunology, but we haven't the slightest understanding of what makes us repeatedly commit the incalculable horrors of the twentieth century's genocides. As I write these words, there is in the Balkans a horror going on in the name of one of histories most vile terms: ethnic cleansing. We are ingenious in the ways in which we can inflict pain, suffering, and death, and no nationality is beyond it.

It appeared recently that old Darwin may provide better clues than Freud as to what makes us tick, but the infant science of evolutionary psychology may neatly combine ethology, biology, and psychology to shed a clearer light on our motivations. The point is neither perfection nor the lack of it. It's not even the ability of our species to make choices. We know only that we like to think we're somehow different from the generations of our grandfathers who measured their hours in the slow, silent eons of agriculture. And perhaps one of the most important things to know about us is that we cannot and will not stand still.

## OUR SOFTER SIDE GIVES US HOPE

We can also look for encouragement in the softer side of our genetic endowment. I hope we are not the planet's "moral animal" simply because we can be. We are a highly social animal. Most of our moral law and social grace comes to us naturally to temper the complexity of our interactions. No matter how sophisticated we become at developing the tools and efficiencies of daily life, mothers will still feel the powerful tug of caring for their young, and fathers will usually need little persuasion to stick around and lend support. We will cooperate and show kindness and decency beyond our immediate circles. We will feel the need to educate our young and venerate our elderly. We will not lose the capacity to feel deep sorrow and great joy. We will continue to create the symbols of understanding that inspire us in the form of art. And many of us will respond to the lessons of a higher calling.

As Daniel Burstein and David Kline say in *Road Warriors* (1995), ". . . perhaps we may take some comfort in knowing that however exotic the landscape of tomorrow's world might become, the felt core of human existence—the urge for family in whatever form, the need for love and belonging, and the desire to live a significant and productive life—will remain as familiar as always."

Brand builders might find even more meaning in the words of William Bernbach, cofounder of the great old Doyle Dane Bernbach ad agency, and Harry's former boss. Bernbach said, "It took millions of years for man's instincts to develop. It will take millions more for them to even vary. It is fashionable to talk about *changing* man. A communicator must be concerned with *un*changing man, with his obsessive drive to survive, to be admired, to succeed, to love, to take care of his own."

## CYNICAL OR SUCCESSFUL?

Harry presented me with this seriously elegant thought, but I wonder if he feels comfortable with such depth of feeling because he found it necessary to add: "That's all very well and good, but the most important thing to remember about evolution is that we share the same DNA with a cockroach."

I tell him he's being flippant and cynical. He replies, "On the contrary, the cockroach is one of nature's most successful creatures. Even RotoRooter can't get rid of it."

# 12

# Missions and Missionaries: Letting Everyone Know What Your Brand Stands For

People joined within a company can be inspired by shared values. But they can also be motivated by a shared purpose. And the two are not the same. Values relate to ideals and principles. Purpose relates to strategy and action. A brand's mission is a specific definition of its purpose.

A lot of business people are turned off by the notion of a mission. They think a mission is something for nuns. But once they get the idea that a mission is a strategic tool that defines purpose, they breathe easier about it. One of the reasons the word "mission" is misunderstood is because a lot of business writers confuse values and missions. Values can and often do exist within a statement of mission, but the primary benefit of such a statement is, very simply, to share a clearly defined purpose, to get everybody in the boat rowing in the same direction. (Perhaps the confusion could be eliminated if we called it a Purpose Statement rather than the fancier Mission Statement.)

## THE MISSION STATEMENT'S PURPOSE

An effective mission statement serves many needs: It can be the glue that cements the brand's focus into the minds of all its stakeholders.

It can capture the brand's emotional appeal. It can be the discipline for a brand's work. It can be called upon to give your fellow workers and you a critical reminder of what business you're really in. It can be the track that keeps a brand from veering off into tempting side issues. It can be the mirror you hold up to the brand to reflect its progress. It can be the deep root from which the brand grows. It can be the ultimate objective for all of its communication. And as Peter Drucker says, "A well defined mission serves as a constant reminder of the need to look outside the organization not only for 'customers' but also for measures of success" (*Harvard Business Review*, 1989).

If you start your brand off with thinking about its mission rather than the sugarplums of reward, so much the better. When the mission works and the rewards finally come, they taste that much sweeter. Starting with the mission before anything else is a lesson businesses can learn from nonprofit brands. Drucker illustrates the point with a quote from one executive who says, "The businesses I work with start their planning with financial returns. The nonprofits start with the performance of their mission." The latter method focuses an organization on action and the defining of specific strategies needed to attain crucial goals (*ibid.*).

**A** mission statement can be the track that keeps a brand from veering off into tempting side issues.

This kind of thinking calls for a mission that relates to the brand's work exactly (as opposed to one that merely offers good intentions). For example, Nike helps athletes maximize their performance. Hallmark cards provide people with a high-quality means of communicating emotion. Apple builds the computer ordinary folks can use. Disney provides quality, family entertainment— for both children and adults. FedEx means overnight delivery you can count on.

On the nonprofit side, the Salvation Army turns society's rejects (alcoholics, criminals, and derelicts) into citizens. The Girl Scouts help youngsters become confident, capable young women who

## THE JAPANESE AND MISSION OBJECTIVES

One of the principal reasons for the success of Japanese business is that Japanese managers do not start out with a *desired* profit; that is, with a *financial* objective in mind (Drucker, 1999). Rather, they start out with *business* objectives, and, especially, with *market* objectives. They begin by asking, "How much market standing do we need to have leadership?" "What new products do we need for this?" "How much do we need to spend to train and develop people, to build distribution, to provide the required service?"

Only then do they ask, "And how much profit is necessary to accomplish these business objectives?" Then the resulting profit *requirement* is usually a good deal higher than the profit *goal* of the Westerner.

respect themselves and other people. The Nature Conservancy preserves the diversity of nature's fauna and flora (*ibid*).

A mission can be specific *and* inspirational. Think of Thomas Jefferson and the Declaration of Independence—a purposeful mission statement that welds the transcendent spirit of the United States of America to this very day.

One has to admire the socially responsible mission of Merck, which says, "We are in the business of preserving and improving human life. All of our actions must be measured by our success in achieving this goal." A cynic might see this as lofty claptrap, but it's actually what makes Merck tick. As Tom Duncan and Sandra Moriarty say in *Driving Brand Value* (1997), "Merck's work in curing river blindness along the Amazon River and helping eliminate the tuberculosis epidemic that broke out in Japan after World War II—neither of which were profitable ventures—are examples of a socially responsible mission. Notice Merck's mission says nothing about making a profit, and yet Merck has been quite profitable over the years." I imagine, too, that such a mission statement helps Merck recruit dedicated scientists to its laboratories.

In *Selling the Invisible* (1997), Harry Beckwith says,

> The test of a mission statement is simple. A mission statement must cause change; it must change how people in your company act.
>
> Three weeks after you reveal your mission statement to everyone, ask five employees: "Have you done anything differently in the last three weeks because of what the mission statement says?"
>
> "And are you likely to change anything you do in the next three weeks?"
>
> If you get ten no's, throw out your mission statement.
>
> If your mission statement isn't producing, fire it.

## MISSION STATEMENT ALTERNATIVES

While skillful executives will not deny the value of espousing and proselytizing the focus of purpose, there are some who think that actual mission statements are rubbish. Former Burger King CEO Barry Gibbons goes so far as to call them a "total crock" (*American Way*, 1999). One of his Top Ten Laws of Business is that "If a business communication doesn't fool your mother, start again." He apparently feels that mission statements regularly fail the test, and he's probably right.

He says, "One of the great quotes of recent history came from Lou Gerstner when he took over at IBM. He was asked to state his vision for the company, and his reply was that the last thing IBM needed was one of those. What it needed was to get out of the rotten mess it had gotten itself into, not a mission statement that could be framed for the employee cafeteria or washroom."

Well, we hear you, Lou, but what could possibly be wrong with giving everybody at IBM the guiding hand of clear purpose? In fact, it can be a confusion of purpose and a loss of focus that gets a brand into trouble in the first place, including IBM. If a CEO doesn't have a clear notion of what the brand represents, how can he or she expect employees to function properly when they deal with customers and other stakeholders?

Focus is like courage: It doesn't work in half measure. A brand that wants to be a little of everything will eventually amount to a lot of nothing. That's why the days of the conglomerate may be numbered. Many of them are shedding extraneous divisions in an attempt to find a core on which they can focus their attentions. Narrow brands work best. Companies no longer grow by expanding into areas that are not part of their core activity. I will talk about line extensions in a future chapter, but anything that takes the focus off a singular mission dissipates the strength of a brand.

> A brand that wants to be a little of everything will eventually amount to a lot of nothing.

### REFINE YOUR STATEMENT

I completely agree with Gibbons, however, that a lot of mission statements are fatuous wallpaper. They do nothing more than self-stroke the egos of the executives who wrote them. An insipid mission statement does more harm than good. You know you've written a clunker when you *don't* see it pinned on the employees' walls. One large organization's written mission was "to enhance the asset base of the owners." Put that up on your company wall and count the yawns. It's not that the owners don't matter. It's just a totally selfish and ignoble example of what might motivate a group to a high level of mediocrity.

Mission statements like these survive in obscurity at the very bottom of the bottom drawer. But surely we can see the value of a written focus rather than the perpetuation of unfocused, day-to-day expediency. Surely we can climb beyond a cynical repression of our better natures. Surely we can see that people respond to clarity of purpose (and sometimes a call to nobility) and that both can be effectively communicated in a statement of mission to propel a brand.

Michael Saylor, the 35-year-old CEO of MicroStrategy, is a big believer in the power of a mission for both an individual and a company. *Fast Company* (April 2000) reports that Saylor says small missions produce small companies, but great institutions survive because their missions are "timeless, ethical, and imperative," such as his personal favorite, the Roman Empire, whose mission was to spread civilization. Of his own organization, he says, "Our mission is to make intelligence accessible anywhere."

He tells new recruits, "Call some friends tonight, and ask what their company's mission is. Then ask yourself, Would I follow that organization to the end of the earth? Or is it a place to simply spend 40 hours a week?" *Fast Company* reports that he then regales the recruits with "the story of the bridge in Alcantara, Spain that has been standing since the days of the Roman Empire—nearly 2[,]000 years. As the bridge's cornerstone attests, Caius Julius Lacer, the architect, intended it to stand for all time. Now that's an admirable mission."

## USEFUL YARDSTICKS FOR SUCCESS

There are several useful yardsticks for a mission's success. One example can be simply an internal audit of how well a mission is understood, how much it is endorsed, and how much it affects *esprit de corps* and a willingness to innovate. Another long-term measure is the degree of attitude change of the brand's constituents, both in and beyond the company. There's nothing fatuous about any of that, particularly if it contributes to a materially improved, broad-based brand perception.

It occurs to me that a CEO charged with responsibility for a brand's financial health might be held equally accountable for a measure of how clearly the brand's mission is understood and acted upon. Surely one has a bearing on the other.

If you're faced with writing a mission statement, don't despair. Start thinking about the mission (purpose) rather than how it is to be expressed. The words will come. Think about what the brand wants to accomplish in the mind of its most important customer. You might think your brand is a gift from God, but *what is its value to the customer?*

Under the best of circumstances, what would your best customer say about you—both the product and the people? If we're talking about business-to-business, what would she say is your core competency, and how would she describe it? What would be her best wish for you as a supplier/collaborator? What is it about your brand that makes your competitors nervous? Asking and answering some or all of these questions will help, but writing your brand's mission will sometimes feel like a "mission impossible." It's not something you dash off over a lunchtime martini. Some companies take months to get it right. But the time and trouble will be worth it.

Another helpful step is to think of the ideal. Remember that a mission is like a journey that never ends. A mission is what you would wish for your brand, not what your physical brand is. It is the brand's ultimate destination.

> Remember that a mission is like a journey that never ends. It is the brand's ultimate destination.

## THINK OUTWARD, NOT INWARD

It is intended to guide the action of the people responsible for the brand, to help them think outward rather than inward, so don't work on it in isolation. And certainly get it out of the boardroom. If you set the guideline that the mission has to be actionable, that it has to invoke the ideal meaning of the brand's work from the customer's point of view, you can get every member of your organization involved. After all, they have to endorse it.

As Peter Drucker says in the *Harvard Business Review* (1989, July-August), "Finally, a clearly defined mission will foster innovative ideas and help others understand why they need to be implemented. . . ." Nothing helps understanding more than involvement in the process of discovery.

Harry Beckwith says that a mission statement should be for internal consumption only. I agree with him to the degree that I don't think a company should take out a full-page ad in the *New York Times* to tell everybody its mission statement. But I also see no reason to keep it a dark secret. Any member of a company should be able to proudly tell you what its brands stand for—the feeling, as well as the fact.

## ONLY PREACH IT IF YOU BELIEVE IT

Senior Chairman of Vanguard mutual funds John Bogle (*Forbes*, 1999) will eagerly tell you, "The mission of Vanguard is not very complicated[,] but anybody who preaches it had better believe it . . . The business of managing other people's money—no matter how an enterprise is structured—must be focused on the human being it serves and the human beings who provide those services. A mutual structure may be necessary to provide both optimal services and maximum return to shareholders, but it is not sufficient. Organizational principles are involved, but so too are human principles."

This practice is Vanguard's fanatical parsimony with customer investment costs; plus, in its 25-year history, Vanguard has never had a layoff. In fact, Bogle says he would allow an increase in the expense ratio for only one reason: to save jobs.

Vanguard doesn't believe in advertising (too wasteful of customer's money), but the brand preaches the low-expense focus of its funds the way a fundamental evangelist might preach eternal salvation. The message gets a lot of attention. Couple a clearly stated mission with index funds that have outperformed most managed funds in the past few years and it's not hard to understand why Vanguard has $442 billion under management, and, in 1998, grew by a whopping 33 percent.

The guys at #1 Fidelity mutual funds can feel John Bogle breathing down their necks. (Mr. Bogle reached the age of mandatory retirement since I first wrote these words, but CEO Jack Brennan appears to be cut from a very similar evangelical focus on parsimony.)

Vanguard mirrors the thinking of a good nonprofit in that it didn't adopt its mission to provide meat for an ad campaign. It's not a marketing gimmick or a public relations stunt. The mission emerged from the beliefs and convictions of its leader long before the brand was successful; in fact, the mission was what motivated the brand's start in the first place.

> Vanguard mirrors the thinking of a good nonprofit in that it didn't adopt its mission to provide meat for an ad campaign.

When that happens, when a mission guides a business to success, it makes a lot of very nice noise. People admire the cut of your jib. The press calls, looking for a story. Analysts rate and respect your integrity. The best workers come knocking on your door. Investment gurus trust and recommend you. There's a buzz on the street that spreads far and wide. People, like me, write about you with a certain awe. Publishers ask you to write about yourself and your brand. You are admired for both your principles and your acumen at home and abroad. Without intending it, you strike fear in the hearts of your less-focused competitors. Your good fortune gives you no place to hide, and the limelight puts an added glow on your brand's mystique.

Everybody who deals with your brand—employees, customers, suppliers, the press *et al.*—are waiting to be your willing missionaries, given the stimulus of a potent mission.

Give them one.

## CHAPTER 13

# What We Can Learn from a New Generation of Brand Leaders

It seems that in the past, a great many brands just happened. To the delight of their inventors, some products were simply made into effective brands by the demand of their customers. Around the time when just about the fastest thing that moved was a horse, these brands evolved and grew over time. Think of Levi's, Coca-Cola, and Ivory Soap. Even today, with a tangible difference and/or a lot of luck, a product or service can capture the imagination and garner an almost accidental success. Think of toys like Beanie Babies and Furby. You wonder how on earth they're able to generate so much ink and word-of-mouth to create such feverish demand.

Today, though, it's much more likely that a brand starts with a specific purpose in the imagination of a leader; it is developed not just as product or service for consumption, but hand-in-hand with the leader's values and convictions.

## THE BUSINESS LEADERS' ROLES

Business and its leaders are much more visible than they ever were. They court our attention more than they ever did in the past. Business leaders now develop the kind of status and awareness that was once reserved for movie stars and politicians. News of them is almost as important as news of what they sell. They are the source of news as futurists. We don't find it at all unusual that they are becoming some of our most important philosophers. It's not just

Business leaders now develop the kind of status and awareness that was once reserved for movie stars and politicians.

business people who devour the words of Jack Welch, Jeff Bezos, Warren Buffett, and scores of others in the limelight of our times.

That's why a few words on the nature of the new leadership are worth your consideration. And along with it, so is a look at the workforce that leaders must court. If we try to understand the best of both, we might even be able to emulate the habits that make them truly effective. We might learn how to attract the best and brightest to our side. With brands that have to adjust to change (or die in the attempt), we might learn something about how the best leaders cope and adapt.

When we think of the old big-time leaders, we tend to think of larger-than-life autocrats, military egomaniacs, and the super-tough guys of the boardroom and playing field. We think of Alexander, Napoleon, MacArthur, Patton, Churchill, Carnegie, Rockefeller, Morgan, Hearst, Ford, Lombardi—I'm sure you can easily name your own stereotype of magical alpha attributes.

This shows what MIT's Peter Senge describes in *Fast Company* (May, 1999) as "our ideas about leadership, and in particular, to the cult of the CEO-as-hero." He says it's a cult that forms a "pattern that makes it easier for us to maintain change-averse institutions. When we enact the pattern of the CEO-as-hero, we infantalize the organization: That kind of behavior keeps everyone else in the company at a stage of development in which they can't accept their own possibilities for making change. Moreover, it keeps executives from doing things that would genuinely contribute to create significant change. The cult of the hero-leader only creates a need for more hero-leaders."

Senge says the hero-leader is the one with "the answers." He says, "Most of the other people in the organization can't make deep changes because they are operating out of compliance rather than out of commitment. Commitment comes about only when people determine that you are asking them to do something that they really care about."

## PRODUCTIVE NARCISSISTS

We tend to think of narcissism as a purely negative personality trait, but anthropologist and psychoanalyst Michael Maccoby uses the term as it was meant by Freud; namely, to describe the kind of person who is independent, innovative, and driven in business to seek power and glory. Such people may be necessary in times of great transition. They are charismatic and gifted in attracting followers, but can often be difficult to work for. They're often skillful orators, and while they seek adulation they are not easily impressed.

One of their negatives is that they tend to be a bit on the paranoid side. Rather than teach, they prefer to indoctrinate. They listen only for the kind of information they seek. Their faults grow as they become more successful. If you work for a narcissist, look elsewhere to bolster your own self-esteem. Work to *his* vision. Shower him with praise, but remember, he's too smart to appreciate a sycophant. Let him take the credit. Disagree only when you can demonstrate how he will benefit from a different point of view. Think of CEO superstars like Bill Gates, Andy Grove, Steve Jobs, or Jeff Bezos. And remember how an executive at Oracle describes CEO Larry Ellison: "The difference between God and Larry is that God does not believe he is Larry" (*Harvard Business Review*, 2000).

### ASK, DON'T TELL

As the nature of work continues to change, asking rather than telling gains more and more leadership credibility. In the past, we had a labor force made up mainly of manual workers. It was a force that could be told what to do in an almost military fashion. But today, we have many more "knowledge workers" in the pool. And they make a very different kind of soldier.

As Peter Drucker (1999) says,

> Employees who do manual work do not own the means of production. They may, and often do, have a lot of valuable experience, but that experience is valuable only at the place where they work. It is not portable . . . But knowledge workers *own* the means of production. It is between their ears. And it is a totally portable and enormous capital asset. Because knowledge workers own their means of production, they are mobile. Manual workers need the job more than the job needs them. It still may not be true for all knowledge workers that the organization needs them more than they need the organization. But for most of them[,] it is a symbiotic relationship in which they need each other in equal measure.

## EMPLOYEES AS ASSETS

A brand's employees and how they interact with the brand's stakeholders are clearly critical to the brand's success. It pays a leader to think of employees as capital assets rather than costs, and, as Drucker goes on to say, "Management's duty is to preserve the assets of the institution in its care."

> **It pays a leader to think of employees as capital assets rather than costs.**

This difference knowledge workers bring to the work force has enormous effect on the nature of leadership. Leaders still have to have the authority of the final say. They can still expect and demand a high degree of obedience in a crisis, but the workplace has changed and, by necessity, leadership is changing with it—from heroic, autocratic, top-down, highly controlling directives to democratic bottom-up necessities and what USC's Warren Bennis (*Financial Post*, 1999) calls "releasing" the brain power of the work force.

Bennis says,

> . . . we have to move from a command and control model to a more flexible, more collaborative, more nurturing kind of leadership. We have to move from a macho style to a maestro style. In the high tech, globally wired, digital world we live in, knowledge workers are in high demand and need to be treated as volunteers . . . Leaders who can release the brain power of their staff, who can energize the know-how and creativity of their work force, are the only ones who can be sure to be in the phone book by 2001.

This is more and more true for the brand-driven company where the customer is king: Those on the frontline of customer relations must be allowed to assume enormous authority. Looking at it the other way around, it's the job of the people at the top to make sure the people at the bottom have everything they need to get the brand job done, including the responsibility, the right tools, the training, the environment, and the value-driven mission. The fact is that as a leader, you don't have to have all the answers. You only have to know where to look for them. One of those places might be right under your nose: It might be in the hearts and minds of the people who work alongside you. Leaders are realizing that the people most able to solve the problems of work are the people doing the work and that giving responsibility is more productive than simply giving orders.

> The fact is that as a leader, you don't have to have all the answers. You only have to know where to look for them.

Harry says, "When I hired somebody, I didn't do so for the thrill of barking out orders. I hired people who were so much smarter, they would walk out on me if I dared to tell them what to do." (I resisted the temptation to ask how hard it would be to hire people who were smarter.)

Of course, business isn't suddenly benign. We still see highly narcissistic and charismatic leaders who have the necessary audacity to get great things done. Some continue to reflect the words of Louis XIV, the Sun King, who said, "My greatest concern has always been glory."

We still see battles for supremacy going on across the new, high-rolling, high-tech landscape, and they're just as dramatically intense as anything out of business history. Internet technology has been called Darwinism on steroids.

## THE NEW BATTLEGROUND—BRAND POWER

But the one thing that makes today's business conflicts different is that they're likely to be a battle for brand power, as much as of personalities and personal power. They are also battles that display the sometimes-peculiar habit of cooperation between the combatants. What we're witnessing isn't the evolution of a new business age, as much it is as a co-evolution, a rebirth of what the father of economics Adam Smith called "connexions and dependencies."

## UNLIKELY PARTNERS

Thomas Petzinger Jr. (1999) writes of Adam Smith, "It is not through benevolence, as he wisely pointed out, that the butcher, brewer, and baker provide our dinner—but neither is it through self-interest alone. It is through their niche-begetting dealings that we enjoy the fruit of a free economy. For more than a century[,] this truth was largely hidden as major corporations filled the center of economic life. But now[,] technology is devaluing the major corporation. The functions that corporations brought in-house are being automated, distributing value-creating opportunities across the landscape to be seized by millions of entrepreneurs—not by acting alone, as big companies once could, but by acting together. Every act of economizing occurs not within but between; every business exists only because, and precisely as a consequence, of its connections to other businesses."

Thus, we see that Microsoft and Xerox form an alliance. Xerox works with Sun Microsystems. IBM, Motorola, and Apple collaborate. A customer lets a supplier control its inventory. A customer lets a supplier's engineers design its products. And those products are then sold to other customers.

Meanwhile, Bill Gates is no less a formidable adversary as he goes to war for the Microsoft brand. Scott Cook plots mightily for the preservation of the Intuit brand. Michael Dell fights for the supremacy of his direct-business model. And their objective is fixed on the ultimate prize: the heart and mind of loyal customers rather than mere personal aggrandizement. The mission is the hero rather than the missionary. As Amazon.com founder Jeff Bezos might say, creating the emotional equity for a brand is everything. Without it, he knows he and his employees are dust on a windy day.

## THE NEW LEADERS

Creating personal wealth today is often a likely byproduct of creating wealth for customers. As I read recently (*Financial Business Post*, 1999), "Michael Lewis, author of *Liar's Poker*, wrote in 1995 what defined the rich today was not conspicuous consumption, the mark of earlier generations, but conspicuous production. The Gilded Age's top one-tenth of one percent made a show of wealth, imitating the landed aristocracy's indolent habits and commissioning gargantuan neo-classical monuments to themselves. But the new generation of rich—mostly young, male and involved in wealth creation through technological processes not easily comprehended by the average person—makes a life of work. The creation of wealth's the thing more than its display."

Author Neal Stephenson (*Inc.*, 1999) says some of the new high-tech leaders seek and enjoy wealth, but he adds, "Clearly, most have motives other than having a big house on the edge of a country club, motives that are incredibly diverse. Some have long-term social goals, and some dream about something they want to build, and starting a company is how you get things done now. These are people who tend to be very active intellectually and whose personal goals go way beyond the desire to be the president of a company. Being the founder and CEO of a company is something they do in order to achieve their real goals."

The new leaders are less likely to see themselves as what Senge (*Inc.*, 1999) describes as merely "the person at the top." He says, "That definition says that leadership is synonymous with a position. And if leadership is synonymous with a position, then it doesn't matter what a leader does. All that matters is where the leader sits."

> In many businesses, planning is virtually obsolete. Reacting replaces it. Ready, aim, fire really is being replaced by ready, fire, aim.

Senge, on the other hand, defines leadership very simply as "the ability to produce change."

I go further and say the new leaders have to have an enormous capacity to also initiate and manage change. In many businesses, planning is virtually obsolete. Reacting replaces it. Ready, aim, fire really is being replaced by ready, fire, aim. Due diligence is being "pretty sure" you're doing the right thing. IPOs take weeks instead of months to mount. Decisions are made in an eye-blink. Companies get bought in a week or sooner. Business is conducted in real time where there's no place to hide.

### TODAY'S BUSINESS GROWTH—UNBELIEVABLE!

We've never seen anything like today's examples of formidable growth. As of 1999, sales in the *Inc.* (ibid.) 500 list of America's fastest growing private companies have increased by an average of 1,715 percent in five years. Incredibly, the number one company on the 1999 list, Roth Staffing (which provides both permanent and temporary help for IT firms) grew 20,332 percent!

As Tom Jermoluk of @Home Network notes, "This stuff moves so fast, you gotta figure out a way to clone yourself. We're doing a deal a minute—it's crazy, and it all happens overnight." Amazon.com's Jeff Bezos compares the rise of doing business on the Internet to the Cambrian era in evolution. "That was when the earth had the greatest rate of new life. What people don't know is that it also had the greatest rate of extinction" (*Fortune*, 1999).

That's why new leaders celebrate individuality and responsibility over conformity and mere obedience in their employees. Thomas Petzinger Jr. (1999) writes, "They deploy technology to distribute rather than consolidate authority and creativity. They compete through resilience instead of resistance, through adaptation instead of control. In a time of dizzying complexity and change, they realize that tightly drawn strategies become brittle[,] while shared purpose endures. Capitalism, in short, is merging with humanism."

The U.S. Navy may strike you as a classic environment for top-down command and control leadership of the most archaic kind. Unfailing obedience is a necessity for men required to put their lives on the line. It would hardly seem to include the listening and questioning model the new economy's enlightened leadership requires. Doing things by the book is *de rigeur*. It's shape up or ship out. If it moves, salute it; if it doesn't move, paint it. Ours is not to reason why; ours is but to do or die. There's the right way, the wrong way, and the navy way. No questions asked as you go over the top, boys. And remember that it's not too many years ago that sailors were pressed into service—literally kidnapped and hauled aboard to serve what must have felt like a criminal sentence as they were tied to the rigging and flogged with a cat-o'-nine-tails for minor rule infractions. It's hardly the ideal environment for what Peter Drucker calls "systematic innovation."

That's what's so impressive about the story of the captain of the *USS Benfold*—a formidable, $1 billion warship, armed with the world's most advanced and lethal computer-controlled combat system. He demonstrates a stunning example of effective leadership for a brand called the U.S. Navy. His remarkable story was reported by Polly LaBarre in the April 1999 issue of *Fast Company* magazine. She writes that Comdr. D. Michael Abrashoff is a model of leadership as progressive as any in the business world. But it's because he's in the military that I think the commander's story is even more astonishing.

The 38-year-old Abrashoff has a sterling service record, including combat experience, but it's his ship and her crew that he talks about with unabashed pride. The *Benfold* is credited with the best record in the Pacific fleet for combat readiness. To keep it that way, he saw his mission as "nothing less than the reorientation of a famously rigid 200-year-old hierarchy. His aim: to focus on purpose rather than chain of command. When you shift your organizing principle from obedience to performance, says Abrashoff, the highest boss is no longer the guy with the most stripes—it's the sailor who does the work. 'There's nothing magical about it . . . In most organizations today, ideas still come from the top. Soon after arriving at this command[,] I realized that the young folks on this ship are smart and talented. And I realized that my job was to listen aggressively—to pick up all of the ideas that they had for improving how we operate.'"

When you shift your organizing principle from obedience to performance, says Abrashoff, the highest boss is no longer the guy with the most stripes—it's the sailor who does the work.

He truly believes that "the most important thing a captain can do is to see the ship from the eyes of its crew." He further believes that there's always a better way to do things, and he probed those better ways in great detail with the crew. He and his men dissected every operation to see how each one helped the crew to maintain operational readiness. There was no reticence about making some stunning changes that seem highly unusual for a military organization. Anything and everything that was done just because "that's the way we always do things" was jettisoned overboard. In his mission to create true operational readiness, Abrashoff pursued a policy of what Peter F. Drucker has called "Organized Abandonment."

Many of his superiors and fellow commanding officers question Abrashoff's methods. He says, "I divide the world into believers and infidels. What the infidels don't understand—and they far outnumber the believers—is that innovative practices combined with true empowerment produce phenomenal results."

One of his confident insights into change is that the more people enjoy the process, the better the results. Spending 35 days in the Persian Gulf is no fun for a crew of very young people, but during replenishment alongside supply ships, the *Benfold*'s crew were known throughout the region for projecting music videos on the ship's side. In purchasing food for the ship, Abrashoff switched from high-cost naval provisions to cheaper, better-quality, name-brand foods. With the money he saved, he sent five of the *Benfold*'s thirteen cooks to cooking school, which made the *Benfold* a favorite lunchtime destination for crews across the San Diego waterfront. Abrashoff's ship has a $2.4 million maintenance budget and a $3 million repair budget. He was able to return $1.4 million of these amounts to the navy's top line, which he credits to a proactive environment in which people simply want to do well.

## YOU CAN'T TOP PERFECTION

On average, only 54 percent of sailors remain in the navy after their second tour of duty. Under Abrashoff's command, 100 percent of the *Benfold*'s career sailors signed on for another tour. He figures this saved $1.6 million in costs related to personnel. He understood that scraping and chipping paint was a hated chore and a waste of younger crewmen's time and talent. He farmed the job out and incalculably boosted morale, while increasing the young sailors' time for training and combat readiness (it also got the ship a paint job that lasts 30 years for a mere $25,000). On his watch, the *Benfold*'s sailors came out winners in the advancement cycle, with promotions twice as high as the navy average. He created an Internet account so that the sailors on sea duty can send and get messages home daily through a commercial satellite. When new crewmen arrive fresh from boot camp, they are greeted with a welcome plan, which includes a hand-picked mentor and the right to call home to let the folks know they've arrived safely (the call is on Abrashoff's nickel). He makes sure he knows every crewman through face-to-face meetings and understands his or her goals. Needless to say, he remembers every person's name.

When he learned that credit-card debt was causing serious trouble for many of the young crew, he hired financial consultants to give the needed advice. He broadcasts new ideas over the ship's loudspeakers. Sailors make a suggestion one week and see it implemented the next.

Abrashoff says, "None of this means we've sacrificed discipline or cohesion on the ship. When I walk down the passageway, people call attention on deck and hit the bulkhead. They respect the office[,] but understand that I don't care about the fluff—I want substance. And the substance is combat readiness. The substance is having people feel good about what they do. The substance is treating people with respect and dignity. We gain a lot of ground by keeping our focus on substance rather than a lot of extraneous stuff."

The examples and sterling results of his intense-listening command go on and on. They would indeed create envy in the best leaders in

> "The substance is having people feel good about what they do. The substance is treating people with respect and dignity."

business today. He says, "In many units—and in many businesses—a lot of time and effort is spent supporting the guy on top. Anyone on my ship will tell you that I'm a low-maintenance CO. It's not about me, it's about my crew."

Abrashoff reveals his six principles that make the Benfold a working example of great "grassroots" leadership:

1. **Don't just take command, communicate purpose.**
2. **Leaders listen without prejudice.**
3. **Practice discipline without formalism.**
4. **The best captains hand out responsibility, not orders.**
5. **Successful crews perform with devotion.**
6. **True change is permanent: once you start perestroika, you can't really stop it.**

I would like to see these principles engraved in stone and hung on the wall of every CEO's office. If no other leadership principles were presented in this or any other book, Commander Abrashoff's would be enough.

He also says, "I'm lucky. All I ever wanted to do in the navy was to command a ship. I don't care if I ever got promoted again. And that attitude has enabled me to do the right things for my people instead of doing the right things for my career.

"In the process I ended up with the best ship in the navy—and I got the best evaluation of my career. The unintended benefit? My promotion is guaranteed."

After completing his 20-month tour of duty on the *Benfold*, Commander Abrashoff reported to a top post at the Space and Naval Warfare Systems Command. I would wish him good luck, but he obviously knows how to make his own.

I was going to give other examples of good leadership in this chapter, but I decided this one is enough. Our intrepid commander provides superb value for his every point of contact, including taxpayers. Before he makes admiral, some smart brand could do worse than to hire him away, and make him rich and famous.

*Fast Company* magazine (June 1999) gives good advice in an article called "Make Yourself A Leader" that appears to reflect Commander Abrashoff's leadership ethic. Its 12 steps are:

1. **Leaders are both confident and modest (you have an ego, but you make the people around you more powerful).**
2. **Leaders are authentic (you know who you are; you believe in yourself; you walk the talk).**
3. **Leaders are listeners (you are curious and know that the enemy of curiosity is grandiosity).**
4. **Leaders are good at giving encouragement, and they are never satisfied (you raise the stakes for everybody; you're always testing and building both courage and stamina throughout your organization).**
5. **Leaders make unexpected connections (you see patterns that lead to small innovations and breakthrough ideas).**
6. **Leaders provide direction (you give direction, not answers; you are in touch and out front).**
7. **Leaders protect their people from danger—and they expose them to reality (you don't insulate your people from change; you mobilize them to face it).**
8. **Leaders make change—and stand for values that don't change (you know what habits and assumptions need to be changed and the values that need to be maintained).**
9. **Leaders lead by example (small gestures send big messages, and you live by principle).**
10. **Leaders don't blame—they learn (you try, fail, learn, and try again).**
11. **Leaders look for and network with other leaders (it's only lonely at the top if you place yourself on a pedestal).**
12. **The job of the leader: make more leaders (you know this is your ultimate job).**

## My Own Vision of Leadership

I have my own vision of leadership. I liken it to the work of the gandy dancer—a job title that hearkens back to the glory days of the railroad. Gandy dancing describes workers who walked the rails with sledgehammer in hand to keep the rails straight and parallel. The powerful locomotives would not have made it far without the watchful eye of the gandy dancer, working on point, keeping things straight with the destination always in mind. A visionary, gandy-dancing leader understands that when you take care of the tracks, the trains will take care of themselves.

The words come from another time, but there was prophecy in what John F. Kennedy said with so much eloquence at his inaugural address: "It is time for a new generation of leadership, to cope with new problems and new opportunities. For there is a new world to be won."

# PART Five

# BRAND BUILDING

# IN THE DIGITAL ERA

CHAPTER 14

# Brands in a One-to-One Marketing World

In a few very short years, we've seen our traditional ways of marketing brands go through an astonishing revolution. We've literally moved from an age of mass marketing to the age of mass customization. It's now possible for brands to communicate with their customers one-to-one. Just as important as the brand talking to one customer at a time, the customer can just as easily talk back to the brand.

It must be difficult for a scion of the old economy to grasp the idea that you can actually deal with one customer at a time without wasting time, and that mass customization is not a contradiction in terms. The fact is that much of marketing has shifted from conducting business as a party of millions to a party of two. It is a phenomenon that will only get bigger as we become more and more familiar with what the computer can mean in our daily lives.

## CUSTOMER DATABASES

In our interactive times of one-to-one marketing, the very rules of brand competition are being rewritten. In *Enterprise One To One* (1997), Don Peppers and Martha Rogers write, "Information technology makes three important new capabilities available to businesses. The database allows you to tell your customers apart and remember them individually. Interactivity means the customer can now talk to you (rather than serve as the passive target for your messages). And mass customization technology enables businesses to customize products and services as a matter of routine."

Phrasing it a little differently, they say in their preface, "Instead of selling one product at a time to as many customers as possible in a particular sales period, the 1:1 marketer uses customer databases and interactive communications to sell one customer at a time as many products and services as possible over the entire lifetime of that customer's patronage. This is a strategy that requires a business to manage customers individually rather than just managing products, sales channels, and programs. While the traditional marketer gauges success in terms of market share growth, the 1:1 marketer also measures share of customer."

## CUSTOMIZATION AND PERSONALIZATION

The brilliant Peppers and Rogers talk about customization, but according to C. K. Prahalad and Venkatram Ramaswamy, writing in the *Harvard Business Review* (January/February 2000), there is a difference between customization and personalization.

Customization assumes that the manufacturer will design a product to suit a customer's needs. It is now standard operating procedure over the Web, where consumers can customize a host of products and services simply by choosing from a menu of features.

With personalization, however, the customer becomes a co-creator of the content of the experience. More and more customers want to play this role. They see the product as no more than an artifact around which they can have an experience—both individually and with experts, or other customers. From the brand's point of view, personalization makes the customer part of its

> Customization assumes that the manufacturer will design a product to suit a customer's needs.

competency. This goes a bit further than customization to court loyalty. It helps the customer to think, "I designed it, so it's mine."

This is how brands engaged in one-to-one marketing can use computers to create formidable customer loyalty. An online grocery store is an example. Along the road, you might use your computer or interactive TV set to buy groceries. Once you've "educated" the grocer's database about your needs, likes, and dislikes over a period of six months or so, you're not likely to want to change.

A second grocery store could come along and offer you the same service, but you would have to spend another six months teaching it what the original store has already learned. The original store has a huge leg-up on your business, now and in the future, because its microchip already knows how to molly-coddle you and the idiosyncrasies of your precious grocery list. It has worked hard to keep you happy and even surprise you with its intelligent suggestions.

This intimate knowledge of you and your weekly order (multiplied over many customers) gives this store what Peppers and Rogers describe as a *"permanent and perhaps insurmountable competitive advantage when it comes to retaining and increasing the business from customers it already has"* (Ibid., p. 10).

Other "vendor-neutral" sites, such as Amazon.com, use the same techniques to keep loyal customers for books and other products, such as music discs. Having a data history of what interests you, they can actually suggest related books or music. Fear of being left behind on the information highway will spur all manner of "vendor-specific," bricks-and-mortar retailers to get into your computer to court your loyalty with a Web site. For example, American Airlines offers its million-strong Net-SAAver subscribers a weekly listing of rock-bottom fares on undersubscribed flights.

What's happening is that you don't have to ask customers what they want. With one-to-one interaction, they tell you. And when you can give them exactly what they want, they're likely to be less promiscuous. We used to talk about the push and pull of marketing, but as *Fortune* magazine (1998, December 8) says, "The Web is not about push; it's about suck: Online consumers can suck out of cyberspace whatever interests them and leave behind what doesn't. You push stuff at passive viewers, and Web users are anything but passive. You may be able to let some uninvited advertiser take your TV screen hostage for 30 seconds, but you'd probably throw a fit if they took over your computer screen. Online customers aren't going to be pushed around."

## PURCHASING POWER

We talk about a phenomenon called purchasing power, and that power has never been so great for the consumer. Power is now firmly in the hands of buyers. It's a time of seller beware. In their book *Net Worth* (*Business 2.0*, 1999, March), John Hagel III and Mark Singer talk about "reverse markets, where consumers seek out and extract value from vendors rather than the other way around." Infomediaries will do the search work for the consumer and sell the information to appropriate vendors. "Today, vendors dedicate the vast bulk of consumer marketing expenditures (about 70 percent) to preemptively capturing the attention of the consumer in advance of the purchase. In reverse markets, customers will shun this kind of intrusive marketing. Successful marketers will learn how to list themselves effectively in search environments, how to engage the consumer at the time of purchase, and how to tailor products and services in ways that reduce incentives for switching to other vendors."

> **P**ower is now firmly in the hands of buyers. It's a time of seller beware.

Portals such as America Online, Excite, and Yahoo perform some of this function. They are entry points to the Web for over 50 million cyber-surfers. Traditional marketers invest in developing products and then marketing them to consumers. Portals invert the process by investing in finding consumers and then selling them to merchants. You can see what this does to our notions of traditional brand marketing. It makes the Internet a lot more than just another channel for distribution.

## THE OLD ECONOMY AND THE NEW

In the old economy, it was/is expensive and difficult to answer the question "Who is my customer, and what does he/she want?" Customer segmentation was/is a real hit-or-miss proposition.

Writing in *Fast Company* (1999, February-March) magazine, consultant Adrian Slywotzky outlines the difference:

If you're the producer, you spend money and time trying to find your customers. You hire consultants to conduct focus groups; you channel your energy into market research—all with the hope that you will learn something about what your customers want. Based on these gleanings, you spend more money on marketing and advertising, hoping to lure customers into your store or to sample your service. And finally the big moment comes: customers arrive *and they don't want what you are selling. Or you don't have exactly what they want.* Or it turns out they're not really the customers you had hoped to attract in the first place.

It's a system guaranteed to produce mismatches. And it is precisely those mismatches that digitization prevents. In fact, the promise of e-segmentation is the promise to turn the old world upside down. Rather than get stuck in a make-and-sell system, you shift into a sense-and-respond mode. The information that was once expensive and difficult to get—and that often turned out to be inadequate, fragmentary, too old, or just plain wrong—now comes to you courtesy of your customers, who deliver it to you both cheaply and effortlessly from online feedback or through their buying behavior.

## There's no escape from technology

The Net has even found its way into church and into your conscience. "At Almundena Cathedral in Madrid, Spain, parishioners make their donations by swiping their credit card through an electronic device mounted right into the stone wall. At Almundena, you have to be a hacker to abscond with parish funds" (*Business 2.0*, March 1998).

### Keeping Your Customers

In this light, the efficiencies of one-to-one brand marketing become awesomely clear. As Slywotzky goes on:

> You save money. You save time. You get a window into the future: By studying the behavior of your most valuable and forward-looking customers, you have the ability to build a predictive capability that tells you where the market is headed next. And, most important, you can then reduce the

risk that your customer will move on, and you don't—which could leave you with an obsolete business model, products, or services that no longer fit your customers' profile, and the daunting task of trying to retrofit your company and its offerings to a customer base that has moved on to new territory and more responsive relationships.

Responsiveness is key for the successful brand, and it has never been easier to execute. Elsewhere in this book, I talk about Levi Strauss & Co. Slywotzky uses the $6.9 billion jeans-maker here to prove that you don't have to be left behind when fickle consumers change the pace: "A few years ago, Levi Strauss saw its core customers declare Levi's jeans decidedly unhip. The company closed eleven U.S. plants, launched a new ad campaign— and moved aggressively into e-segmentation, using digitization throughout its retail system to reestablish customer relevance.

> Responsiveness is key for the successful brand, and it has never been easier to execute.

In 1994, the company initiated its Personal Pair program: Women who were willing both to pay an extra $10 to $15 over the usual price of jeans and to wait an extra week or two for delivery, could go to certain Original Levi's Stores and have themselves "digitized"—that is, have their measurements taken and a pair of jeans custom-made, and then have the information stored in the company's database for future purchases. And the result? The Personal Pair program achieved a repeat-purchase rate that was significantly higher than the 10 percent to 12 percent of Levi's typical customers; by 1997, the program accounted for 25 percent of women's jeans sales at Original Levi's Stores.

The article quotes Sanjay Choudhuri, Levi's director of mass customization: "The goal is not to sell a pair of jeans; it's to build a relationship. . . . We're not marketing to the customer—the customer is acting as a styling consultant to us. The customer says, 'I know your pants fit me; now let me tell you what I want the jeans to look like and how I want to look in the mirror.' It's getting personal. The customer is starting to design."

It's sad that in spite of this interactive success, Levi's has decided to abandon most of its online sales efforts. The problem is that Levi's traditional sales channels began to complain that the brand was taking away their bread and butter. A big retail store can hardly find pleasure in Levi's attempts to sell custom jeans directly to the customer online.

## Nowhere to Hide

An inferior brand has a tough time hiding on the Internet, where brands become more and more transparent. It's too easy to go to neutral sites that tell you what you want to know about brands within just about any product category. They tell you how Brand A compares to Brand X, feature for feature and dollar for dollar. If the comparison favors Brand X, it will impact your feelings simply because third-party endorsement is always more powerful than anything a brand can say about itself. One such site is Compare.net. As the above-quoted *Fortune* article states, "Whether it's lawn mowers, camcorders, or treadmills, skeptical consumers can read unbiased product reviews and participate in on-line discussion groups. In this environment, it's pretty hard for a vendor to spin a second-rate product into a first-rate buy."

> An inferior brand has a tough time hiding on the Internet, where brands become more and more transparent.

It's worth noting another difference: the information is available 24 hours a day, 365 days a year. You have to go to your local electronics store to compare TV sets at the store's convenience. With the Internet, you do it at yours. Of course, you can also buy 24 hours a day, which is a boon to those with no time or an aversion to shopping.

We keep hearing stories about how the numbers are growing to form a veritable tsunami of online shoppers, and it's apparently getting there. Techno-seer Nicholas Negroponte anticipates between

850 million and 1 billion people online, generating between $1 trillion of e-commerce worldwide by year-end 2000 (*Financial Post,* February 1999). He says the developing world is always underrepresented in online population figures. This seems like a highly optimistic number, but of one thing we can be sure: there's no doubt that business-to-business marketing is much more prevalent than business-to-consumer.

## ROCKETING SALES

Forester Research estimates that business-to-business Internet commerce will rocket to $1.3 trillion by 2003, from just $43 billion in 1998 (*Financial Post,* ibid.). It will account for 90 percent of all commerce conducted over the Internet. And the incentives to get in on the action are considerable. For example, with Boeing's Web-based parts system, any airline with a computer and an Internet connection can now check on the availability of parts, and place orders by merely pointing and clicking. Systems manager Tom DiMarco says, "The mechanic can make the decision right from the hangar." Just think how quickly a grounded plane can be returned to service at huge savings for the airline.

Even more exciting, Boeing designs its planes entirely online. The millions of parts that make up a plane used to be blueprinted from pen-and-ink design. No more. The parts are created, ordered, and paid for by computers dealing with suppliers all over the world.

The efficiencies of this kind of commerce can hardly be tabulated. As important as that is, the opportunity for communication that a brand craves is just as stunning. The incentive to develop user-friendly, highly informative sites that encourage feedback could be as important to a winning supplier as lower prices, particularly if the site's offering is backed by sterling service.

Writer Leslie Helm says in *The Cutting Edge* (*Financial Post,* ibid.):

> The biggest advances in productivity, over time, could come when the Web allows customers to conduct transactions from among a broader universe of suppliers than they would have originally considered.
>
> Later this year, Portland Oregon-based Integrated Food Sources, a large trading company in the processed food

business, will launch a Web site for matching buyers and sellers of processed foods around the world.

To streamline the process, the new site will handle customs paperwork required for exports and imports, assure that suppliers are properly certified by the Food and Drug Administration, and eventually translate messages so that buyers and sellers around the world see the transactions in their own languages.

## THE COST OF E-COMMERCE VERSUS BRICKS AND MORTAR

Matt Hyde is Vice-President for online sales (rei.com) at Recreational Equipment Inc.(REI)—a powerful retailer of outdoor gear and apparel. He debunks the idea that a physical store is more expensive to run than a Web store (*Financial Post*, May 29, 1999). For one thing, it costs about the same to hire 300 part-time store clerks for a bricks-and-mortar store, as it does to hire 60 programmers and systems managers at the industry average of $80,000 each. And the cost of Web site upgrades (often $500,000 a crack) never ceases. It costs $6 million to build an REI store, but rei.com has cost $15 million in upgrades and site remodeling since 1996. Hyde says selling both ways simply serves REI's customers better, and customers who use both the Web site and the physical store spend an average of $150 more than single-channel shoppers. One apparently feeds the other, regardless of comparative costs.

This is yet another example of how the Internet shrinks time to nothing, relieves us of clerical tedium, helps rid us of bureaucracy, and speaks many tongues, to boot. But more than anything, it shows that business-to-business brands' use of the Net might turn out to be more about saving huge amounts of money rather than making huge amounts.

Technology writer Jim Carroll says the real estate industry can save some $2 billion annually by re-engineering its paperwork process through the Net (*Marketing*, 1999). He tells of an energy company that will use the Internet "as the foundation of a system for its gas pump convenience stores to re-order inventory—with resulting cost savings of $50 million in the first year."

*The Economist* (1999, June 26) quotes Cisco Systems CFO Larry Carter, who claims that 55 percent of orders pass through Cisco's system without being touched by anyone. "'We just collect the money,' he says. He reckons that Cisco is saving well over $500 million a year by using the [W]eb; indeed, it could not have maintained its growth without it."

## Technology's Role in the Economy

Global stories of such economizing multiply into impressive ways of keeping a lid on brand prices. They also go a long way to explaining how technology can take a lot of credit for the lack of inflation in our super-efficient domestic economy.

One cannot help but be dazzled by the utility of the new information economy. We used to fear technology's ability to make us slaves to George Orwell's idea of an omnipotent and vengeful Big Brother, but technology has become our tireless, ever-jolly servant and we, its impatient ruler, greedily absconding with all the goodies it has to offer.

## Eschewing Internet Hyperbole

Warren Buffet may be admired for his investment acumen, but I like him for his sense of humor. He says he doesn't invest in categories he doesn't understand, particularly technology. He prefers what he sees as predictable. He favors understandable companies that dominate their category, such as Coke and Wrigley. As he said on a PBS program where he appeared with Bill Gates, "I don't think the Internet is going to change how people chew gum."

But as the tech gurus keep telling us, interactive technology has barely scratched marketing's surface. If we are to see it grow to be as popular as sliced bread, we must bid our best engineers to find ways to make it more inviting to those who shun it—like Harry, who is in awe of anything more technical than a can opener. He still visualizes electricity as ants running up and down a wire. He once told me that he sees his telephone answering service as a dozen well-spoken ladies crawling around on the floor, tending to a hundred ringing telephones. When he moved to a new house, he actually wanted to hire someone to explain the fancy new electric stove. It seems strange to suggest that Harry could be representative of anything, but I think there are many more technophobes out there than we care to think about. A new brand of computer preloaded with software that is ten times simpler to use than Macintosh would receive a hero's welcome from the technically fearful.

The need for greater simplicity doesn't stop with the technology. As an example of human ingenuity, technology has the ability to astonish us. But we must be on guard against the raging hyperbole of its effect on our lives and on brand marketing.

Obviously, technology offers many new opportunities to capitalize on a brand and its ability to talk and learn one-to-one. But we must not allow it to distract us from the real issue. Wired and unwired, we still live in one world. Technology is hardly destiny. A brand's best defense will always be to produce bulletproof products and services that carve out clear, emotional territories you can own in your customers' minds, regardless of the communication format. This is the opportunity and protection of a vibrant brand in cyber-territory. And it would be the opportunity and protection of a brand if cyber-territory were still Dick Tracy comic-book fiction.

## CHAPTER 15

# How Technology Impacts Traditional Brand Communication

It's easy to see how a move from mass marketing to mass customization is going to have a profound effect on brand communication. It prompts a parallel shift from mass communication to communication that is more personally involving because it can be one-to-one. You and I can no longer be thought of as unwitting pawns in a brand's quest for dominion. Unlike Rodney Dangerfield, we all get respect.

In our recent age of mass marketing, advertising was just about the only branding game in town—at least as far as the consumer was concerned. We were introduced to brands by what the ads said, and we had little or no opportunity to talk back. As Agency.com's Chan Suh (*Business 2.0*, 1998) says, "It's not so much that the old advertising was dishonest as it was that it could make certain claims without fear of being contradicted. A wired world, in which almost a million people could read the Starr report before TV and newspapers could filter it for them, has changed the rules . . . The new game is about the transparency of a company . . . My mouse is an extension of my fist, and I'm knocking on your door."

Brand communication can no longer afford to indulge in hyperventilated spin. People who have grown up with advertising as a fact of life are smart enough to know the difference between genuine communication and genuine hype. Brands cannot hide behind made-up claims of superiority or pretensions of cool. The average

> Brands cannot hide behind made-up claims of superiority or pretensions of cool.

teenager hanging out in a mall knows more about cool than any executive hunched over a desk cluttered with marketing statistics. With interactive technology, the teenager is the one likely to be telling the brand what's hot and what's not. If she isn't, it's now easier than ever to ask her, and a few thousand others just like her, to do so.

## BRANDS MUST BE ACCOUNTABLE

It's a new ball game where brands are more accountable than they ever were. Brands not only have to be careful of what they say, but also what they do. We don't like it when we hear of Nike's alleged exploitation of child labor in the third world. Reverse word of mouth can be a killer. Any consumer can now protest a brand's behavior with the huge megaphone of the Internet and get other disaffected consumers to join in. Some angry consumers have been known to set up Web sites for just that purpose.

Bad press has always affected a brand's popularity and its consequent performance in the stock market, but public participation in the debate has never been so quick or so ubiquitous. The 1989 Exxon oil spill in Prince William Sound depreciated the company's stock by 10 percent, or $6 billion, partly because the company was so vigorously condemned for slow action, shunning responsibility, expressing little concern for victims, and poor communication. And it's not just good citizenship that can be called into question. Ugly manners can be just as damaging.

## TECHNOLOGY AND THE MEDIA

Technology is changing the way we learn about all kinds of things in our lives, including brands. When you change the media, you change our habitual way of looking at everything. Consider this thought about the new media from *Road Warriors* (1995): " . . . the most significant development of all is the fact that the world is going digital. The words in our books, the pictures on our TVs, and the voices in our phones are being converted from the printed type, light waves, and sound waves first utilized by Johannes Gutenberg, Alexander Graham Bell, and Thomas Edison into the digital ones and zeros that computers read. And when books, movies, TV, phones, libraries, and news media all speak the lingua franca of digital ones and zeros, they can be mixed and matched, accessed and utilized in ways never before thought possible. For example, we'll be able to watch our favorite TV shows when we want, not just when the network wants. And consider this not-unlikely future scenario: you pause a TV news report on new treatments for heart disease to call up an animated illustration of the function of a heart valve from your network service's online encyclopedia[;] then video-call your doctor for a consultation. Is the device in front of you a TV, a telephone, or a computer?"

If you think about this interactive media scenario in terms of how a consumer might learn about a brand, you get the idea that the times that brands live in are indeed a-changing.

## CHANGING TIMES FOR BRANDS

Advertising a brand on the Web has powerful advantages (*Financial Post*, 1999, February). It allows you to be taken straight from an online ad to the advertiser's "virtual" retail outlet with a click of the mouse. You don't have to dial an 800 number and be left on hold, and you certainly don't have to venture out from the comfort of home. Just click and it's done. Advertisers who can sell their brands digitally, like software makers, can even sell their products and collect payment entirely over the Internet—no courier companies, and no waiting at home for UPS. Your purchase just gets downloaded into your computer. And while demonstrating the effectiveness of conventional print advertising is difficult, an ad on the Web makes tracking simple, accurate, fast, and highly detailed. Measuring advertising value simply cannot be matched by any other medium.

Paul Kemp Robertson of Leo Burnett in Chicago (*Financial Post*, 1999, June) says, "It takes on average 44 weeks from brief to final cut to produce a television commercial—that is Jurassic. On the Net, if an ad isn't working it gets changed the very next day."

It's also worth noting that Forester Research (*Financial Post*, 1999, August) says online advertising will be the fourth-largest medium in the United States by 2004. It's predicted to trail only television, newspapers, and direct mail in popularity for advertising spending. This isn't good news for radio, magazines, or the Yellow Pages.

## THE WAY IT WAS

In conventional marketing, scarcity often means higher value. When a widely used commodity like coal was scarce, it had greater value. If you owned the world's only Rolex, it would be worth millions (you would also be the only person on earth who is always on time)! With technology, on the other hand, when the product is scarce, it often has no value at all. For example, one fax machine is totally useless. But the Web gives us a powerful new phenomenon called the network effect. As Wall Street firm SG Cowan, Reamer's Jeff Reamer says about America Online (*Fast Company*, September 1999), "The great beauty of AOL's service is that, like any network, its value grows to the nth power of the number of people that use it. A telephone network is meaningless with 1 phone on it. With 2 phones, it begins to be useful. With 1,000[,] phones its important. With 100,000[,] it's incredibly important. AOL works the same way. The value of its service grows with every single person that joins it."

## THIS WAY IT IS

The network effect was largely responsible for the success of the Hotmail brand—the first free, Web-based e-mail service, which had a million registered users after only six months of its launch. This unprecedented, mind-blowing performance was accomplished with

## DOT.COMS STILL SUPPORT TRADITIONAL MEDIA

While we can expect the new media to become more and more a factor in brand communication, a surprising number of dot.coms count on analog media to get their stories across. Ad spending rocketed in 1999, and the blast-off was due in large part to dot.com use of print and broadcast. Traditional ad agencies may have every reason to worry about the longer term, but for now, they're worrying all the way to the bank.

a marketing budget of less than $50,000! Think of Yahoo, with 65 million users after only six years, and eBay, which went public in 1998 and now has 3.8 million registered users (Ibid.). Attaining such critical mass is positively viral.

Marketing and advertising had better get used to it. Marketing people didn't create these successes. The brands' customers did it by themselves, with online chat that begets online chat. We've simply never seen anything like it, and by all accounts, we ain't seen nothin' yet! I heard a guest on a financial network say recently that we have tapped only 3 percent of the Internet's potential.

Technology pokes its busy nose into every marketing area.

Researchers will have a field day with some of the new measurement techniques they can impose on the efficacy of a brand's TV commercials. In the newsletter *INSIDE 1to1*, Stacey Riordan writes,

> According to Ted Livingston, a consultant at Woodstock-based Next Century Media . . . technology and demographic viewership information similar to Nielsen data are being used to develop systems capable of mass customizing television commercials on the fly. Livingston said this technology can be used to send multiple versions of commercials for a single product to various viewers or to send commercials for different products to different viewers based on their profiles. In addition, Livingston said Next Century is developing an interactive remote control with what he terms an "applause/boo" button that enables viewers to respond to various commercials.
>
> The potential benefits for such systems are numerous: [C]able providers have the ability to build Learning Relationships with end users based on feedback from their interactions[,] while saving costs on poorly targeted commercials. Meantime, consumers perceive a greater value from advertisements that are consistently relevant to their needs and interests. According to Livingston, implementation of these systems will begin in the near future.

I love the applause/boo button. It might do more for viewership than a nude remake of "Charlie's Angels." I wonder if technology could be advanced to such a degree that we could actually nuke all the commercials we love to hate? Can you imagine what a charge it would be to zap the stilted beauties for the toenail fungus product whose name I'm glad I can't remember?

## BLENDING MEDIUMS

All those who profess an understanding of branding must grasp how analog and digital communications can and will work together. They both have a role to play in a brand's communications. Chan Suh, CEO of the interactive agency Agency.com, puts the roles into the context of the four major components of the customer-brand relationship. These are: assertion, demonstration, transaction, and fulfillment. He says, "Assertion is the product claim: 'new,' 'better,' 'longer lasting.' Demonstration consists of supporting testimony, often in the form of word-of-mouth approval. Transaction is the purchase—an exchange of value for value. The fulfillment stage is where the rubber hits the road: Is the customer happy?"

> While traditional brand communication is good with emotional appeals, digital media is better at delivering information and service.

Analog media is best at the assertion phase, but the scenario gets more difficult elsewhere. While traditional brand communication is good with emotional appeals, digital media is better at delivering information and service—particularly during the phases of transaction and fulfillment. As Suh notes, the old and the new media are complementary, but the way things stand, if you want to reach men 18–49 and you want to make an assertion, you still can't do better than buying 30 seconds on the Super Bowl . . . we (digital media) are complementary to analog media. Few media have come along and completely erased the other (*Business 2.0*, 1998, December).

They are indeed complementary, but the problem is that those who specialize in analog communication don't have much to do with those in digital communication. And vice versa. The disciplines are obviously different, but it's as though the people who practice them even speak different languages. And they probably do. The people creating the commercials you see on TV seek most of their inspiration in the right side of the brain. The people providing digital communication tend to dig around in the left side.

Chan Suh doesn't run an ad agency; he runs an interactive ad agency. Presumably, if you want to get the rest of the package through him, you have to go to one of the regular ad agencies in the $3.1 billion Omnicom Group, of which his Agency.com is a member. On the other hand, the analog guys often know virtually nothing about being digital. Ad agency J. Walter Thompson's top executive Charlotte Beers says of digital advertising, "It's a totally new vocabulary for me" (*Business Week*, 1999).

## A Place Called Media Heaven

In an ideal world, the same communications people who create your commercials would conduct your brand research; create your consumer and trade print ads; design your packages, your direct mail, and other promotion material; create your Web site; and build your one-to-one database and all your Web advertising. It would be a world in your dreams called Heaven. The people populating it would be called angels, and you know how hard they are to find and hire! It would be just as delightful, however, to get all the disciplines of modern branding sitting at the same table to work on your branding problems and opportunities. This is what you get from the best brand consultants who are equipped to help you do the total branding job.

The new whiz-bang technology should make it easier than ever to integrate all of a brand's communications in one seamless package. But this can only happen if each discipline starts with the brand and its mission as the guiding hand. I can't think of anything more vital to the cause of branding. In fact, it's so vital that the day may be fast upon us when the CEO rather than the marketing director accepts it as his primary function. That will be the day when he willingly changes his acronym from CEO to BEO—Brand Executive Officer—as a badge of the highest honor!

## CHAPTER 16

# The State of Brand Communication Consultants

Harry and I were in Mike Ditka's restaurant in Chicago. We were in the upstairs bar having a quiet *digestif* after a great steak dinner. Harry said, "See that woman at the bar? The one in the green dress?" I looked and saw that Harry was pointing out a blonde stunner. Harry went on, "She's the most beautiful woman I've seen in a year. And just think. Beneath all those clothes, she's just a bunch of double helix DNA strands."

This typically bizarre comment from Harry reminds me in a funny way of how many communication consultants confuse brand issues.

## THE LAYERS OF A BRAND

A brand is not something you clothe with communication. It's not the communication that dresses the brand. It's the brand that dresses the communication. But in many cases, communication consultants show us the outside of the brand without letting us see the core.

Building a brand in the mass-marketing age was about building an image. Building a brand in the mass-customization age is about building a reputation. Ad agencies can and do create attractive images that contribute to the positive perception of a brand, but as business writer Charles J. Fombrun (1996) says, "Unless those images are anchored in core characteristics of a company and its products, they will decay. A brand needs to sustain its reputation with a strong supportive infrastructure of interwoven management practices."

Advertising agencies have been slow to grasp this distinction. They seem to be stuck in a rut of "doing ads" rather than involving themselves in the larger issues of brand building with all the insight and tools we now have at our disposal. Your traditional communications suppliers don't know or refuse to admit that advertising can be an important ingredient in the branding process, but it's never *the* ingredient—that creating a brand is a great deal more fundamental than creating an ad campaign, and that a brand exists within a broader construct than the 30-second TV spot.

> Building a brand in the mass-customization age is about building a reputation.

## THE FALL OF ADVERTISING

This is more than my opinion. Advertising has dramatically dropped its standing in the list of branding tasks. Asked to rank marketing tactics in order of importance, only 10 percent of major corporate clients put advertising at the top. *Business Week* (1999, July) reports that at the June '98 meeting of the American Advertising Federation, "clients stunned their ad agencies by ranking advertising sixth out of seven marketing strategies, trailed only by legal counsel . . . While not openly hostile to their agencies, it's clear that companies no longer consider traditional advertising as crucial . . . Over the past decade, corporations have taken the concept of brand building to a new level that the TV commercials only partially address."

It appears that creating emotional connections with consumers is bigger than the broadcast break signaled by the announcement "and now a word from our sponsor."

In the same article, ad agency consultant Alvin Achenbaum says 20 years ago "companies devoted 90 percent of their marketing budget to advertising and the rest to other promotional efforts. Today, advertising commands maybe a third of the budget."

Public relations was once advertising's poor-and-distant cousin, but the corporate execs at the AAF now rate it well above advertising.

My bet is that they're thinking plain old publicity rather than the more high-falutin' PR. Launching a new brand in a high-interest category can get a lot more mileage out of publicity than paid advertising.

## NO NEED TO ADVERTISE

The food brand Newman's Own has never felt compelled to advertise, and after a dozen years, it still gets all the publicity it needs. Wal-Mart and Sam's Club don't seem to be hurting from a lack of significant spending on advertising. Starbucks launched its coffee empire with virtually no media advertising. Richard Branson seems to feel he can get along very nicely with very little of it for almost all of the Virgins in his stable. The Body Shop became a brand with publicity generated by Anita Roddick's obsession with the environment.

Hotmail's launch relied on the viral effect of Web buzz and free publicity to get a million customers for its free Web-based e-mail service in just six months (as I said earlier, its promotion budget was less than $50,000)! Hotmail shows that if you're first out of the gate with a valuable new promise for a product or service, you get all the publicity you want from the press and from word of mouse. It's not only a lot less expensive, it's also a lot more persuasive. One executive says of high-tech services that you don't have to persuade people to try new stuff; if you tell people about it, they will try it.

Occasionally, you even come across a brand that goes out of its way to avoid any kind of limelight with great success. London's venerable Connaught Hotel never advertises, and its managers even avoid the press. You can almost hear the marble-voweled, upper-class accents saying, "Chaps don't do that sort of thing," and they have no trouble filling the grand old joint on nothing more than gracious reputation and unsolicited publicity from people like me.

## REINVENTING THE AD AGENCY

I suppose you can't expect people who make a living from creating advertising to go around recommending free publicity as the way to launch a brand. It's natural for them to sell what is, after all, their bread and butter. It's like asking a barber if you need a haircut. But they might think more about other ways of gaining recognition if they saw their role as creators of brands rather than suppliers of a support activity. An ad agency can be a formidable ally that often helps a brand develop a persuasive point of view. Advertising is an undeniably powerful tool for *maintaining* awareness after a brand's novelty wears a bit thin, but it doesn't necessarily have a lot to do with a brand's bigger reality, or even the truth. In our transparent times, that's simply not good enough.

Of course, some very good ad agencies see and hate the diminution of the agency's role in marketing and are fighting to reverse it. The much-admired Martin Puris of the ad agency Amarati Puris Lintas synthesizes the point by finding it necessary to start what *Advertising Age* (1998) calls a revolutionary reinvention of the modern ad agency. He writes, "The current model for ad agencies is broken."

Another of the agency's executives said, "We have to migrate upstream and reclaim a seat at the executive table." He adds that Amarati Puris Lintas wants to have a role not only in advertising but in all marketing areas, which is why the agency is going through

## BANDWAGON COOL

Harry came into my office with a copy of *Vanity Fair*. He flipped the magazine open to a fashion ad and said, "How come all the models in these fashion ads look like their puppy just died?"

What he was pointing out was "bandwagon cool." This is the phenomenon of ad guys keeping their eye on each other rather than on a brand's customers.

Somewhere along the road, one art director thought it would be cool to hire a sad-looking model who looked like she had just escaped from heroine rehab. It stood out and was indeed cool because it took us by surprise. But it stops being cool when it multiplies like rabbits at stud. Look out for bandwagon cool that makes your ads look like everybody else's. Singular, human communication is always better and more important than cool.

sweeping management changes intended to recapture the strategic role many agencies have ceded to management consultants.

## THE WORK AHEAD

I fear that's going to be a tough row to hoe. *Business Week* says of J. Walter Thompson's Charlotte Beers' efforts to get her old-line agency back into the branding scene, "Plenty of other ad chiefs are fighting the same battle, as the industry becomes increasingly marginalized in the marketing universe" (*Advertising Age*, 1998). Brands seek help more than ever from consultants who have no particular axe to grind in how the branding job gets done. A good consultant offers all and any of the tools needed for building brand relationships. You can buy the expertise in total, or in pilot-sized chunks. And you can be sure it will be offered without prejudice or favoritism for any one method.

> A good consultant offers all and any of the tools needed for building brand relationships.

## LOGOS ARE NOT BRANDS, NO MATTER HOW MUCH THEY COST

In light of their historical connection with branding, you can feel the painful plight of many good ad agencies as they struggle to regain lost luster, but I have no sympathy for the specialist outfits that want to charge you a million dollars for a logo. I talked earlier about the false notion that a logo is a brand. I go further: The company that wants to charge you a million dollars for a logo should start the Scoundrel's Hall of Fame. These identity geeks would have you believe that creating logos and letterheads is a brand's foundation. As you may have gathered from reading this book so far, this is pure nonsense. Ask yourself when was the last time you bought anything because of the logo graphics? Has anybody ever refused to buy Coca-Cola because they don't like the typeface? For your million dollars, the logo and letterhead merchants will even give you a real left-brain runaround about the exact placement of art on your office walls, as though it ever mattered to anybody but their compulsive selves. I would love to ask them what they think of the fact that founder Phil Knight paid all of $35 for the world-famous Nike Swoosh. And what about Richard Branson, who thought $200 for the Virgin logo that goes on everything from 747s to bridal shops was more than generous?

## SAVE YOUR MONEY

Not far below the corporate-identity peddlers, in my estimation, are the giant consulting firms that claim to offer branding advice. These include firms like Anderson, McKinsey, Ernst & Young; KPMG Peat Marwick; and Deloitte & Touche. They do very well at a lot of things, but certainly not branding. The question to ask them is, "How, on God's green earth, are they going to acquire the right-brain cells to create an emotionally driven brand promise?" If you ask them, "But how does it make you feel?"—they're likely to start patting their suit pockets in the hunt for a calculator. The main thing to admire about these guys is the staggering fees they feel more than willing to charge for the services they render. When hearing the numbers from one of their transactions, Harry said it sounded like the GNP of Belgium. We should all have so much moxie.

The same big firms are now talking about merging with law firms, which could produce a huge conflict of interest between auditing and legal advice. Cumbersome conglomerates in the making? You bet. You have to wonder if our consummate consultants have heard that the world is trending toward specialization.

As *Business Week* reports (1999), "It is increasingly challenging to effectively manage any conglomerate these days. In a firm such as PricewaterhouseCoopers, with 155,000 employees in 150 countries, imagine the problems of coordinating disparate businesses, implementing new strategies, monitoring quality control, and melding different professional cultures and compensation systems."

It's difficult to see how clients will benefit from dipping into such a plate of scrambled disciplines, but of course, management consulting and legal work provide fatter fees than the accounting that got the big consultants into business in the first place. I can see them tripping over their own underwear simply because it's hard to do one thing well, let alone everything. Growth is fine and dandy, but a mania for growth at any cost provides its own form of madness and a kind of corporate bedlam that can be hard to fathom.

## THERE'S ALWAYS ROOM FOR THE GOOD GUYS

There will always be room for the ad agency that puts a focus on creating highly involving advertising that touches and surprises us, and furthers the goal of creating relationships with customers. Such advertising needs the benefit of focused strategic direction, but it doesn't matter if the direction is developed by the agency working with the client, or by a brand consultant working with the client.

It might even be that the agency that offers a bit of everything to do with communications—media advertising, media planning, PR, direct mail, and branding advice—ends up the loser because it lacks focus. I may sound like a broken record, but it's impossible to be all things to all people and also be effective.

In any event, the real advances in branding simply aren't coming from the traditional communication consultants. They are driven by the brands themselves. The title of Brand Executive Officer I referred to at the end of the last chapter is very near reality. Brands are, more than ever, taking responsibility for their good names, their focused missions, and the emotional connections that comprise the stuff brand loyalty is made of. Just as you would be loath to let anyone set the agenda for your personal identity and reputation, they see it also as a brand responsibility that cannot be abrogated. The management of a brand's essence is simply too crucial an issue to hand over to anybody on the outside. AmEx Executive Vice President John D. Hayes, responsible for global advertising and brand management, expresses the principle well when he says, "Your brand has to live inside your company. We hire partners who best suit our needs, not ones who do everything" (*Business Week*, 1999).

**PART Six**

# BRAND BUILDING:

# KEY ELEMENTS

17

# The Power of the Name

The name is the brand. It is the quick-as-lightning source of all that is in the question, "But how does it make you feel?"

The name brings to mind all the brand's fact and feeling. It's the distillation of the brand's promise and emotional value. That's why naming a new brand is marketing's most exciting assignment. It's an unprecedented opportunity because you may be getting a chance to write business history in a single word. That one word (maybe two) could be the most significant thing the company ever does, simply because it becomes the brand. You can change certain things about a brand over its lifetime, but the name is likely to remain untouched.

## A BRAND'S ORIGINS

Think of Ivory Soap. It started back in 1879 when one of the founders of Procter & Gamble, Harley Procter, went to church and heard a sermon based on the Forty-fifth Psalm: "All thy garments smell of myrrh, and aloes, and cassia, out of ivory palaces." The word "ivory" stayed with him and became the name of P&G's first white soap. Next came the genius claim that Ivory floats and is 99 44/100 percent pure.

Since women had been using harsh soaps that were very hard on hands, Ivory must have seemed a miracle—a miracle of pure gentleness that never vanished below the water's surface.

The brand promise of Ivory hasn't changed in 118 years. And all I can say is, "Wow!" If that isn't testimony enough to the longevity of a well-conceived brand name, consider that Ivory has contributed profits to P&G somewhere in the neighborhood of $2 billion to $3 billion over its lifetime (Aaker, 1991).

Maybe we should all follow Harley Procter's pious example. It seems that going to church every Sunday pays an unexpected earthly dividend.

I doubt that the founders of Yahoo! took their brand name from such a divine source, but it's easy to see how some feisty, young upstarts would go for a name that's outlandish, to say the least. You can see them sitting around Mom's confiscated garage with beer and empty pizza boxes, halfway through their working day at midnight. Somebody says, "Hey, dudes, we gotta have a name, so like, let's call it Yahoo!." And the others give their assent with a diffident, "Cool, man."

> You can change certain things about a brand over its lifetime, but the name is likely to remain untouched.

## THE THREE RULES OF BRAND NAMES

The same might be true of Excite, Red Hat, Ion Storm, and Amazon.com. These exotic brand names all have three things going for them: they're different, they're easy to remember, and they scream for attention.

What they lack in relevance, they gain in a kind of surprise that's impossible to ignore: What has the name Yahoo! got to do with the product? What kind of a promise is Yahoo!? What emotion does Yahoo! express? Does anybody know that Jonathan Swift invented a separate race called Yahoos in *Gulliver's Travels*? What would you guess are the brand values of a company called Yahoo!?

You've got to like a company with the guts to call itself Yahoo!. And while it doesn't take itself too seriously, it seems to express the founders' joyous youthfulness and conviction about their endeavor.

Yahoo! is a lot more interesting than a miscreant word like Microsoft. And it's hard to imagine that it went through any elaborate testing or research mumbo jumbo in order to reach a consensus that it is, indeed, cool. I guarantee that submitting the name Yahoo! to a focus group would have proved it to be the dumbest name in corporate history.

Of course, names don't have to be as outrageous as Yahoo! to get the job done. We get a kick out of seeing the name Profile carefully placed next to the GE logo on household appliances. Arian Lowe & Travis people worked on the development of it with GE's Vic Alcott a few years ago. GE was becoming more and more of a commodity name in the appliance business—a good name, but no longer one that could be sold at the premium it once commanded.

One solution was to develop a spinoff that promised cachet in an upscale line of appliances designed to give a slimmer, more flush-with-the-cabinets appearance. The word Profile suggested this physical benefit and communicated to women shoppers the elegant and desirable trait of slimness. It's funny to think that a woman confronted with a Profile refrigerator might say it makes her feel thin! The product line was launched with immediate trade and consumer success in the mid-1990s.

## HANGOVERS TO HEDONISM

I like hearing about names that drop from the blue. Just ask him, and Harry will tell the story of the development of the name Hedonism, the resort that has become so linked with the western part of Jamaica called Negril.

He and colleagues Alan Murphy and George Whitfield were standing waist-deep in gentle, blue Caribbean surf one very bright morning, near the construction site of the new resort. They were nursing fierce hangovers. They had their eyes shut to keep out the pain of the sunlight bouncing off the water into their addled brains. They were drinking cold, hair-of-the-dog Red Stripe beer and trying to talk with thick tongues about the resort they were about to launch. They had already decided to make it the first resort to copy the Club Med business model. One of them—Harry thinks it was George Whitfield—said, "God, this is hedonistic." Harry and Alan Murphy put away their hangovers and jumped on the word, and Hedonism was born as a vibrant brand.

In one happy accident, a one-word name sums up the entire experience, both heart and soul, for the customer and the travel agent who has to sell it. And strangely enough, the fact that it's an exotic word few people could accurately define was never a hindrance. It actually helped because its strangeness made it stick out.

Most Caribbean resorts in those days were named after places. They had nice names, such as Frenchman's Cove, Round Hill, Malabar Beach, and so on. It never occurred to anybody to choose a name that described the *feel of the experience*. In that way, Hedonism made tourism history. Its expressiveness filled a new resort in very short order and continues to do so to this day.

Hedonism is a very different kind of name for a resort, and the difference is what makes it forever memorable. It's a little like Xerox, a name we now take for granted as synonymous with copiers, but was daring in its day. I like what Al and Laura Ries say about it in *The 22 Immutable Laws of Branding* (1998). They say marketers often disparage the importance of a name, so the old Haloid Company could have come up with a generic name, such as Paper Master. They might have compounded the error by making it a line extension and calling it the Haloid Paper Master.

Few know what Xerox or xerography means literally, but even today, it says high technology in copiers in a much more memorable way than the Haloid Paper Master ever could.

Less than a year after the launch of Hedonism, the same three people came up with another one-word masterpiece. Their next resort launch was for the rejuvenation of a dead hotel near Jamaica's Ocho Rios. The new, all-inclusive business model was to be the first resort for couples only. If Hedonism was somewhat racy, the new place was to be highly romantic. The name they came up with was, very simply, Couples—another case where one evocative word sums up the essence of the resort's experiential *raison d'être*.

> **F**ew know what Xerox or xerography means literally, but even today, it says high technology in copiers in a much more memorable way than the Haloid Paper Master ever could.

## THE NAME AND THE EMPLOYEES

You have to believe that a name has an effect on the people who work for it, just as a name has an effect on a person. Lance and Barney are two different kinds of people. Hortense and Kelly are on opposite poles. Working for General Dynamics has got to feel different from casting your lot with Ion Storm on the basis of the names alone.

Narrowing a brand's promise and/or emotional content to one or two words is the most difficult communication discipline, but the trick is to go at it as though it was a walk in the park. Your strategy will undoubtedly come from the left side of the brain, but a great name will undoubtedly come crashing into existence from the right.

Sometimes a name like Hedonism just pops out with little work and unerring instinct from the unconscious. It may indeed be significant that Hedonism came out of a meeting between three horribly hung-over guys, standing waist-deep in water and drinking beer at 11 A.M. It's a graphic example of what lateral-thinker Edward de Bono calls "walking away from the problem."

## Names and Naming

Harry Beckwith (1997) (once again, not to be confused with our Harry) has some interesting things to say about names and naming. He says:

*Monogram your shirts, not your company.* IBM is good for IBM, but can you remember ADP, DMM, ETI, ADC, APC, ABC, CBC, or BCW? Don't feel badly. Neither can anybody else.

*Don't get funny with your name.* If you start a hair transplant clinic, don't call it Hair Apparent. Potential customers might also think it's a joke and stay away in droves.

> "**D**on't get funny with your name. If you start a hair transplant clinic, don't call it Hair Apparent. Potential customers might also think it's a joke and stay away in droves."

*Generic names encourage generic business.* Three Twin Cities companies call themselves Financial Services Inc., Financial Specialists Inc., and Financial Counseling Inc. It's impossible for these companies to separate themselves. "A generic name is not your name; it is everyone's."

*Never choose a name that describes something that everybody expects.* Don't use a word such as creative, as in Creative Design. It is highly uncreative. Or a word such as Quality, as in Quality Cleaners. As Beckwith says, "Doesn't that sound like a cleaner that might break your buttons?"

*Be distinctive and sound it.* "In a world filled with me-too company names, companies with distinctive names like NameLab, Federal Express, and Prodigy quickly create the association that they are not me-too services . . . "

With NameLab, he applies the Information-Per-Inch Principle. NameLab is a San Francisco company that specializes in naming products. Their name demonstrates they know what they're doing. He says, "With lightning speed, NameLab's name suggests the company takes a near-scientific approach to developing names, something distinct in its industry . . . If you needed a name for your service, whom would you call first? Names Inc., The Name Company, or NameLab?"

He suggests that, indeed, names such as NameLab and Federal Express are winners in the Information-Per-Inch test and that they should be the standard you use to measure the effectiveness of your name.

## OOPS! DIDN'T MEAN THAT!

Founded by Naseem Javed with offices in New York and Toronto, ABC Namebank specializes in names that will fly in places, such as the Middle East, as easily as in Middle America (*Financial Post,* 1999). As reported in the *New York Times,* "Mr. Javed claims multinationals risk international embarrassment when they fail to call in a specialist. And he rhymes off a slew of corporate brand blunders that sounded good in the marketing department but were unintentionally hilarious in translation. There's 'Chevy Nova,' which in Spanish comes out as 'no va' or 'won't go.' Then there's Vicks cough drops, which were introduced to the German market only to discover that 'vicks' is slang for sex."

There are now a slew of naming outfits you can call for help, but I sometimes wonder if you're not better off getting a few good people around the boardroom table to come up with a name through mouthfuls of pizza. For every different, involving name that comes along, there are just as many that actually sound as though they were all spit out of the same computer.

## HERE, THERE, AND EVERYWHERE

Marc Babjec of the New York ad agency Kirstenbaum Bond & Partners says (*Financial Post,* December 1999) that as naming becomes professionalized, names sound more and more alike. "You can imagine how, at one time, Livent might have sounded new and hot. Well, now we have Lucent. And we have Aquent and Avilant and Agilent and Levilant and Naviant and Telegent. What's next, Coolent? What you have here is clients being taken for a ride."

> EyeWire seems to do a good, memorable job of relating the name to the content of the site.

I value names that attempt to tell you what the product or service is and what it *feels* like. For example, Eye-Wire.com is the Internet's first portal for the graphic design industry, featuring such visual content as video, animation, photography, type, illustration and clip art, and related graphics software and services. EyeWire seems to do a good, memorable job of relating the name to the content of the site: If you have an eye for design, you have an eye wire for online design. Bingo! It suggests acute vision and eye-blink speed. It's a name that makes you think.

## VISUAL NAMES

Some names succeed because they express the feeling of a brand in a highly visual way. An online grocer, such as Peapod, comes to mind. So does Amazon. And how about The Beetle? Or Jaguar? Visual names like these reach into our long-term memories and associations the way a purely intellectual name like Microsoft can't.

The rise of the Internet has spurred the need for creativity in naming products and services. The need for brevity and quick description seems to prick the imagination, and the iconoclasm of the new age often turns up names that are downright cheeky. The new names are also full of feeling, and they tell a story.

A net venture-capital firm calls itself garage.com, which mirrors the start-up habit of commandeering mom's garage as office space. An education toy company calls itself Noodle Kidoodle. The previously mentioned Ion Storm invents computer games. A search engine calls itself HotBot. An MIT research project for developing tech-smart kitchen appliances calls itself Counter Intelligence. An Internet dating service goes by the name of match.com. When the

# IN THIS RING, FRENCH WINS OVER ENGLISH

What's in a name can make all the difference. When Montreal-based *Cirque du Soleil* expanded to the U.S. market with its superb fare of entertainment, it used an English version of its name (*Cirque du Soleil* means Circus of the Sun). But as business writer Peter Diekmayer (*The Montreal Gazette,* 1999) points out, "Some customers were disappointed because they had expected a traditional circus. It then started using its distinctive French name . . . and achieved rapid acceptance, at least in part because that name gave it an exotic flavour [*sic*] and indicated it was a circus like no other."

*Cirque du Soleil* is a fascinating story. It started as a group of Quebécois street performers. It's now a global company worth $150 million with offices in Montreal, Amsterdam, Las Vegas, and Singapore. It staged seven shows on three continents in 1999. While it has remained creatively independent, Disney World just built *Le Cirque* a permanent theater with a ten-year contract. It has two permanent shows also in Las Vegas.

*C'est magnifique!*

couple using it gets married, they can seek the help of theknot.com. A high-tech system for retrieving a stolen car calls itself Boomerang.

## IF THEY COULD SEE US NOW

You wonder what tycoons-of-old, like John D. Rockefeller and J. Pierpont Morgan, would have thought of such names. Their generation favored the stolid genre of handles that usually began with the word General. Would they have looked down their noses and called the new names fripperies? I suppose when electricity was a new consumer force, a name like General Electric served its purpose and communicated a certain dull reliability, but the word "general" always seemed to me a copout—an excuse for our olden-days tycoons not being able to think of something a little more specific. If GE were just coming on the scene today, it would probably be called something like Zap City.

> If GE were just coming on the scene today, it would probably be called something like Zap City.

With more than 7,000 Internet domain names registering every day, a site brilliantly called Namestake.com performs the increasingly necessary task of helping you legally protect online branding. With so much volume, disputes cannot help but arise. For example, Yahooka is an Internet guide to marijuana that was recently threatened with legal action by Yahoo! (*Financial Post*, February 1999). (Shane McGee, a trademark and technology lawyer with the Columbus, Ohio, firm of Vorys, Sater, Seymour and Pease LLP, says an "amicable" settlement between the two is near.)

## CLOSE CALLS

Some names were nearly mistakes. Richard Branson came up with Slipped Disc at the same time he came up with Virgin for his mail-order records years ago. It was his first company, and all of us can be glad that Virgin won. Virgin is used with great effect to give a distinctive, cohesive name to Branson's brand in all its forms. Can you imagine flying on Slipped Disc Airlines?

Founder Jeff Bezos toyed with "aard" and "cadabra" before settling on Amazon. He can hardly be sorry. As the *New York Times Magazine* says, "Amazon suggests great size, of course, and a compendious database . . . But it's also flowing with so much third-world, underdog, eco-conscious goodwill that every click on Amazon.com feels like a vote for the rainforest. And even as its market valuation soared past that of Barnes & Noble and Borders combined, the company clung tenaciously to that image of a principled David, pluckily battling its much less-principled rivals."

## FAMILY NAMES

Naming a company used to be a lot simpler. You could use your own name and then maybe add "& sons" when the next generation joined the firm. The only company name I know of that includes daughters is Russ & Daughters, which, since 1914, has been famous for fine schmaltz herring in New York's Lower East Side. Founder Joel Russ had no sons and thought bringing his girls in would give him a different shtick. It worked.

Last names are still the choice of law firms, brokerage houses, and a lot of ad agencies. It's as though putting your name on the door is like extending your hand in a pledge of personal integrity. It suggests tradition and filial values. A father who values and honors his sons (or daughters) has just got to be an honest guy. Family members presumably don't cheat each other and the family name is their troth not to cheat you.

In that respect, a surname still works well, like Dell Computer, named after its founder Michael Dell. But I wonder in the age of the Internet if we will have time for such monikers as www.batten/barton/durstine&osborne&sons.com in comparison with www.yahoo.com. And just think, if Yahoo! had used its founder's names instead of Yahoo!, we would have Yang & Filo Inc., and a bit of naming magic would have been lost to the world.

CHAPTER 18

# Logos and Other Elements of Style

When medieval kings went into battle, they bore a flag (called a standard) to differentiate their "brands" from their allied barons' brands. This was more than vanity or a way to promote *esprit de corps* among the ranks. They did it to combat illiteracy. The ordinary soldier couldn't read. Rather than carry a banner that said, "Seventh Cavalry Division," the king had a standard-bearer fly his colors, often in the form of a distinctive coat of arms. All the troops had to do was look up, and they could identify where they were supposed to be and (hopefully) who not to put to the sword.

Even today in England, pubs use pictures to illustrate names like The Swan, The Lord Nelson, The Dog and Gun, and so on. This also goes back to a time when most people couldn't read. A cobbler would hang the sign of a boot outside his shop. A fishmonger hung a model fish. A gunsmith hung a representation of a gun. You still sometimes see signs like these used as quick signals.

### THE NAME AS THE LOGO

But in an age when just about everybody can read, there is no better symbol of your name than your name itself. IBM's logo is just plain IBM—the one monogram that is just as powerful as the spelled-out name itself. Borders Bookstore's logo is the word Borders. Ford is an evocative script of the name Ford. Sony uses its name only. The logo for Coca-Cola is Coca-Cola in a nostalgic, old-fashioned script, as well as the less ornate word Coke. I can't remember if Yahoo! uses anything other than its name, but if it does, it's most surely gilding the lily!

Using just your name to form your logo is particularly appropriate for a new brand. It's hard enough to seed your name in the minds out there. Why complicate the effort with trying to also communicate a graphic symbol? And as far as the Internet is concerned, you can just forget about a graphic until you get to your homepage. When you log on, you can't even get your name in upper and lower case.

You might well ask, what about the flags of countries? The United States of

> IBM's logo is just plain IBM—the one monogram that is just as powerful as the spelled-out name itself.

America is a fine name, but would we want to give up Old Glory? Of course not. Your company, too, can have a flag that flies proudly from your company flagstaff to rally the troops. Just don't confuse it with clear communication.

## WHICH ONE DO YOU REMEMBER?

What about such memorable signs as the Mercedes-Benz three-legged star? It's terrific. But remember it has been around for several generations, and as symbolic as it may be, it's still not as clear as the name Mercedes-Benz. Shell might indeed use a shell, but why bother when you can use the word Shell? How recognizable are the graphic logos for Honda, Toyota, Nissan, Mazda, and Hyundai in comparison with spelling the names out? Lucent Technology appears to center its advertising around the Zen-like circular brushstroke it uses as a logo. While it's a comely abstract graphic, I don't know why they make such a fuss over it. Lucent is a mellifluous name that suggests light and lucidity. Does the graphic add to it in any way?

I don't think there are any hard and fast rules for all this, but I once again call on the muse of common sense. If you were starting a shoe store called Wedgies, you could probably think of a good graphic. But why bother when you can use the name Wedgies in a strong typeface that avoids any confusion and requires little or no thought?

Wells Fargo and its stagecoach are inseparable even when the stagecoach is only in our mind's eye, but once more, it's a historic connection. The two are often used to great advantage on an outdoor billboard. Couple the name with the emotional jolt of a stagecoach and four horses going full tilt across the Nevada desert, and you touch a lot of buttons in the western psyche. But if you were forced to choose between the symbol and the name itself, I don't think there is much to think about. The name Marlboro and the Marlboro man are inseparable, but if you had to ditch one, which would it be?

## EXCEPTIONS TO THE RULE

There are bound to be exceptions to the "rule." National flags—the British Union Jack, Old Glory, the French and Italian tricolors—are familiar enough to be clichés, but they are also highly evocative and not even slightly abstract. They literally touch us where we live. If you were starting a raincoat company called London Fog, including the Union Jack in your logo might work harder than the name alone. So would using the Italian flag for such obvious products as Italian-made pasta. Virgin Airlines is about to include the Union Jack in its red logo design (after British Airways abandoned it for something more contemporary).

My friend Tony Hilliard designed a logo for a new retail concept called O Canada! He put the name under the familiar outline of a Mountie on horseback. Using the two together works harder than the name alone. The inventor of the concept, Alan Murphy, had it made into a memorable flag. It's curious that the Royal Canadian Mounted Police is as evocative of Canada as the Canadian flag. As Tony said, "Canada is the only country in the world that can use a police force as a national symbol."

Sometimes a graphic can help explain or expand the meaning of a name. HUD has a logo that incorporates a roof over the word to suggest housing. Travelers' red umbrella symbolizes the security of rainy-day insurance. A little girl in a raincoat makes the point that it never rains, but it pours for Morton Salt. These aren't graphics for their own sake. They have a relevance, which helps involve you. They add a bit of character as they stimulate your memory and communicate brand values.

## A BRAND'S STYLE

A good brand leaves as little as possible to chance when it comes to style. It establishes a narrow selection of typefaces that represents it. It chooses a color—hopefully, one that's different from the competition's. It sets guidelines for the use of its logo on letterheads, on the side of trucks, on business cards, in advertising, and so on. Setting up these guidelines is big business—too big in my opinion—that reaps huge profits for its practitioners (my views on this highway robbery are expressed in chapter 16). Companies like IBM used to extend style to regimental-type rules for how its employees dress and cut their hair, and what kind of art was allowed to hang on office walls. But even IBM is now less likely to require the formality of a jacket and the dreaded necktie. Women are as likely to wear jeans and a sweatshirt as skirts and blouses, and in the name of productivity, why not?

> Logos add a bit of character as they stimulate your memory and communicate brand values.

## AROUND THE WORLD WITH YOUR NAME

Going beyond style, companies see how important it is to promulgate and protect their identity. Presenting the same face to the world around the world becomes more and more important as geography shrinks.

You simply don't want others to mess with your carefully groomed reputation or use any part of your good name for their own purposes. For example, try opening a corner convenience store called The GE QuickStopShop near the GE plant in Louisville and see how fast a bevy of corporate lawyers comes to stomp on your welcome mat. They will tell you that QuickStopShop is fine and dandy, but you get rid of the reference to GE, or suffer consequences that originated with the Spanish Inquisition.

## EQUALING THE WORK ENVIRONMENT

Nowadays, we see the work environment as a more level playing field when it comes to office size as status. My office is smaller than my assistant's. The multimillionaire CEO of Intel, Andrew Grove, works at the company's headquarters in a standard 8 ft by 9 ft cubicle. He does, however, have a wonderful view of the parking lot, where he has to cruise around, looking for a space just like everybody else. He also lines up in the company cafeteria for his lunchtime tray. The message is that he sees no need to isolate himself from his employees and their problems. By choosing not to set himself apart with fancy executive office perks, he communicates a sense of "we're all in this enterprise together." His egalitarian behavior speaks more coherently than anything he could ever say. It also tends to squelch complaints from the troops about their offices.

> As Peter Drucker teaches us: management is a function and a responsibility rather than a rank and a privilege.

Your company's real style must emerge as a product of your organization's culture, and that, in turn, is likely to emerge from your style as a leader. If you're stuck in a hierarchical mode, you're likely to have an office about the size of Versailles, while your vassals toil in broom closets. You may even have (heaven forbid) a private washroom that cuts you off from the satisfying fraternity of a hand-washing chat! As Peter Drucker teaches us: management is a function and a responsibility rather than a rank and a privilege.

## How the Public Sees You

From the setting of a company's tone to the provenance of the art on the walls, style is something with which you have to come to grips. But it finds its true source of inspiration in the real issues beyond facade and spin. Remember that technology makes you and your brand transparent. The time between a thoughtless act in the name of the bottom line and being exposed for it in public has shrunk to nothing.

It used to be that companies were more concerned with what the public thought of them than what the companies actually were. The jump between reality and fantasy was often a long one. Image was something for the public relations department to worry about, not something that necessarily had to have any basis in fact. You could almost hear the old CEO saying, "Integrity's a highly valued commodity, and by golly, we've got the wherewithal to buy as much as we need of it."

Maybe Harry is right when he says style says it all.

## CHAPTER 19

# Advertising: Telling the Brand Story to Customers

Advertising is nothing more than a means for you to control your communication with your customers. And as a famous British ad man named Jeremy Bullmore (great name for an ad man) once said, advertising is a little like the telephone: it doesn't do anything until you use it. When a bad man in a dirty raincoat starts breathing heavily into your ear through the receiver, you can hardly blame Alexander Graham Bell!

## MAINTAINING BRAND AWARENESS

You use advertising to help maintain brand awareness. It's the price you pay for staying in the game. It's the expensive alternative to the cheap publicity that launched a lot of famous new brands in the past decade. But it's still one of the powerful ways to maintain an emotional connection with your customers.

When you run an ad, you are putting out a stimulus in search of a response. The trick is to structure the response so you get the desired reaction, and it's here that we often run into an unfortunate situation: people don't always respond as you would wish.

It may show great irresponsibility on their part, but customers often refuse to do what you want them to. You've just paid a zillion dollars to splash your commercial over practically every TV screen in America, and they just sit there rather than rushing down to the store to buy the amazing new-and-improved toothpaste that your career depends on. Consumers can be downright arrogant in their refusal to accommodate your marketing efforts. They hear what they want to hear and very often, close their minds to the brave attempt you make to influence their point of view.

This is why I sometimes surprise prospective clients when I tell them that you don't run an ad to sell something unless you're in the classified section of the newspaper. Some kind of sale is, of course, the ultimate objective of all advertising. You don't advertise because you enjoy the expense. But before you can begin to make the register ring, you have to make the mind ring. You have to be firmly planted in your prospect's head and/or heart, whichever comes first. Advertising can help you seal your brand promise, and it can help you remind your customers of it, again and again.

> Consumers can be downright arrogant in their refusal to accommodate your marketing efforts. They hear what they want to hear and very often, close their minds to the brave attempt you make to influence their point of view.

## GETTING THE DESIRED RESPONSE

Sometimes an advertiser is so eager to get the right response that he makes the response his message. The advertiser provides one instead of evoking one. If I want you to think I'm a nice guy, I don't walk up to you and say, "Hi, my name is Daryl Travis, and I'm a very nice guy." You might think I'm a conceited weirdo, but you would not give me the desired response.

Now look at this scenario: I walk into your office an hour late for a meeting with you. I'm angry. I'm cursing. I'm so agitated that I can hardly get my story out. On the way to your office, I saw some hit-and-run jerk knock an old lady down with his car. I felt obligated to take her to the hospital emergency room. Then I had to wait around to find out if she was okay. She turned out to be just a bit bruised. Boy, if I could get my hands on that hit-and-run jerk, I'd lock him up and do violence to his sensitive parts.

I haven't *told* you I'm a nice guy, but you might conclude it. I demonstrated it laterally. And what's curious is, on the surface, the stimulus has nothing to do with the response. How can a guy who is angry communicate that he is kind? Such is the complexity of effective communication.

## AIM FOR THE EMOTIONS

You can't make an emotional connection with a customer without using some form of emotion. Winston Churchill knew he wanted to thank the young pilots who fought the Luftwaffe so bravely over England's skies in the Battle of Britain. To make his point, he might have said, "I sincerely want to thank the brave young guys who saved our bacon in the Battle of Britain. They did a swell job, and we all love them for it." This is a decent sentiment, but think how much more feeling he evoked from Britain's embattled citizens with his actual words: "Never, in the field of human conflict, has so much been owed, by so many, to so few."

> You can't make an emotional connection with a customer without using some form of emotion.

Only one of these statements sends a shiver up your spine. The difference is emotion; feeling; sentiment; reaching into oneself to find the stuff that reaches out in a genuine way that can only be heartfelt.

Communicating facts with feeling makes the facts live like fire. The ability to accomplish this in advertising is why many copywriters and art directors have bigger annual salaries than the President of the United States.

General Electric does it with touching TV demonstrations of "We bring good things to life." Sears does it with "Come See the Softer Side of Sears," in its infinite and delightful variations. Hallmark gets to us with demonstrations of "When you care enough to send the very best." Chevy trucks do it with "Like a Rock." Coke has been known to do it with heart-stopping enactments of "It's the real thing." (Coke hasn't used "It's the real thing" for years, but it's amazing how it still sticks; as I said earlier, one wonders why the brand people don't simply submit to its power.) And Motel 6 does it with a simple, down-home promise to "keep the light on for you" that cannot help but warm the coldest heart.

## BRAND PROMISES

Notice that these aren't "clever" lines; rather, they are brand promises, and they are promises that matter. I like to think of a brand promise as a kind of liquid cement that fills in a small crevice in the brain. After a while, if it's well focused, it hardens and stakes out a position in the mind, one that belongs to you and that your toughest competitor will find difficult to dislodge. This is only possible with promises that matter, promises that give us something we can value. You value that a package entrusted to FedEx will be delivered "When it absolutely positively has to get there overnight." You value that Avis "tries harder." You value that when you eat at the The Olive Garden "you're family."

## A TOUCH OF WIT

Humor can be used to express value and invoke a response that can often be highly involving. Humor isn't a technique; rather, it's a powerful means for communication.

New York's Post House restaurant runs a large newspaper ad that shows a life-size steak knife, surrounded by a lot of white space. Over it is the headline, "Horrifying vegetarians since 1979." It doesn't show a steak, but I can feel my teeth biting into one with sinful pleasure after I appreciate how much the restaurant recognizes my intelligence and appreciation for wit.

Humor shows you don't take yourself or your brand too seriously. A position presented with humor is easier to defend because the consumer is less likely to raise a question of authenticity. If Miller had said, "Lose weight with a great-tasting beer," it might have opened up a can of worms that doesn't exist with "Everything you ever wanted in a beer. And less."

> Humor isn't a technique; rather, it's a powerful means for communication.

Ads for these brands *involve* us. They either *surprise* us, or *touch* us, or both. Involvement by surprise is what I believe should be the yardstick by which we measure the effectiveness of all advertising. When you're flipping through a magazine, an ad must somehow make you do a double take. An outdoor billboard should involve you enough to cause traffic accidents. A TV commercial has to own your mind for its half-minute lifespan.

Surprise often comes from looking at the familiar from a saucy new angle. An old ad for the VW Beetle had the headline, "After we paint the car, we paint the paint." When Harry did an ad for the Hedonism resort, he ignored the obvious allure of sea, sun, and sand; instead, he invited you to come and "Be Wicked for a Week."

## A Trickier Track

Involving you with a deeply emotional appeal—a story—is trickier. Hallmark's story of an old woman going to a birthday party among her children and grandchildren is a fine example of a commercial that has you reaching for the Kleenex. Coke used to do it with a combination of music and picture. Remember the international array of young people on a mountainside, each holding a candle with the camera slowly pulling back to reveal that they form a Christmas tree? They sing what I call the Coke anthem—"I'd like to teach the world to sing in perfect harmony"—and even the worst Scrooge could not help but respond with a small tear. I think it's the best, heart-tugging jingle ever written. It translated amazingly well into a popular song.

Former Coke marketing executive Sergio Zyman prides himself on pulling the famous and universally admired "Mean Joe Greene" commercial off the air (*Fast Company*, 1999). That's the one where Mean Joe gives his football shirt to a little kid, who is trying to cheer him up by giving Joe his Coke. Zyman pulled the spot because he said it generated more good will than it did sales, which I find astonishing. Coke *is* a good-will relationship with its customers. Unless a Coke bottle is featured in a cents-off retail ad, advertising doesn't *sell* Coca-Cola.

Traditional media advertising's job is to reinforce the emotional relationship people feel for a great and favored brand. It's like perpetuating a mythology. As I said earlier, to get into people's pockets, you first have to get into their minds and stay there. Few commercials in the history of advertising do that better than "Mean Joe Greene," or "I'd Like To Teach the World To Sing."

Of course, pulling the Mean Joe commercial reflects what I believe is Mr. Zyman's wrong-headed definition of marketing. In his book, *The End of Marketing As We Know It*, he says, "The sole purpose of marketing is to get more people to buy more of your product, more often, for more money" (*Fast Company*, ibid.). This sounds to me like a speech you make at a stockholder meeting. They love hearing that kind of macho stuff. But it's mass-market thinking in a mass-customization environment. It's thinking that looks in rather than out.

> Marketing is no longer about selling. It's about creating relationships with customers that cultivate emotional preference for your brand.

The marketer as all-powerful and the consumer as all-accepting is dead. Marketing is no longer about shoving things at people on TV. Marketing is no longer about selling. It's about buying. It's about making it easier and more palatable to buy. It's about creating relationships with customers that cultivate emotional preference for your brand.

## THE ALL-IMPORTANT MIDDLE STEP

*Of course* it's marketing's job to build sales. To this end, *of course* advertising's ultimate objective is a sale, but between running an ad and making a sale, there's a critical step that has to take place. An ad is a stimulus in search of a response, which means the ad has to create a thought or a feeling that translates into preference.

In a broader context, before any business can create a profit, it has to create a customer. Before an ad can create a sale, it has to provoke a response. That's just like horses go before carts.

Customers aren't empty vessels into which we can pour our marketing desires. They never were. They never will be. We have to engage them before we can marry them. We say we live in The Information Age. Maybe we should call it The Customer Age. (To his credit, Zyman goes on to say that the Net's effect on democratizing the customer and speaking to them directly is what will produce big results in future.)

## SURPRISE AND TOUCH

Surprise and touch are often the words to think of when you want to sort out mere product advertising from dynamic brand advertising.

It's possible for a product to get over the facts of its performance without giving you a feeling for it. But if a product communicates mechanically without involving you emotionally, it will stay a product rather than becoming a brand. A product might have a safely registered trademark and logo, but it might not create the value of an emotional connection with you. Go into your local hardware store, and you see dozens of products that aren't brands. A surprising number of patent medicines and personal care products seem to commit this marketing crime.

> If a product communicates mechanically without involving you emotionally, it will stay a product rather than becoming a brand.

When an ad doesn't connect well, it could be that it concentrates too much on the product and not enough on the promise. It may seem unfair, but the best product in the world won't succeed against an okay product with the best promise in the world. Marketing is about perceptions, not products. People buy promises, not products. And people buy promises that are highly focused. When it comes to promises, fence-sitting doesn't work. Faint hearts fail to win fair maids and loyal customers.

## FOCUS

In a book called *Focus* (1996), Al Ries goes as far as saying that a consistent brand promise gets boiled down to one word that distinguishes one brand from another in the mind of the consumer.

Volvo equals safe. BMW equals sporty. Mercedes equals prestige. Ragu equals thick (spaghetti sauce). Heinz equals thick (ketchup). FedEx equals overnight. These words are "owned" by the brands that represent them, and it's difficult to dislodge that ownership. A brand is vulnerable when it lacks this intense focus.

When brands flirt with other, extra promises; when they lead themselves into the temptation of a broader, more all-inclusive appeal; they simply create a dissonance in the minds of the consumer because what they say conflicts with established feelings. It doesn't matter that a Volvo probably isn't any safer than a BMW. Volvo means safe and that's all there is to it!

## THE *TOTAL* MEANING OF THE BRAND

This is a larger issue than advertising. It involves the total meaning of the brand. For example, it seems to me that recently, Volvo has been flirting with a promise of cars that are sexy and safe. If true, this is a dangerous dichotomy. Jaguars are sexy. Volvos are safe. Automakers used to say that safety wouldn't sell, but a consistent promise of it has made Volvo one of the big-selling luxury imports. Don't mess with a Godsend.

Another reason for an ad not connecting well could be that the promise is full of advertiser wish fulfillment rather than customer wish fulfillment. Or it simply offers a stilted view of reality that suits the advertiser but aggravates the viewer.

Procter & Gamble commercials used to rely on a "slice-of-life" formula that cried out for cruel parody because of stilted dialogue between two women culturally tied to life in a suburban kitchen. Brand people used to defend these commercials with testimony to their effectiveness, but America's viewers can all heave a sigh of relief that such inanity from P&G no longer seems to sully our evening entertainment, and P&G brands don't seem to suffer without it.

> Another reason for an ad not connecting well could be that the promise is full of advertiser wish fulfillment rather than customer wish fulfillment.

Annoying gets attention. That's true. But should it be the measure of effective communication? I think not. When I say surprise is an effective measure for communication, I don't mean "white knights" galloping across the screen, shouting that the Ajax laundry detergent is stronger than dirt! I hear old ad people say, "It worked." But how did it work? The brand has been deader than doornails for longer than I can remember. (To be fair, other factors may have killed the brand, but we certainly don't miss the advertising.)

## CELEBRITIES AND ADVERTISING

The use of celebrities in advertising seems to me to be more deftly handled than it used to be. The old days of the star performer woodenly holding the package to the camera and saying how good it is are long gone. The problem for me was always one of relevance—such as, what has the star got to do with either the product or the promise?

Now Candice Bergen talks to us with genuine wit and endearing self-deprecation on behalf of Sprint to communicate an essential feeling for the brand. Michael Jordan and his cartoon pals cavort with glee as they pull heartstrings for MCI. To the dismay of his fans, the gentleman that is Michael may have retired from basketball, but I see no reason why he can't stretch his authority out for yet a few more years in MacDonald's, MCI's, and Nike's favor. (Of course, there are those of us in Chicago who think he should either buy his own team or run for president, whichever comes first. Since he bought a team, we now think he can do both!)

## PRICE AND PROMISE

Brand advertising rarely concentrates on price. When it does, it is usually connected to the brand promise. If Hallmark ever did a price promotion (I don't think it ever has to), an ad might include the specific cents-off offer with a line that reads, "Now it costs a little less to send the very best."

Of course, some brands like Wal-Mart exist because of low price. In that case, price is the featured benefit. It's sometimes gussied up with the promise of friendly, down-home service, but Wal-Mart means price. (Harry is such a snob, he wouldn't be caught dead shopping in a Wal-Mart store; he always wanted to write a price ad for the brand with the headline, "Wal-Mart, the lowest of the low.")

A real example of brand advertising combined with a promotion was one for good old Ivory soap. It promised to pay you $100,000 if you could find a bar of Ivory that sinks. The offer ties in to a long-lived Ivory claim that its pure soap floats. It appeals to your sense of humor and encourages you to buy the product in a way that is so much more clever than a cents-off coupon.

## AN AD'S LIFE

Brand advertising has staying power. Clients and their agencies get tired of a good campaign long before the rest of the world. And sometimes, new copywriters and art directors come along and want to change everything so that they can be original. It's a human desire that must be watched.

Dove has been pouring moisturizing cream into its bar on TV for decades. You've seen the demonstration hundreds of times. Are you tired of it? Does it ever fail to communicate gentleness and moisture? Do you think Dove would be insane to abandon it for something more cool? I read recently that Dove's market share is 9 percent, but its dollar share was 13.8 percent—proof of a good brand's pricing power.

Another example is Maytag's Old Lonely Repairman, played by actor Gordon Jump. He provides a simple, feel-good way to get over the promise of reliable, long-lived, hard-working washing machines as an attainable benefit. The gentle humor of the campaign

> Clients and their agencies get tired of a good campaign long before the rest of the world.

serves also to make the brand approachable and human. Old Lonely is always welcome in your viewing room. The campaign is an example of an idea that's really just okay, but it gets its power from prodigious longevity; in fact, one commercial about a repairman with nothing to do simply wouldn't work. Having nothing to do for the past 20 years is what counts. Maytag is happily stuck with him. The campaign reminds chop-and-change artists that consistent, long-term focus still makes powerful communication.

An example from my own career came when our client GE Appliances gave us the assignment to introduce RCA Home Appliances to the market. This was a tangled brandscape, to say the least. GE had sold RCA Electronics, along with the GE small appliance business, to Thompson Consumer Electronics, a French company. GE had retained the rights to RCA kitchen appliances, refrigerators and ranges, the major appliances, to be released as a flanker brand to their own leading line.

Our client had advised us that the only thing we should consciously avoid was the RCA icon, Nipper the dog. Thompson was contending with the high-tech imagery from the likes of Sony and Mitsubishi, and was trying to forever lose the dog from their communications.

As our team developed a brand scheme for the new line, we quickly discovered that the consumer had a very positive and affectionate response to Nipper. We didn't have a lot else to work with, and if we listened to what our consumers were telling us, it seemed ludicrous to kill off a brand icon with such a demonstratively positive legacy. Amidst objections from RCA Electronics, we brought Nipper to life (heretofore he had always been an illustration, never a real dog) and had a successful launch of the RCA line of major kitchen appliances.

About a year later, RCA Electronics brought Nipper back in their advertising. They used the very same dog we had found and specially trained, and added their own slant with Chipper, son of Nipper. Now more than 15 years later, this canine team still leads the way in RCA Electronics communications and has helped forge a very successful resurgence of the RCA brand. It's a literal case of teaching an old dog new tricks.

## BRAND LEADERS

Leading-brand advertising often defines its product category. Hallmark is a good example. Can you even name another brand of greeting card? (If you can, it's probably a Hallmark spinoff, but in fact, the other big card company is Carlton.)

Brand leaders get strength in advertising their category. Doing so reminds you that they "own" the category. If you say you're the bestselling brand, it means a lot of people obviously use the product to make it true. If you weren't "the best" (so the logic goes), you couldn't be number one. I was surprised to find out recently that the Nissan Maxima is the bestselling 6-cylinder import model. I would think this would be a reassuring thought to somebody on the cusp of buying one, but I've never heard it mentioned in any Maxima ad.

## NUMBER ONE'S VULNERABLE POSITION

Leading brands are vulnerable to comparison precisely because a comparison puts the secondary brand in good company. Coke doesn't challenge Pepsi. On the other hand, Pepsi had every right to attack the leader with The Pepsi Challenge. It's not that Pepsi stands a chance at knocking Coke off its number-one, emotional position. But often what you are against defines you just as much as what you

## CONSISTENCY AS A CUSTOMER MACHINE

Sometimes a single piece of communication is so powerful and so right that it can run for years without change. When Harry and Tony Hilliard were a writer/art director team at Arian, Lowe & Travis in 1992, they were asked to prepare a full-page ad for LeSPORT—the spa/resort in St. Lucia. The ad was to appear in the *London Times Magazine*.

They worked on the problem for a couple of weeks and then submitted only one ad for the client's review. The headline, "Give us your body for a week and we'll give you back your mind" so captured the brand promise that none of their other quite worthy attempts came close. The ad is now practically the only ad the resort runs, and it has run unchanged in the *London Times Magazine* at least once a month for eight years.

LeSPORT CEO Craig Barnard says, "We often think about how we could improve it but we end up leaving it alone. It continues to pull very good response and it serves as a reminder to people who have been to the resort that they should come again. It's an urbane communication that beautifully states the resort's mission and promise. I will change the ad only when we change the basic promise of the resort."

are for. Seven-Up should make a millionaire out of the genius who came up with The Uncola.

Changing ads in a campaign from time to time may be necessary to keep it fresh, but such changes don't have to interfere with the consistency of the brand's voice. The "Wait 'til we get our Hanes on you" campaign has seen dozens of executions without changing its core identity. The same is true of McDonald's. Consistency of voice is money in the bank. If a person projects a different personality every time you meet, you never get a sense of what she's all about. You can change your clothes, but you don't change yourself— unless, of course, you want to be put down as irrelevant. Brands are the same.

I've never gotten a good sense of Mazda because the brand chops and changes its communication (or so it seems to me) with every season. The same is true of Nissan. Could a lack of consistency in their brand communication be partly why these brands lag behind Toyota and Honda? It certainly has nothing to do with the efficacy of their products. It could be that new COO Carlos Ghosn is right when he said, "One of the biggest surprises is that Nissan didn't care about its brand. There is nobody really responsible for the strategy of the brand" (*Business Week*, 1999, October).

> You can change your clothes, but you don't change yourself— unless, of course, you want to be put down as irrelevant. Brands are the same.

Staying in the automotive field a moment longer, Volkswagen advertising finally got it right with the "Drivers wanted" campaign. For years, they seemed intent on boring customers to death by reminding them of their German heritage and something called *Farfegneugen*, which I can hardly pronounce and doubt I can spell. Talk about talking to yourself! And talk about spending tens of millions to buy your way into near oblivion! With a new and intelligent product alignment also came new communication that involves its young audience with what could be lasting consistency.

## Stay Consistent

Sticking to one's personality guns rightly extends into all of a brand's communication—direct mail, promotions, collateral material, in-store POP, and so on. When you integrate all your communication, when all your advertising and promotion efforts speak with a common voice, you amplify the power of your voice by an incredible factor. This becomes even more important with all the new tools at our collective disposal through the courtesy of technology.

It's not just outside the company but also inside it that brand communication finds its power. And it's not just with your customers, but with all your stakeholders, that it finds its emotional voice. There will be more about integration in a later chapter, but the point can be made here that integration is more about creating and managing a brand's relationships than merely creating and managing a brand's advertising.

## LOOK AHEAD

People (like the dear, departed David Ogilvy) gave us a lot of rules for advertising that well-meaning clients sometimes shake in my face. I have to remind them that those rules were tantamount to waging Desert Storm with the weapons and tactics you might have used in the Korean War.

What worked yesterday might work just as well today, but for the larger issue of integrating a brand's communications among its various constituents and interest groups, I prefer to look at tomorrow.

## CHAPTER 20

# Telling the Brand Story to Other Stakeholders

Customers aren't the only source of success for a brand. They aren't the only ones who need to be asked the question, "How does it make you feel?"

Certainly the way employees feel about the brand they represent will have a bearing on how customers and other stakeholders learn about it and feel about it beyond their own experience.

## THE INFORMATION VIRUS

Harry never had any problem dealing with Bell for his phone service until one of his friends was "downsized" from the company in a very shabby manner. Listening to the sad story of the way an employee was let go made Harry a lot more receptive to Sprint when they came calling with an offer of lower long-distance rates.

Any employee who is less than enthusiastic about the brand he or she works for will influence outside feeling for it. This is particularly true of the front-line troops, but those who toil in the back room also live in a world populated with co-workers, friends, and relatives who have friends with relatives, and so on. Even without the kind of information virus that can spread with unprecedented alarm on the Internet, a contagion of bad feeling doesn't take long to incubate.

The antidote is, of course, to treat employees with respect within a culture where good manners count. But other than the obviousness of such a pearl, you can help create a feeling of belonging by chat, by natter fests, and by keeping everybody informed about everything that's going on. When I say everything—I mean *everything*.

Why shouldn't the girl in the mail-room of a private company know about its quarterly P&L? Why not tell her about the big order you just missed, along with why you think you didn't get it? Why not tell her your most recent idea for changing an operational procedure that has nothing to do with the mailroom? Or better yet, tell the whole company about a procedural improvement she successfully suggested. Think back to Commander Abrashoff and how he communicated with his crew and—even more important—how its members communicated back.

> Intranet technology makes it easier than ever for the person at the top to coalesce the work force with information that encourages a feeling of pride in belonging.

In a big company where personal contact is a limited possibility, Intranet technology makes it easier than ever for the person at the top to coalesce the work force with information that encourages a feeling of pride in belonging. Once the technical installation is done, it's also inexpensive to operate. With a click of a mouse, the CEO can talk to everybody every day, as many times a day as he or she wants (although I would suggest not becoming an overexposed nuisance).

## START TALKING

If you put out a regular company newsletter, you can do a lot more than publish the facts of births and weddings. Editorial content can tell people what's really going on. You can recognize accomplishment. You can express your feelings candidly as you would as a member of any family.

When you think about it, there's not much to hide. Only sworn confidences need to be kept close to the chest. Half of what most companies consider secrets don't die in a shredder. Companies are so close nowadays that a lot of them share plans without fear. Harry says he's had a dozen great ideas (his adjective) in his life that he's never feared sharing with would-be competitors for feedback. He says not one was ever stolen. I'm not suggesting that you broadcast your plans to your competitors, but this isn't World War II, where walls have ears and loose lips sink ships.

Executives also have to get out of their offices and talk to people to find out what they're feeling and what they need to do their jobs better for the good of the brand. Nothing beats your personal contact.

I think it was Tom Peters who called it, "management by walking around." But it doesn't need a label. We have to remember that communication doesn't go one way except in a monologue. What you want is to get feedback; to get a dialogue going that never stops. Learning what your employees think, feel, want, need, and absolutely have to have will only help you do a better job of management and leadership. By the same token, it makes it easier to speak candidly about what you need from them. A CEO often has access to a company's numbers, but it's even more important to have access to how the people associated with the brand feel about it. Understanding the feelings helps ensure the numbers.

## Don't Lose Touch with Those Around You

It's so easy to become isolated from the larger reality of life in the trenches. I'm reminded of Hillary Clinton running for a senatorial seat. She's appalled to find out how much Westchester residents are obliged to pay in property taxes. There are products in the dairy section of the supermarket that she has never heard of. She almost had to learn all over again how to drive a car. The perquisites of power should never include a loss of touch with the life that goes on around you.

The objective is to always see the brand clearly; to always have a view of the inside of the brand, with outside vision. The obvious way to do this is, of course, to get physically outside the company and talk to customers and all the other desired recipients of a brand's communication.

As Peter Drucker (1999) reminds us, ". . . it is a very old observation that few things improve the performance of a physician as much as being a hospital patient for two weeks."

I've never met anybody in any company that didn't absolutely love a feeling of close belonging, and it simply doesn't happen in a vacuum. It happens when you have a feeling of connection with a brand's leaders. It's as important as competitive wages.

And, as Stanford professor Paul Watzlawick says, "One cannot not communicate."

Your inactions speak as loudly as your actions. What you don't say often says as much as what you do say. The more candid you are, the less people will guess and gossip, the less they will spread rumors, and the less your brand will fall victim to false witness.

## COMMUNICATION AFFECTS EVERYBODY

Communication drives this process. And it drives support for your brand among all the other groups that have a stake in your brand for whatever reason. Suppliers nowadays are often as much a part of the brand (and a factor in its success) as employees. They can do exactly what is asked of them, or they can contribute beyond the call of duty—all depending on how they feel about the brand. The press can kill you or caress you. Its members are much more likely to value the latter if they actually know you and get a feel for what the brand is about—its values, its mission, its ethos.

Investors can make or break you by jumping in and out of your stock. If they understand you and your intentions, they might take a longer view. Wall Street listens to financial analysts who will do a better job if they can feel free to consult you on their analysis. Government and its bureaucracy can help you or hinder you, but even it is starting to show the hopeful signs of humanity that needs your personal attention. And we see that nowadays, competitors are also likely to be partners, and deserve to be courted with feeling and informed with fact.

> The more candid you are, the less people will guess and gossip, the less they will spread rumors, and the less your brand will fall victim to false witness.

While dialogue between the brand and all these stakeholders is often spontaneous, it's important to have a plan for your communication with each brand influence—a plan that is just as important as one you would devise for media advertising. One thing you don't want is different brand people on the inside telling different stories, particularly different stories to the same people on the outside.

Communication benefits from structure. It can also save money. In a big company, it's not unusual for departments to publish their own brochures, spelling out an issue from their specific angle. Cut that out. Departments can have different audiences with different informational needs, but there's only one basic brand story.

*Driving Brand Value* (1997) says, "The accumulated support of all stakeholders is what produces brand equity." The book gives us a diagram that illustrates that communication equals brand relationships equals brand support equals brand equity. The relationships attached to your brand make up its ecosystem.

## THE PARTS OF A BRAND

Profit is indeed the juicy fruit of a brand, but relationships are the root. The nourishment for the root that grows the plant that grows the fruit is communication. And it doesn't always have to be a complicated process that relies on Intranets and Internets. Sometimes, the good old phone will do the trick.

I heard recently that Michael Dell of Dell Computer personally calls detractors in the press and asks them to check with him before they write what he thinks is a wrong angle on the brand. He gives reporters his personal number and promises he will always get back to them as fast as he can.

I hope he also calls them when he thinks they did a good job. I regularly call or e-mail writers of what I think are brilliant books to express my genuine admiration. They appreciate it, and I benefit from having a personal connection to a future source of information in the area of their expertise. It doesn't matter how powerful or famous a person becomes, experience tells me that everybody likes hearing a genuine expression of feeling for a job well done. Harry became a quite famous ad man, but if you call him to say how great you think his headline *du jour* is, he will fall on grenades for you.

A personal, snail-mail letter isn't yet quite as dead as the dodo bird. It's still an effective medium and may become more so as we rely too much on the short, often clipped exchange of e-mail.

A story of simple communication with stakeholders I like is one *Driving Brand Value* tells about former Coke chairman Roberto Goizueta's involvement with financial analysts: "To most corporate executives, financial analysts are a group to be feared. Goizueta pores over every word analysts write about the company. He frequently writes letters back, blasting analysts who denigrate Coke's stock. His letters pick apart their calculations and gloat when their forecasts don't bear out. It's an intimidating approach, but it has earned him the respect of the industry and the assurance that analysts treat stories about Coke very carefully."

There are two lessons here. One is that good communication comes armed with a full set of teeth. The other is that if a brand hates anything, it hates silence.

## CHAPTER 21

# Integrated Marketing: There's No Better Time to Meet the Future than Now

The last time I went to a performance of a symphony orchestra, I was struck by the analogy that can be made with the integrated marketing of a brand.

Before the conductor (CEO) appears, all the different sections (departments) go through the dreadful warm up. The violins aren't playing together, and they're certainly not in synch with the awful noise coming from strident trumpets and shrill flutes. The musicians (the brand team) are intent on doing their own thing. They blow and saw and bang on their instruments with no concern for the audience (the customers and other stakeholders). It's an ear's nightmare. Even worse, it's close to how I have perceived the operation of some brands.

However, with a stroke of the CEO's baton, the thirty people in a half-dozen departments turn chaos and cacophony into a single voice. The CEO and all the members of each department are reading the same message from the same script in perfect communication with each other. This integrated internal communication serves the mission of communicating with the customers in perfect harmony. Emotions resonate back and forth between the participants and the customers. On both sides of the baton, everybody has a grand time. A bond of mutual appreciation takes palpable form between all the participants.

## THE FUTURE IS HERE

This isn't just a pretty picture. It's the story of the integrated brand of the future—a future that is, for many brands, already here.

A brand that practices integrated marketing pulls all its values, functions, promises, and processes into a seamless whole. Every brand task feeds on the idea that the customer is not an abstract concept dreamed up by the marketing department; in fact, the lines between departments grow dim as all structural considerations of the company start with the customer and work their way back into the brand organization.

The drive is to look ever outward toward the brand's relationships. The fuel for that drive is communication—internal and external—that finds its purpose in furthering relationships with the brand's stakeholders.

It's not an abstract. It's what is done daily at Harley-Davidson, Saturn, Dell Computer, and many others. These companies don't just make money. They make meaning. It's telling that integration and integrity spring from the same Latin root.

## BRAND INTEGRATION

Brand integration is a company-wide process, not a department. A striking example is Radio Shack's service story that involved many of the brand's departments working together (Duncan and Moriarty 1997).

Radio Shack sells some quite complex electronic products that customers might need help with after they get them home. Store employees were therefore trained to expect and welcome calls from customers seeking help after the sale. This meant operations had to work with marketing to develop a system that provided easy access to instructions for the products on the frontline. Even advertising got in on the act with the theme, "You've got questions, we've got answers . . . 20,000 of us at Radio Shack." You can see how all the members of the Radio Shack "orchestra" had to sing in tune with each other to create improved communication and involvement with the customer, which in turn cannot help but result in forming a stronger loyalty bond.

The Radio Shack example from *Driving Brand Value* is an actual demonstration of Duncan and Moriarty's definition of integrated marketing: "Integrated marketing is a cross-functional process for managing profitable brand relationships by bringing people and corporate learning together in order to maintain strategic consistency in brand communications, facilitate purposeful dialogue with customers and other stakeholders, and market a corporate mission that increases brand trust."

They go on to say that communication is the lifeblood of integrated marketing and that "The creative frontier of the 21st century will be in defining and refining purposeful two-way communication in commercial relationships."

Communication is central to a brand because a powerful brand is more likely to be promise-centric rather than product-centric. Products obviously matter, but they can also be a dime a dozen in a single category. It's their overriding promise of value that attracts and keeps customers loyal.

> The more candid you are, the less people will guess and gossip, the less they will spread rumors, and the less your brand will fall victim to false witness.

For example, you can't communicate a car. You can only communicate a car's promise of value to a particular person. Almost by definition, a promise cannot exist without communication and (hopefully) reciprocation. If the people who represent the brand from top to bottom do not have a clear, shared knowledge of the brand's promise, there's likely to be an internal fuzziness that finds its way to the outside and results in less-than-optimum reciprocation. Poor internal understanding of brand value can result in confused and broken ranks. It invites the hostility of customers and the invasion of competitors.

## THE RIGHT WAY OF BRAND INTEGRATION

An article in the *Harvard Business Review* (1999) states, "The fundamental difference between a product-centric and a brand-centric company lies in the attitudes of the people throughout the organization—not just the marketing department—in their understanding of what it means to shift from selling products or services to selling a promise of value." From this point of view, you can see how a brand's lifeblood is pumped by the engine of communication.

Listen to what the designer of the iMac says about what integrating internal communication can do to help the external communication of the product (*Fast Company*, 1999):

> What drove the design of the iMac was a vision and a commitment to create the best consumer computer that we could . . . we made the needs of the customer the highest priority. And when you do that, it places significant demand on different parts of the company.
>
> For example, we found that the right place for a lot of the cable connectors was on the side of the iMac, which is where they are most accessible . . . but from the engineering perspective, the easiest place to put them is on the back. Putting them on the side was actually very difficult and would mean elevating the concerns of the user way above those of the engineers . . . (but we) spent zero energy to cajole the people at Apple into believing that what we were proposing was right . . . by genuinely trying to design a product for people in a very natural way, people were intrigued by the product—whether they were our managers or our customers.

The opposite of Radio Shack's and Apple's integration can be found in the example of brand fragmentation by the phone company, US West (Duncan and Moriarty, 1997). It wanted to improve customer service and cut costs. An $880 million reengineering project attempted to create greater efficiency by dramatically cutting smaller-service offices and substituting megacenters. The company also spent $50 million a year in advertising to promote the concept of improved customer service. The problem is nobody could get through to the company on the phone! In its home state of Colorado, some 2,000 people were forced to wait over 30 days for new phone service. People in Iowa accused the company of missing installation and service appointments. New orders were incorrectly provisioned, and repairs took too long.

In 1995, the Colorado Public Utilities Commission fined US West $4 million as public restitution. Arizona set service standards that US

West had to meet or face fines of up to $5,000 per occurrence. This tale of woe goes on, but it shows you that poor communication can signal disaster. It's a simple but sorry example of one hand not knowing what the other is doing. If you want to know how a company supposedly in the communications business could fail so badly in its fundamental mission—both in its own house and in broken promises to customers—you can always ask the executives whose heads rolled in the affair. They obviously forgot to integrate, not separate.

## LOYALTY TO YOUR CUSTOMERS

Baxter International is a $9 billion health care products and services company that even integrates with customers for mutual benefit. Baxter actually negotiates risk-sharing partnerships with hospitals and health maintenance organizations to set cost targets for supplies and shares the savings, or the additional costs, if expenses overshoot targets. As reported in *Driving Brand Value*, "Participants in Baxter's ValueLink inventory management program cede ownership and management of inventory to Baxter, which will deliver supplies direct to hospital floors and departments. Baxter has even taken over the task of cleaning and sterilizing equipment, freeing hospital staff to care for patients. At some hospitals, Baxter employees are on site 24 hours a day!"

> **M**ore than 50 percent of all U.S. capital expenditure is now for information technology.

This is a superb case of Ask not how loyal your customers are to you, but how loyal are you to your customers? It shows how a brand that organizes itself to deliver superior service makes itself literally indispensable.

Many of the successful high-tech firms have similar working relationships with their business customers. It's a thing of beauty, and there's no reason why it can't be a universal model for conducting business between brands and the consumer.

## IT'S HOW YOU USE WHAT YOU HAVE

As I said in an earlier chapter, database technology gives us new ways to pursue the two-way communication with customers that integrated marketing demands. Duncan and Moriarty continue, "A company with a warehouse full of products isn't nearly as rich as a company with a database full of profitable customers, prospects, and other stakeholders."

This goes a long way to explaining why more than 50 percent of all U.S. capital expenditure is now for information technology. But having valuable information is only as valuable as the spirit in which it is used. The information gives us the means to pursue closer customer relationships, but it won't do it without a helping human hand. Amazon.com might have an amazing database dossier on you and your tastes in reading, but if it doesn't approach you with human brand manners, it will fail to keep you engaged (nobody knows this better than Amazon's founder, Jeff Bezos).

## THE ORGANIZATION OF A COMPANY

Promise-centric, integrated marketing calls for a good look at how a company is organized to make its mission successful, but it doesn't necessarily mean tearing up the organization chart. An integrated brand like Gateway Computer Systems, for example, organizes itself by starting with the customer and working back into the brand. That simply means a promise of outstanding service must be backed up with efficient help lines, and effective order and service fulfillment to make sure the promise is kept every time it is called upon. In some ways, it means that everybody in the company is on the frontline and ready to go over the top together. But as the previously quoted *Harvard Business Review* article reports, "Business-planning processes and topics are the same in a promise-centric company as they are in a product-centric organization. A brand plan is a business plan."

> A promise of outstanding service must be backed up with efficient help lines, and effective order and service fulfillment to make sure the promise is kept every time it is called upon.

Integrated marketing plans should start with a zero-based planning process. This means that the tools you use are based on an assessment of what needs to be done now rather than the needs of last year's budget allocations. It likely involves a situational analysis that uses SWOTs (Strengths, Weaknesses, Opportunities and Threats) with a customer focus.

The four Ps of traditional marketing (Product, Price, Place/distribution, and Promotion) take on a greater customer focus with the four Cs (Customer, Cost, Convenience, and Communication) (Duncan and Moriarty, ibid.).

## The Synergy of Integrated Marketing

In a broad sense, the synergy of integrated marketing gives us an organic view of business and its brands. Integration is natural in the literal sense of the word. It is the ultimate way for business to create the most productive economies, and it's a giant step in the evolution of how we can best achieve them.

When I say integration is natural, the study of it is like exploring the anatomy of survival and organic growth. *The New Pioneers* (1999) talks of William C. Frederick, who helps us to see the origins of business and its role in that growth:

His decades of research ultimately persuaded him that all living things harbor an impulse to economize as a bulwark against the universal propensity toward the loss of energy and form, a force called entropy. 'This economizing process is the only way to survive, grow, develop, and flourish,' he wrote in a landmark 1995 study. 'Overall, life on earth has been a roaring economizing success story.' In the case of us humans, business is the tool we use to lighten our loads, 'the main economizing vehicle on which organized human life depends,' Frederick says. The corporation thus is 'as Darwinian as a frog.'

# PART Seven

# MANAGING
# YOUR BRAND

# 22

# Conceiving: Launching a New Brand

A clean slate is an exciting slate. It's an opportunity to get everything as right as it ever will be. So what we're going to do in this chapter is actually launch a new brand. We're going to start a business the way so many others do nowadays—right out of the garage. Imagine this:

I'm a highly skilled carpenter/contractor who hurt his back. I'm by no means crippled, but I can't handle a lot of the heavy stuff that building requires. I had to look around for an opportunity where I could use my skills in a less physically stressful way.

I live in Mill Valley in Marin County, California, and it's obvious that real estate is a booming business. People are selling and buying houses at an unprecedented rate. I think about light renovation work, but worry that even that is going to be too hard on two damaged spinal discs. Then a friend, who is thinking about buying an old house, asks me to go along with him to give it a once-over. My new business idea is suddenly born.

I do a little research by looking in the yellow pages and see that there aren't as many house inspectors as I thought there would be. There are quite a few, but by the look of their ads, I get the sense that they are mainly mom-and-pop operations. They have names like Bob's Home Inspection and Acme Inspection. Only Ameritech stands out as a possible big guy.

I nose around a little more and find out that there are no real standards for being a qualified house inspector, but there is a well-thought-of school in Los Angeles that gives a short course on the subject. I sense that house inspection is ripe for somebody to come along and be a leader in the field.

My wife used to have a marketing job with a publisher, but she quit to care for our kids. Fortunately for me, she has never lost her interest in the field. When I tell her my idea for a new enterprise, her eyes light up, and she says, "We could make you a brand!"

She calls a dozen or so house inspectors to get a feel of what the competition might be like. My initial feeling is confirmed. She reports, "These may be people who know something about inspecting a house, but I don't get the feeling they know much about how to market themselves." An idea is born.

From there, we asked ourselves what we thought a prospective home buyer would want from a building inspector. Looking at it from their point of view, we remembered our own feelings about buying our house. We were very excited at the prospect. We thought about it so much, we sometimes couldn't sleep. We had the house renovated and furnished a dozen different ways a dozen different times long before we ever owned it. We drove slowly past it at every opportunity. We worried about getting the money together for a down payment and whether or not we could qualify for a mortgage. We found the process daunting, and, finally, we certainly wouldn't want to feel we were buying an incredible headache.

We ended up writing down three things:

1. **Customers would like to feel they are dealing with a professional like no other.**
2. **They would want to feel they were dealing with a company that had a profound, visceral integrity.**
3. **They would want to deal with a company that was highly approachable and accommodating—one that would not feel that any question was too dumb to answer; one that was on their side rather the side of the agent or the seller.**

With this in mind, we hammered out a possible mission statement. "Our mission is to provide home buyers with a totally thorough inspection that gives them true peace of mind over the most important purchase decision of their lives: An informed buyer is an empowered buyer; we don't settle for less."

We put our minds together to come up with a name that would quickly communicate the mission, that would stand out, and that

> $I$t was the name we most remembered and liked best. We thought it was a happy expression of the business and acted like a kind of promise all on its own.

would reflect the value of peace of mind. We spent an entire Sunday writing a page full of names, but narrowed it to two: HousePro Inspection and Home Sweet Home Inspection.

We let them simmer for a week and finally settled on Home Sweet Home Inspection simply because after a week, it was the name we most remembered and liked best. We thought it was a happy expression of the business and acted like a kind of promise all on its own. It was also sufficiently different from the other names in the yellow pages that we thought it would make a memorable and distinctive logo.

I got really excited about it when my wife showed me what it would look like in a warm serif typeface she found on her computer. But then, she showed it to me with a line under it that said everything that I thought would "grab" a house shopper and cause them to pay attention. It looked like this:

**Home Sweet Home Inspection**
**Don't Make A Move Without It.**

I thought these two thoughts with a phone number attached would be all I would ever have to put into an ad. But my wife reminded me that, more importantly, it gives customers all they need to get out of an ad. It was kind of like an outdoor billboard in its economy of communication.

Of course, house shoppers aren't the only customers for a house inspection service. There are also real estate agents, who play a big role in recommending inspectors; in fact, this recommendation ingredient may be the most important one. Everything we did had to make them look good in the eyes of their customers—including our independence. So far, we thought we were on track; in fact, my wife met with and talked to several agents for feedback on the name and logo line. The reaction was positive. It made them smile and nod in agreement immediately.

By now, my course was clear. I was going into the house inspection business. As a licensed contractor, I knew I had the qualifications, but I decided to go to the school in Los Angeles for the course I had researched earlier. I'm glad I did. I learned a few things about the business and got a diploma that gave me the boost of extra credentials.

When I got back from the course, my wife said no house inspector she contacted had a professional brochure. She thought having one would give house shoppers and real estate agents a feeling of confidence. And, if we were the only ones to give the agent a brochure that they could give to their clients, we would probably get preferential treatment from both. I began to see that I had married well!

## LOOK PROFESSIONAL

She and I collaborated on a full-size 8 × 12 brochure that covered inspection of the site, the outside, and the inside of the house, with a general idea of what to look for. We decided to get it done right and hired a freelance art director to do the layout (including a few simple line drawings) and oversee the production. It was expensive, but we got a very professional job that makes us look like we actually know what we're doing (which, of course, we do).

The day we went around our area in Marin County to leave off copies of the brochure with agents, we got terrific response. Two days later, we got our first customer.

By giving agents a high quality brochure they can hand out and that makes them look good, they act like an unpaid and unbiased sales force. But the funny thing: The day we got our first customer is when we realized we hadn't nailed down exactly what to charge for the service!

Other things we did: My wife wrote an article for our community newspaper titled, "What to Look Out for When You Buy a House," which gave us free publicity. Another newspaper liked our brand name and wrote an article about our family business. We took out an ad in the yellow pages.

We insist on giving written reports to our customers, and the reports are properly dressed in a very good binder with our logo on it. If and when the person buys the house, we go and put a welcome mat outside the front door (no logo; just a mat with Welcome on it). My wife keeps track of all customers and sends them a card on the anniversary of the day they bought the house. She calls it her database. Eventually, she even designed a Web site and got it up and running with good results. People turn more and more to the Web for information. No other home inspector is there to compete with us.

## WE DID IT!

Results speak. I can't handle all the inspections and now have a guy I've worked with for years handling half the calls. My wife and I can actually see the day when we may be running a franchise operation. We're actually working on a pilot project to see how well it would take. Home Sweet Home is a rewarding and fun success. I knew that for sure when a customer said to me, "When we looked at our house, I got the feeling you were buying it with us!"

This story isn't quite fiction.

Home Sweet Home is a brand Harry designed for his son-in-law and daughter, Glen and Kitty Edwinson. It's small potatoes compared to a brand launch by somebody like Procter & Gamble. But principles have nothing to do with size or affluence. Branding simply doesn't care how big you are. Just look at what this family business did.

> **P**rinciples have nothing to do with size or affluence. Branding simply doesn't care how big you are.

They found a hole in a product category: the need for a brand (rather than just another service) in a category where product expertise is abundant but relevant, stated promises aren't.

They entered a category crying out for a brand leader that has a chance to become dominant (at least in a geographic area), with no obvious challengers.

They based everything about the brand on what its prospective customers *feel*; in other words, they started with the mind of the customer and worked back to form the brand's purpose.

They looked for the brand's meaning, not just its function.

They developed a highly specific mission before they thought about how much the brand could make. (A lot of people think capitalism is about taking. It's not. It's about serving.)

The mission is based on values—values of integrity, professionalism, and plain human approachability.

The mission is the conviction from which all strategic considerations will grow.

They developed an involving, memorable name that's totally relevant and completely clear.

They work closely with the distribution channel (agents are important stakeholders) and make it easy for the channel to sell the product with a unique and welcome brochure. The agents might give buyers other names at the same time they give the name of Home Sweet Home, but only Home Sweet Home has a developed valuable communication tool that customers are eager to read (an example of communication delivered at the right time and place).

They developed a simple database and stay in touch with past customers. Any past customer who recommends them to a new one gets a note of thanks.

They stay in constant touch with both the trade and their consumers by simply "walking around."

They use technology in the form of a simple, informative Web site to further communicate with prospects and keep the news of the brand alive. No other inspector does this. It gives the brand the perception of high tech, along with its high touch.

They see that style counts. You might be advised to not sweat the details of daily life, but for a brand, the details are where one finds religion. The brand van is kept neat and fresh all the time. The logo and logo line are painted on the door. The mission statement is printed on the back of business cards. There's a brand uniform—sturdy brown shoes (no sneakers), clean khakis, khaki socks, a navy-blue golf shirt with the logo discreetly on the left chest, a navy-blue sweater and windbreaker for winter, and no hat. (Kitty believes an angry feminist invented baseball caps to make all men look like pinheads.) The business has portable cell phones. Messages are easily accessible from anywhere and answered fast.

Cost of the service is the least of their problems, but they stay on the high end of the spectrum because it serves to demonstrate the fact of their quality. It's a cash business; they get paid on the spot before commencing with the inspection. No bad debts. No huge accounting task.

They get further communication mileage by writing a highly detailed evaluation of the condition of the house. Some inspectors charge less for a purely verbal evaluation. Home Sweet Home never does one. They feel strongly that the customer needs the security of a written statement. There's likely no slip between the pen and the lip. Besides, the customer never throws out a written evaluation and will look at it from time to time to see how they're doing with progress on house features that need attention.

Glen asks that the buyers stay close to him, so he can explain the inspection as he goes. But the written evaluation serves as an occasional reminder of how thorough Home Sweet Home really is; for example, the evaluation gives a rough cost for each recommended repair.

It all adds up to a different feeling for Home Sweet Home than for any other inspector—a more tangible feeling of competence, commitment, and trust—that is well justified. This feeling gives agents complete confidence in their recommendation of the service. Other than the brochure, there is no planned promotion effort for agents, but Kitty and Glen occasionally leave off flowers as a mark of appreciation to their loyal agents. Around the Christmas season, they will individually invite favored agents to a restaurant for lunch. Once again, no other inspectors do these things.

Any new brand that follows the principles of the above steps will demonstrate the value they place on all stakeholders, the power of two-way communication, and the commitment to values that are no less than eternal. It will be a brand that sees the value of being promise-centric rather than product-centric. It will be a brand that gets an enthusiastic answer to the question, "How does it make you feel?" It will, in effect, be just like the big boys, who work in office towers rather than an attached garage.

## BEWARE CONFLICTS OF INTEREST

Lastly, our intrepid brand builders are thinking about a sister business called Home Sweet Home Repair and another called Home Sweet Home Inspection School. Harry strongly advises against them. He says they may seem like logical steps, but no matter how honest the intention, the repair business could be construed as a conflict of interest with the core inspection business. The real reason for not doing either of them, however, is focus.

A powerful brand never yields to the temptation of adultery. It's a one-promise affair that brooks no distraction. All the brand's energy and resources must be concentrated on and committed to building a reputation in one narrow brand, and one narrow brand only. Home Sweet Home must aspire to be synonymous with trustworthy home inspection. Period. Dilute that, and it will likely die.

A**ll the brand's energy and resources must be concentrated on and committed to building a reputation in one narrow brand, and one narrow brand only.**

CHAPTER **23**

# Gardening: Bringing on New Shoots from Existing Roots

$F$ew subjects in marketing are as confusing as the effectiveness of growing a new offshoot from an existing brand. It starts with what seems like a logical decision and the best of sense to stick a famous brand name on an offshoot brand. The logic goes, "Everybody knows the name of the core brand. Its reputation will rub off on the offshoot brand." In real life out there in brand land, it simply doesn't work that way.

Just look at Miller beer. When Bill Backer and his team at the McCann Erickson ad agency helped the brewer to "move Miller High Life from the champagne bucket to the lunch bucket without spilling a drop," they were highly successful. For one thing, it's a lot easier for a premium brand to move down than it is for a cheaper brand to move up. But as Al and Laura Ries say in *The 22 Immutable Laws of Branding* (1998), "With a powerful marketing program, Miller High Life was rapidly gaining on market leader Budweiser. (It got within 20 percent of the King of Beers.) Then Miller introduced a bevy of line-extension brands and stopped Miller High Life cold."

What happened?

Well, Miller took the focus away from its vibrant core brand with Miller Regular, Miller Lite, Miller Genuine Draft, Miller Genuine Draft Lite, Miller Reserve, Miller Reserve Light, Miller Reserve Amber Ale, and so on.

204

It ends up that nobody knows what Miller stands for other than a hodgepodge. The Miller promise in the mind of the consumer gets totally garbled because it *is* totally garbled. Nobody needs or can handle that many brands and subbrands (and subbrands of subbrands) of beer. The confusion became further debilitating when Budweiser and Coors also brought out multiple brands, to say nothing of Schlitz, Michelob, Heineken, Amstel, Pabst, and Busch with their subbrands.

## JOINING THE CLUB

The real problem was that people who like the Miller brand generally bought the new Miller products. Miller was no further ahead, except in the cost of promotion. Beer consumption didn't go up just because there were a lot of new brands. The brewers brought out all these beers because the other guys were doing it, and they were afraid they would get left behind.

It's a little like the problem with Coke when they brought out Diet Coke. It simply stole business from regular Coke. And think about it. Can Diet Coke even remotely be "the real thing"? Coke would have been much better off to promote Tab as a separate brand with "one crazy calorie" rather than muddy the regular Coke waters with Diet Coke. Only Coke's market dominance keeps it from being a real problem—at least for now.

## CONSUMERS FOLLOW THEIR OWN LOGIC

Consumers don't follow the logic of marketers. They follow their own. Once they fix a brand in their heads, they don't like disturbing it. I'm not suggesting that Diet Coke represented any kind of tragedy to Coke drinkers, but why would Coke risk even a smidge of dilution of its primary brand's promise? Why wouldn't it simply stick with Tab or another new brand name for a diet soft drink?

It goes back to the marketer's logic that says, "Everybody knows Coke. Its reputation will rub off on Diet Coke. And it will rub off quicker than if we use a new name." But what it mainly does is dilute the Coca-Cola focus.

American car brands are hopelessly unfocused and are inexorably losing ground to more focused marques. How is anybody supposed to feel about Chevrolet or Oldsmobile or Buick? These brands simply don't stand for anything, either in their own minds or in the minds of the consumer. And Ford and Chrysler are no better.

## DRIVING INTO OBLIVION

As Al and Laura Ries continue in *The 22 Immutable Laws of Branding*, if you ask, What is a Chevrolet?, the answer is "a large, small, cheap, expensive car . . . or truck. When you put your name on everything, that name loses its power . . . Chevrolet used to be the largest-selling automobile brand in America. In 1986, for example, the Chevrolet division of General Motors sold 1,718,839 cars. But trying to be all things to everyone undermined the power of the brand. Today Chevrolet sells fewer than a million cars per year and has fallen to second place in the market behind Ford." (Ford may be leading Chevy because it has eight separate car models, as opposed to Chevy's ten. Less may indeed be more.)

> Trying to be all things to everyone undermined the power of the brand.

It's by no means impossible that GM is headed for slow but eventual oblivion because of its lack of focus. Even the potential of Saturn is watered down because its original small-car focus is now blurred with a mid-size model.

The only distinctive brand in the Chevy lineup is Corvette. Can you imagine a Corvette limo? Probably you can't, but knowing GM's potential for garbling brands, I wouldn't be surprised if one were on the drawing board. After all, GM is thinking about a Cadillac pickup truck under a new model called Evoq.

Evoq is going to be a new Cadillac car model that's supposed to take Cadillac into the heady realm of Mercedes-Benz and BMW. Cadillac's General Manager John Smith feels he has the clout to make Cadillac an international marque. I always thought customers were the ones with the clout. If GM wants to persuade the world that it can make a car like a Mercedes or a BMW (and there's no *logical* reason why it can't), I would strongly suggest a new name that doesn't carry Cadillac's heavy baggage, not just a new Cadillac model name like Evoq. All the advanced engineering in the world will not change what people feel about Cadillac, good or bad. I would also suggest that a pickup truck in the Evoq luxury lineup is closer to insanity than GM has ever come. It's as if a Cadillac kind of guy, like George Bush, decides he can be a professional wrestler, as well as an ex-president.

Foreign cars fare much better at focus. For example, Volvo stands for safety. The brand owns this focus—one, simple word. Other cars are, of course, just as safe, but this long-lived, unwavering focus is largely responsible for Volvo's position as the best-selling luxury import. It's to Volvo's credit that it adopted the word years before any other manufacturer believed safety had any potential as a profitable marketing position. It separates the Volvo brand from all the other cars—foreign and domestic. They should not be tempted to go for sexy, or sporty, or luxury, or prestige. They should hammer away at dull, old safety.

## USE A NEW NAME WHEN ADDING TO YOUR BRAND

If you see an opportunity for an addition to your line, you're usually better off with a completely new name. When Honda saw an oppor-tunity for a luxury Japanese import, it called it Acura, not Honda Plus. Honda simply doesn't mean luxury. Honda was fortunately not tempted to confuse the meaning of its core brand. It's the same with Toyota and Lexus. Different names keep clarity intact, for both the core brand and the offshoot brand.

One of the smart things Levi's has done is to bring out Dockers. Levi's means blue jeans, not khakis. Levi's

> Different names keep clarity intact, for both the core brand and the offshoot brand.

khakis sounds and feels wrong. Dockers works. When Levi's brought out Levi's shoes, they had a branding failure simply because Levi's means blue jeans, not shoes.

Gillette has admirably avoided the name-extension trap. It would appear perfectly logical for Gillette to make an electric shaver with the hope of great reputational rub-off. But Gillette very wisely sells electric shavers through the Braun brand. Same for oral care products. Not one consumer in a dozen knows that Gillette owns the Oral-B name.

## DON'T GET COCKY

Brand people often overestimate the power of their brand name, but they have to always keep in mind the mind of the customer. The customers know what Levi's means and nobody is going to tell them different. Violate the principle behind this thought, and you risk expensive failure.

Nothing could appear more logical to the management mind than Tanqueray Vodka. It failed because in the mind of the consumer, Tanqueray feels like gin and will never feel like vodka. Harley-Davidson feels like the epitome of a motorcycle, but it will never feel like a car. Xerox is copiers, not computers. IBM is computers, not copiers. With all the money and management brains in the world, Xerox and IBM can't (and shouldn't want to) change ingrained perception.

> A lot of marketing people don't understand that it's what people think and feel that drives the value and acceptance of a brand in their lives.

Marketing is littered with hundreds of examples of dead line-extensions that push credibility beyond what the customer can handle or is willing to accept. A lot of marketing people don't understand that it's what people think and feel that drives the value and acceptance of a brand in their lives.

It's also true there are just as many success stories of brands that changed by narrowing their appeal. Toys "R" Us used to be called Children's Supermart. It sold children's furniture, as well as toys, but focusing on toys and nothing else gives shoppers a very easy destination to remember when they think about toys. Furniture just confused the issue. People don't have time to be confused. That's what's so smart about Footlocker. It sells only athletic shoes—no brogues, no penny loafers, no high heels or rubber boots, just athletic shoe brands in all their gaudy panorama.

## SIMPLICITY OF FOCUS

Simplicity of focus breeds a following. If the guy who opened Subway sandwich shops starts flipping burgers because he thinks it will expand the appeal of the brand, he might well be on the road to killing it off. Kentucky Fried Chicken went into rotisserie chicken, but has gone back to a focus on fried. KFC means fried, not roasted. Roasted may be healthier, but the colonel's traditional fare is what people want from a brand with an acronym that spells Kentucky Fried Chicken.

Focus is that simple and that serious an issue. A lack of it erodes a brand's power. A lot of it works. All of the above brands dominate their category.

Management often believes that good management is the only quality needed to make a success of any good offshoot product or service, but without singularity of name and purpose, good management will flounder.

Williams Sonoma, Pottery Barn, and Hold Everything are retail concepts that seem to have nothing in common except that one very smart company that understands focus owns them all. They are stores that might be right next to each other in a mall, but they don't get in each other's way. Can you imagine what a hodgepodge might have been created by having all these retail concepts under the name Williams Sonoma?

Even in a singular field like publishing magazines, *Time* doesn't have *Time for Business*, *Time for Sports*, *Time for Finances*, and *Time for Celebrities* (Ries and Ries, 1998). *Time* spins off *Fortune, Sports Illustrated, Money,* and *People*. By not confusing the focus of its core brand and by launching separate brand names with separate identities, multiple success stories have made *Time* the world's largest magazine publisher.

Al and Laura Ries say further (ibid.), "Customers are never wrong. That's one of the many human traits that is so endearing and yet so frustrating from a branding point of view. When you try to tell customers that your brand is different than it used to be, they will reject your message . . . What you think your brand is doesn't really matter. It's only what your customer thinks your brand is that matters."

## CHAPTER 24

# Virgin: An Exception to the One-Crop Garden

Just when you think you might have a good handle on raising off-shoot brands, along comes somebody who purposely, and with mischievous aforethought, defies conventional wisdom and sets the tongues of brand gurus clacking. Nobody is more qualified to do this than Virgin's Richard Branson, the happy, grinning Englishman who never appears to do much of anything by the book, including branding.

There are those who accuse him of recklessly stretching his Virgin brand beyond the breaking point. But you're less likely to join them after you decipher the Virgin promise, and see how it pulls the whole empire of about 200 loosely associated companies together into a cohesive whole.

The promise takes the form of a pure and simple feeling in the minds of Richard the Lionhearted's loyal and admiring followers—a feeling verging on a certainty—that he would never offer them anything unless it was different, or better, or more imaginative, or less expensive, or more comfortable, or more fun. In fact, every Virgin brand offers you *all* of these qualities under the personal protection of Richard's responsive word. If you trust Richard, you will favor a Virgin brand, and it's easy to trust Richard for his values of honesty, fair play, respect, hard work, and above all, fun.

But there's another very important aspect of the Virgin promise that says there is no area of business (including not-for-profit) that is beyond Richard's crusading grasp. That's because British consumers now *expect* him to come to their rescue. They delight in his ability

---

## TAKING IT SITTING DOWN

I've been struck by Richard Branson's lack of stuckupedness and surfeit of good humor. I once overheard someone ask him ask him if it was true he had a British Airways seat in his hot-air balloon. When he said it was true, they asked him why. He said, "Sitting in it comes in handy when you have to stay awake all night."

---

to burst the balloons of corporate fat cats who have been taking them and their patronage too long for granted.

A deep streak of publicly approved iconoclasm allows Branson to tilt at diverse windmills from airlines to condoms (called Mates), from financial products to railways, from retail stores to property management, from entertainment to publishing. His hit list of potential Virgins is apparently endless. And every time he goes forth to conquer, the public cheers him on as some good knight in shining armor.

When the big guys fall asleep at the tiller, Richard is the little-guy pirate in a paper party hat, waiting to board the opposing ship to prod the pompous with his silly wooden sword. He's the people's champion, a fun-loving version of a Ralph Nader with an eccentric John Cleese twist. If you think this is a reputational exaggeration, remember that Britain's youth chose him over Mother Theresa as their most likely choice to rewrite the Ten Commandments!

Virgin simply wouldn't be Virgin if it didn't cast such a wide net. It's as though Richard can't pass a puffed-up establishment he doesn't want to deflate, and his penchant for pouncing on opportunity started when he was a puppy.

He was the first to stir up the entertainment pot by offering young people in England a new way to buy music for less of their hard-won pocket money: through the mail. When a postal strike nearly sank the business, he quickly opened music stores that offered a social experience different from anything England's young people had ever seen—stores where you could hang out, lounge around on beanbags with friends, and stay as long as you wanted.

He did these things at an age when most of us are still in high school.

He loves being different. For years, he operated his corporate headquarters out of a houseboat, where he also lived with his wife and children. He only moved when his wife finally put her foot down about living in a madhouse. Even today he has a loathing of formal offices. His staff of 20,000 that aren't working in his stores or airplanes are in a multitude of odd houses all over the map. Corporate headquarters has fewer than 20 people in a house in London.

"Small is beautiful" could be a Branson invention, and it's another definitive difference that allows Virgin to venture into so many areas of business. He believes in the opposite of central planning, or command and control. Each Virgin company is its own small unit. When a company gets bigger than sixty people, he splits off a new one and appoints new management from within the ranks to run yet another company in its own house. The new people make their own decisions and get on with them. Managers get a share of the business they run.

Everybody has Richard's personal phone number and can call him at all hours (people who call him are surprised to find he usually answers his own phone). Smallness and a feeling of personal responsibility and human dimension permeate every aspect of the Virgin brand—all this without the time and energy a lot of similar-sized companies waste on bureaucracy.

> Smallness and a feeling of personal responsibility and human dimension permeate every aspect of the Virgin brand.

He says (1998), "Virgin is not a big company—it's a big brand made up of lots of small companies. Our priorities are the opposite of our large competitors'. Convention dictates that a company looks after its shareholders first, its customers next, and last of all worries about its employees. Virgin does the opposite. For us, our employees matter most. It just seems common sense to me that, if you start with a happy, well-motivated workforce, you're much more likely to have happy customers. And in due course the resulting profits will make your shareholders happy."

Common sense is a quality with which Richard seems inordinately well endowed. He is likely to rely on it as much as any sort of market research. For example, he says, "When it comes to setting up new companies one of my advantages is that I don't have a highly complicated view of business. When I think of which services I want to offer on Virgin Atlantic, I try to imagine whether my family and I would like to buy them for ourselves. Quite often it's as simple as that" (ibid.). But an earthy common sense has never prevented Richard from indulging an outrageous sense of fun.

I get the feeling that we in the USA don't appreciate Richard as much as his British brothers and sisters. We tend to see the nutcase, dressing up in a bridal outfit to launch his brilliant Virgin Brides retail outlets. Or we see a newspaper photo of Richard in the full-drag dress and makeup of an airline hostess, serving drinks to passengers on Virgin Atlantic, and wonder if his elevator goes all the way to the top. Or we ask how the guy who gave us the Sex Pistols has any business launching Virgin Direct banking products. And of course, we're astonished that such a shameless "exhibitionist" sells a billion pounds worth of pension and investment plans in the brand's first two years.

The one thread that goes from one Virgin brand to another is that people believe that the guy who dresses up in a kooky buccaneer outfit to goad British Airways with real competition is unlikely to let them down.

Richard is not the fool who goes where angels fear to tread. He and two of his fellow Virgins look at fifty new business proposals a week. When they decide to go into any of them, it is always with a joint venture partner. It is always a new organization rather than one that is bought. It is always with a manager who has expertise in the new product's field. It is always with both upside and downside protection. It's always with the uncanny ability to follow Napoleon's advice when he said, "Never interrupt your enemy when he's making a mistake."

It is always with speed and energy and the complete understanding that making an error is not the end of the world; rather, it is a condition of living in it. I don't know if it's true, but I've read that

---

## TAKING ON #1

It's well known that Richard Branson doesn't lack courage. He actually sold the record company that made him successful, so he would have enough funds in his Virgin Airways war chest to take on behemoth British Airways.

This intrepid course flies in the face of basic marketing advice, which touts that Davids are crazy to go up against Goliaths. While such an admonition is enough to get Richard riled and ready, he does indeed appear to feel some strain in trying to make hay against big BA. When asked how to become a millionaire, he says through his famous grin, "Start as a billionaire and then buy an airline!"

---

Richard has killed off more than 200 companies. It's not a number that would surprise me.

The ability to flirt fearlessly with failure proves that he was right to buy back the company after it had a brief stint as a publicly traded entity. You can do things when you own the joint that you would have a tough time doing when you have to answer to shareholders. Being answerable for his decisions and antics, or curbing his wacky sense of adventure is simply not Richard's cup of tea. Being a private company is another great advantage in allowing Virgin to diversify with impunity. When Virgin loses, it comes primarily out of Richard's pocket, but the brand's finances are kept in a private (and perfectly legal) offshore trust.

The man did not become a famous billionaire by possessing a faint heart in the face of error. His exploits in small-craft Atlantic crossings and near-death hot-air ballooning are well documented. They are an integral part of the jolly, daredevil brand called Branson. But I maintain that it takes just as full a set of guts to pull off all the goofy publicity stunts, such as driving a tank down a New York street to launch Virgin Cola.

You have to hand it to the chairman of a world-renowned brand who doesn't get any takers for a bet that he will ski down a Swiss hill naked, but goes ahead and does it anyway. It's his lack of pomposity that attracts us. A willingness to look like a complete fool is part of Richard's appeal.

The brand called Branson and the brand called Virgin are just about inseparable. With either one, you never know what surprise will be pulled out of the hat next. And we eat it up.

The practical side of Richard's high jinx is that it stands him in good stead. It gets Richard and Virgin into the press, and it costs a lot less than paid advertising. His stunts allow him to compete against giant ad budgets like British Airways' for our attention, and they remind us how much fun he has taking the mickey out of conventional brand management.

I can't prove it, but I would argue that Richard's tomfoolery is largely responsible for the present, popular shift from paid advertising to publicity for launching a new brand. Over and over again, he certainly shows us how it's done.

> I can't prove it, but I would argue that Richard's tomfoolery is largely responsible for the present, popular shift from paid advertising to publicity for launching a new brand.

His quest for fun and his egalitarian style of management are becoming more and more evident in the world's start-up companies in the new millennium. But when Richard espoused such values 25 year ago, he was way ahead of us all. His caring for staff and promoting partnership is legendary. He demands a lot of his Virginites, but they get a lot in return, including the feeling that they are part of a crusade led by a plucky Robin Hood.

When Richard won a whacking 610,000£ libel judgment against British Airways for playing "dirty tricks," he shared it among Virgin's people, with each one getting 166£. Gestures like this say more about the promotion of solidarity and esprit de corps than the peptalk rah-rah of executive chest thumping. He simply believes in treating people well.

The best thing about his entrepreneurial dash and verve is that it seems to come naturally. Richard never went to a university and certainly never to a business school. If you read his autobiography, you get the feeling that he has learned by lurching from one catastrophe to another, while enjoying every minute of it with amazing good humor and the certainty that nice guys do indeed finish first.

You get the feeling also that he's utterly resourceful. He's what the French call "*un débrouillard*," which means something like "a person who is never stuck for a good solution."

He and his wife once had a flight canceled on them when they were trying to get to Puerto Rico from a small Caribbean island. He says it was his first attempt at an airline. "The airport terminal was full of stranded passengers. I made a few calls to charter companies, and agreed to charter a plane for $2,000. I divided the price by the number of seats, borrowed a blackboard, and wrote VIRGIN AIRWAYS: $39 SINGLE FLIGHT TO PUERTO RICO. I walked around the airport terminal and soon filled every seat on the charter plane. As we landed in Puerto Rico, a passenger turned to me and said: 'Virgin isn't too bad—smarten up the service a little and you could be in business'" (ibid.).

Apart from just another humorous Branson story, this speaks volumes about Richard and the old saw about when the going gets tough, the tough get going. He gleefully gets on with what life brings on and has a jolly good time into the bargain. This is the magnet of his remarkable leadership. Add an unassailable reputation and you have an equally remarkable brand.

It's a combination that makes Virgin such a movable feast in defiance of the conventional wisdom about narrowing a brand's focus. I can't wait to see where the Virgin king will take us next.

## CHAPTER 25

# The Gardeners: Managing the People Who Manage the Brand

Peter Drucker (1999) says, ". . . central to my writing, my teaching, and my consulting has been the thesis that the modern business enterprise is a human and social organization. Management as a discipline and as a practice deals with human social values . . . only when management succeeds in making the human resources of the organization productive is it able to maintain the desired outside objectives and results."

This leads me to believe that there's no more valuable asset than the workers who toil in the brand vineyard. This was true in a time of plentiful labor, partly because recruitment and turnover carry an enormous cost, even under the best of conditions. But in a time of labor shortage, attracting and keeping good help has reached critical importance.

Marx and Engels might say, with surprise and high-five rejoicing, that the workers have finally won. But they would be more surprised (and less likely to rejoice) to see that workers and management often sup from the same bowl; that the workers are more and more likely to also be the owners. The growing idea in the post-industrial age is no longer that each one takes from the other; rather, it is that each one serves the other.

## EXTRAVAGANCE IN THE CAUSE OF EMPLOYEE LOYALTY IS HARDLY NEW

Peter F. Drucker (ibid.) wrote:

In managing manual workers, we learn fairly early that high turnover, that is losing workers, is very costly. The Ford Motor Company, as is well known, increased the pay of skilled workers from 80 cents a day to $5 a day in January of 1914. It did so because its turnover had been so excessive as to make its labor costs prohibitively high; it had to hire [60,000] people a year to keep [10,000]. Even so, everybody, including Henry Ford himself (who had at first been bitterly opposed to this increase) [,] was convinced that the higher wages would greatly reduce the company's profits. Instead, in the very first year, profits almost doubled. Paid $5 a day, practically no workers left—in fact, the Ford Motor Company soon had a waiting list.

### TIMES ARE CHANGING

We're beginning to free ourselves from the straitjacket of what Thomas Petzinger Jr. (1999) calls "Newtonianism"—a mechanistic view of business that says output is exactly proportional to input; that management is an act of calibration and control; that the whole always equals the sum of the parts.

We've come to see that the process of taking things apart (analysis) is not nearly so intellectually profitable as putting them together (synthesis). The rise of thinking in terms of systems, rather than one-way causality, gives us a better view of "the big picture" (18–23).

The big picture shows us that the employer-employee relationship has changed radically since our WWII and Korean War fathers and mothers started out in their careers. They faced toe-the-line, mechanistic thinking and collar-and-tie conformity, and learned how to put up with it. This is not derision. The period of history for which they are responsible was split between those who did and those who did as they were told. People were needed who could accept orders to build industrial might and fight a world war.

Top-down management and hierarchical organization was the order of the day (to a certain extent, it still is). Many of them aspired to be The Organization Man, who perpetuated the rule of conformity in the ranks, and commanded and controlled from the top. There was something wrong with the idea that business could be enjoyed, that work could be fun. Security was often cherished at the cost of fulfillment as a job's most desirable asset.

> We've come to see that the process of taking things apart (analysis) is not nearly so intellectually profitable as putting them together (synthesis).

Our parents were likely raised under the dictum that sparing the rod spoiled the child, along with a woman's place was in the home. They didn't argue with daddy. They were brought up with so much respect for authority, it's amazing how they learned to raise their Boomer offspring with more *laissez-faire* spirit and a healthy sense of individuality. They (and Dr. Spock) gave us the opportunity to learn that, indeed, real men do cry and real women can grow up to be cowgirls.

As Harry S. Dent (1998) writes, "The Bob Hope generation tends to view individuality and self-actualization as self-indulgence and narcissism. In their era, the prevailing ethic was conformity, or being outer-directed. The more advanced [B]aby [B]oomers and [G]eneration X view self-actualization as a new level of freedom, *and a higher level of personal responsibility.*"

Thomas Petzinger Jr. (1999) says of new pioneers entering management from the ranks of the Baby Boomers, "Many of these new leaders also had an inkling that happiness and fulfillment in the workplace might actually devolve to the benefit of the organization itself; indeed, in surveying their employees, MCI, Sears, and other giants found a significant link between morale and revenue. What a concept: Treating people individually and with dignity—the tenet of virtually every religion in the history of the planet—turns out to be good for business!"

## THE GOLDEN RULE FOR YOUR WORKFORCE

It appears that the golden rule is golden, after all, and it turns out that keeping the workforce happy and stimulated is one of a brand leader's most important functions. "But how does it make you feel?" isn't only a question for customers.

## FINDING GOOD EMPLOYEES

Our Harry says that being a leader is an easy job; that all Mr. or Ms. Leader has to do is find the best people and turn them loose, so Mr. or Ms. Leader can go to lunch a lot. This over-simplification has some merit.

Bill Taylor and Alan Weber, founders of the award-winning *Fast Company* magazine, relate how much time and energy goes into finding and keeping good people (*Financial Post*, 1999).

They talk about a "free-agent nation" of 25 million self-employed North Americans as some of the best minds waiting to be found.

Some already run their own companies in Silicon Valley. These people are often the products of downsizing—"a new breed of self-employed, high-tech-savvy, performance-driven individuals" with great ideas who need elbow room and headroom to grow. Taylor notes, "Free agents are now asking companies what kind of work experience a firm will offer them and how their job will bring meaning to both their professional and personal lives."

These people are joined by "Passive Job Seekers"—those who are the very best, but already have good jobs and are difficult to reach through traditional search methods. Taylor suggests going to places like home shows and college football games to connect with them—places where the competition isn't.

A third group is the "Boomerang Club." Don't stay bitter with good people who are lured away by a competitor. Instead, start an alumni club, with a monthly newsletter and invitations to social events. If you stay connected, they might come back to you some day.

## KEEPING GOOD EMPLOYEES ONCE YOU HIRE THEM

Once you get people on board, growth through learning and training is now more important than security. Employability is just as
important as employment. There is no longer any stigma to job
hopping, and people who jump from job to job (either in or out
of the same company) are called fruit flies (with no pejorative
intended).

It would seem that one of the jobs of the modern brand is to
turn the valued fruit fly into a leech that doesn't want to let go.

One of the ways to do this, for the sustenance of both the brand
and the employee, is to offer learning
that never ends. It no longer matters so
much what you know as how and what
you can learn.

In *The Learning Paradox*, Jim Harris says that today, knowledge has a
half-life, with the amount of information on the Web doubling every eighteen months (*Montreal Gazette*, 1998).
"If you have your Ph.D. you know a lot
about old stuff. Microsoft assumes that
half the computer codes they write today will be garbage in three
years. This means it is no longer information or knowledge that
counts, but learning. We have entered the fourth wave—the learning[-]based economy."

> **I**t no longer matters
> so much what you
> know as how and what
> you can learn.

Futurist Marian Salzman (*Fast Company,* 1998) says, "Perma-
nence used to be the quality of greatest value . . . People collect skills
and work experience with an emphasis on self-improvement and
self-advancement. Which means that they no longer bond perma-
nently with a single organization. It also means that companies get
workers who are more eclectic and experienced[;] more focused on
learning than on security."

## LIVING AT WORK

It may be that reengineering, downsizing, and just plain massive lay-
offs and the resulting insecurity have forced workers to think this
way. It may be also why so many people seem bent on working
themselves to death. The separation between rich and poor may be

growing, but the so-called rich are working harder than ever to be included in the category. The separation between work and life is much narrower than it was for the Bob Hope generation; in fact, for a lot of people, work has just about become life, particularly in the sometimes-wacky world of high tech. It seems that a lot of us get so involved with our work that we simply forget the time.

> For a lot of people, work has just about become life, particularly in the sometimes-wacky world of high tech.

A computer-gaming company in Dallas called Ion Storm provides what to me is an astonishing example (*Fast Company*, 1998): "Most of Ion Storm's top designers and programmers spend more than 16 hours a day at work, creating monsters and how to dismember them. Employees have been known to arrive at 11 A.M. and leave at 5 P.M.—18 days later."

Ion Storm provides all the comforts of home: a Crash Room with beds, couches, and a wide-screen TV with VCR for movie watching. A gaming area includes arcade machines and a ping-pong table. There are shower and changing rooms. Corinne Yu, 28, director of advanced technology, spends every other night in the office. "I don't go out much, because everything I need is here," Yu says. "Soda pop. A shower. My pillow. It's like home."

This kind of extraordinary work ethic and apparent carelessness with one's personal life may seem extreme. It may make you wonder when people like those at Ion Storm find time to reproduce. But it's well-documented behavior in proliferating, high-tech land.

There's a saying that Microsoft's idea of flextime is letting its people name their own hours—any eighteen hours a day they like. Of course, the rewards are often nothing to sneeze at.

On a single day (December 16, 1998), Jeff Bezos made $914 million when his Amazon.com stock went up 20 percent (*National Post*, 1998). In another case, Excite is a company that produces software to manage the Internet. It started out five years ago with six guys from Stanford University working in a parent's garage. (Why is it always a garage? Why not a bedroom or a basement for a change? Is it because houses in California don't have basements? And where do Mom and Dad park the car when the kids confiscate their garage?)

They also used parent seed money of $15 grand. The company now has a market cap of $2.4 billion. Joe Kraus, one of the founders, just cashed in $2.8 million of his share and holds another $22 million in stock. (I hope he remembered to pay back the loan from Mom and Dad, now that he can afford to give them back the garage.)

## WORK AND A LIFE, TOO

Some brands attract employees by making normal life a valued perquisite. They go against the grain of crippling work hours and stupefying stress. According to Charles Fishman in *Fast Company* (1999), SAS Institute near Raleigh, North Carolina, is the "sanest company in North America." SAS produces very expensive software that makes it possible to sift through mountains of information to find patterns and meaning. With sales of $750 million, the company employs 5,400 people worldwide. But growing success isn't what separates SAS from other hi-tech enterprises. It is fanatically devoted employees.

Fishman writes, "In an age of relentless pressure[,] this place is an oasis of calm. In an age of frantic competition[,] this place is methodical and clear-headed. In a world of free agency, signing bonuses, and stock options, here's a place where loyalty matters more than money."

People leave the office by 5 P.M after a 7-hour workday, but you might find them in the company's 36,000 square feet of gym space at 6 A.M. You might find them getting a massage or taking classes in golf, African dance, tennis, and tai chi. And you might see them dropping kids off at the company daycare center. The company even launders and returns employees' sweat-soaked workout clothes with next-day service. The result is an employee turnover rate last year of 3.75 percent. CEO Jim Goodnight proves that there's profit in benevolence, and his employees love it enough to join him, sometimes for less money than what they're used to making.

SAS may be on to something. Using the intuition of a person who lives by keeping his ear to the rails, I sense a backlash against

## MAKING LONG HOURS AGAINST THE LAW

If you're a reluctant workaholic, you might think about moving to France, where an employer can be prosecuted and fined for employees who work more than 39 hours (soon to be 35 hours) a week without overtime pay (National Post, 1999).

The idea behind the law is that unpaid work has to be curbed to lessen unemployment (France has 3 million unemployed). A sort of work police goes around, checking out company parking lots to see who is working late.

The director of an electronics firm near Paris faced going on trial after inspectors discovered his employees were working too hard. He faced a fine of $50,000 and a suspended prison sentence, if found guilty. He now shuts his plant at 7 P.M. on the dot, 15 minutes after an alarm sounds to tell employees to clear their desks.

Other firms that have ended up in the work police's bad books are Siemens, IKEA, and Alcatel. The latter came close to paying 3,000 fines of $1,200 each after inspectors noted down every daily and weekly infraction of the work rules.

While the mind boggles at such dense bureaucracy, I wonder how Bill Gates would react to such a ruling in the United States? Certainly, his professional employees, who were suddenly forced to work only 35 hours a week, would feel like vacationing sloths.

the crippling work hours of the 1990s. I sense that being responsible for one's life is becoming just as important as being responsible for one's work. The balance is simply too far out of whack.

A lot of workers are now afraid to assume "normal" hours for fear they will look like slackers. Harry is convinced that most people are consistently capable of no more than four hours of concentrated work a day, and he swears this isn't a reflection of his personal work ethic. He says it's particularly true when you include all the day's necessary distractions, such as useless meetings, getting coffee, calling home, healthy daydreaming, lunch, clicking on to computer games, swapping juicy (often productive) gossip, and playing basketball.

> I sense that being responsible for one's life is becoming just as important as being responsible for one's work.

He says, "A company installs a basketball court, so exhausted workers can get some relief by playing with each other. Wouldn't it be more restful to send them home so they can play with their kids?" He also thinks that people use how much time they spend at work as a badge of prestige. According to Harry, "The guy who works 18 hours a day is driving his time the way others guys drive a BMW. He wears his hours the way he wears an Armani suit or a $20,000 watch. He has to overcome the idea that the guy with the least time is the most important!"

With unemployment below 4 percent (and a lot less than that for the technically skilled), you can compete for employees with all kinds of incentives that include better pay, hot tubs, massages, naps, child care, manicures, exotic trips, and, of course, the usual array of benefits and stock options. You can base compensation on contribution and skill scarcity, not on seniority or rank. You can lease a BMW for every employee who has stayed with you over two years.

> You don't hire people so that you can tell them what to do. You hire people so that you never have to tell them what to do.

You can do all of these things (as many companies do), but it seems to me that nothing works better than making everybody the equivalent of being their own boss. You don't hire people so that you can tell them what to do. You hire people so that you never have to tell them what to do. You are then needed for the keeping of the faith; for making final, final decisions; for leadership in emergencies; and for plotting your brand's future. You might also be needed for playing the trombone in the brand band.

It's a good idea to remind yourself that you're not Stalin and your company isn't Russia. You and your brand are better off without the burden of leadership based on stultifying command and control.

Koch Industries is the second-largest, privately held company in the United States. It's a $30 billion-a-year empire in energy, agriculture, and financial services. In *The New Pioneers* (Petzinger, 1999), we learn that Charles Koch credits much of its success with realizing very early that, "America was full of miniature totalitarian regimes. They were called corporations" and that, "A business is a vehicle for integrating knowledge."

He took a political idea that states, "The free society is the form of social organization most in harmony with reality and the nature of man," and he turned it full force on his company. He relied on the knowledge of employees and gave them the freedom to act on it. This gutsy course of action required management to give up huge chunks of control, but it worked. A refinery employee, who was suddenly freed to use his judgment when certain valves had to be turned on and off, improved the performance of the refinery by a quantum 20 percent. Allowing refinery employees to act on their own knowledge and judgment has added hundreds of millions of dollars to the company's books every year!

Koch inspires gumption in another way. He's a good example of leading from carefully developed principles and values; in fact, at Koch Industries, the values *are* the business. Koch proves that having a big moral view doesn't mean you ignore profit.

It means that you understand meaning. It means that you grasp that people want to work for—and do business with—people they can respect and admire. Koch studies and thinks about meaning. One of his favorite quotes is from the historian Daniel Boorstin: "The greatest obstacle to discovery is not ignorance, but the illusion of knowledge" (ibid.).

We really get it right when we absorb the advice of Mary Parker Follett, who wrote way back in 1918, "The leader guides the group and is at the same time himself guided by the group, is always part of the group." She later wrote, "Authority, genuine authority, is the outcome of our common life. It does not come from separating people, from dividing them into two classes: those who command and those who obey. It comes from the intermingling of all, of my work fitting into yours and yours into mine" (ibid.).

If you could run a company and manage its brands based on the leadership values of Commander D. Michael Abrashoff, Peter Drucker, Charles Koch, and Mary Parker Follet, nobody would ever leave you—no matter how many complimentary BMW's you put in their garage or stocks in their portfolio. And last but not least, you would have found the way to enjoy yourself, to boot.

## CHAPTER 26

# Nursing: Managing Brand Crises

My good friend Tony Hilliard is a Londoner—a born and bred Cockney—who knows the rhyming slang that was practiced by the workers in London's food markets (like Covent Garden) as a secret language. "Trouble and Strife" is slang for wife. "North and South" means mouth. Feet become "Plates of Meat." Shave is "Dig-In-The-Grave." A beer is a "Pig's Ear." And lies become "Pork Pies."

It's a huge vocabulary of an ingeniously colorful language that shows the resourceful, poetic brilliance of the Cockney mind. After a while, the entire phrase became too cumbersome, and it was shortened to the first word. For example, "Whistle and Flute" (which means suit) got shortened to "Whistle," as in, "'Ullo, luv, d'you like me new whistle?" The phrase "pork pies" got shortened to "Porkies," and I once heard Tony asking Harry (who often exaggerates his accomplishments), "'Arry, boy, are you telling little porkies?"

When you manage a brand, this is a question you should frame and hang on your office wall. Few businesses tell really big porkies, partly because it isn't ethical, and partly because they fear getting caught. The idea of seeing a big porkie plastered all over the press, or on the TV screen for the consumption of a big audience, is indeed daunting.

## A FEW MILES SOUTH OF STERLING

Nowadays, disillusioned customers can even get mad enough to open a Web page, and broadcast their dissatisfactions and disgusts to others. But it's not just the big gaffes that count; it's the little exaggerations and half-truths and saying things you don't really mean that can also add up and come back to haunt you. Couple them with small, broken promises and a tendency to fudge, and your brand can acquire a reputation a few miles south of sterling.

You're always late for meetings, both in and out of the office. You promise a customer you will call her back this afternoon and somehow, forget to get around to it. You swear a refund check is in the mail, and it just plain ain't. You preach customer service, but the evidence says your record on it is less than adequate.

You put out a piece of software that's still got bugs in it. You make a grapple grommet purported to last forever, but 20 percent of them regularly break down. You run a hotel (or an airline) that is often overbooked. You spout lofty values, but treat your employees like commodities.

I was once driving with Harry from Danbury, Connecticut, to New York City. He was going faster than I like for comfort. I said, "You're doing eighty and the signs say fifty-five." He put his foot down a little harder and answered, "I know what the signs say, but they don't really mean it."

## DO YOU REALLY MEAN IT?

The question is, do *you* really mean it? Do you walk the talk, as the saying goes, and talk the walk? Do you mean it, or do you just pay lip service to the things a brand holds dear? Do you hide behind the fine print? Do you deliver what you say you will deliver when you say you will deliver it?

A friend sent me this comment from a weekly newspaper that expresses the gap between lip service, real service and customer frustration (*Hour*, 1998):

"I used to think that capitalism had won the Cold War because of service. The products, essentially, were the same. It was good old capitalist service with a 'have a nice day,' that made the difference.

"Recently, I found out how badly I was deluding myself . . . Fact is, no one gives a care about service. Mark my words: Unless service improves, all the new technology ain't going to be worth squat. Apple's new iMac might be great but Apple service sucks. Windows 98? Microsoft service sucks too. People will hang on to their old stuff and the bells and whistles the web offers (but for which you must have top-of-the-line machinery) will be largely ignored because the new gadgets come with pitiful service . . . Moscow, pre-Yeltsin, is starting to look good."

When you don't deliver, you break the basic covenant of trade. "Capitalism is promises," wrote the libertarian columnist John Chamberlain, years ago.

"The promises are everywhere, and rarely is one broken." This quote from *The New Pioneers* (1999) is followed by, "Long before there were contracts or even laws, trade occurred on word alone. Those who kept their word were rewarded by others keeping their word. It was through trade that humans discovered trust—'the conviction of things not seen,' in one biblical definition; 'the residue of promises fulfilled.'"

Too bad too many are unfulfilled.

## THE MOST POWERFUL ADVERTISING

Everybody knows that the most powerful form of advertising is word of mouth. When somebody you know says a particular product or service does its job well, we believe it more readily than a paid endorsement from a credible star.

Our friend Paul Downing took his dead father's watch to a jeweler to have it repaired. The repair guy called him a few days later to tell him that he could buy a new watch for less than it would cost to fix the old one. Paul said he wanted it fixed because it used to belong to his father, and he didn't care about the cost.

> When somebody you know says a particular product or service does its job well, we believe it more readily than a paid endorsement from a credible star.

When he went to pick up the watch, the jeweler was so touched that Paul was willing to go to such expense in the cause of sentiment that he fixed the watch for free. I didn't have to ask how that made Paul feel. I'm sure I'm not the only one Paul has told the story to. And I'm equally sure the jeweler has a customer for life in Paul, plus others influenced by word of mouth.

## WOM AND WORM (NOT THE CRAWLY KIND)

But while WOM works hard in your favor, WORM can kill you. WORM is Word-of-Reverse-Mouth. And it's more powerful in a negative sense than WOM is in the positive. People hold on to and retell bad experiences for years after they occur.

If your next-door neighbor tells you how the corner garage ripped him off on a valve job, you will likely never darken that garage's door again. There's a restaurant in my neighborhood I've never tried because a friend says the food is lousy.

Harry tells everybody not to drink a certain Mexican beer because he swears the brewery workers pee in it to get back at the gringos. Like much of what Harry says, this is pure nonsense, but I can never bring myself to ever buy that beer.

Take a good, hard look at your brand. What can you do to protect it from your own porkies and other self-inflicted disappointments? Perhaps the best answer is to remember that a brand starts and ends with a promise—a promise that cannot be broken without some kind of penalty.

Most people will forgive a mistake, but most people are also too smart to forgive a con. H. L. Mencken said that nobody ever lost a nickel underestimating the American people. But whenever I hear this I always answer, "No, but I bet they lost a dollar or two."

Doug Grant, our managing partner at Brandtrust, sums up the reasons for staying straight when he says, "You are your brand and everything it promises—nothing more, nothing less. It's reflected in everything you say and do. How you answer the phones, whom you hire, the color of your building, the music in the hallways, the attitude of the staff, the way your product works (or doesn't), and the face you present in all your communications. That's it. Essence of Business = Promise = Brand."

Harry shortens this by saying, "You are your brand in everything; from the way you answer your phone to the way you answer your conscience."

> "You are your brand in everything; from the way you answer your phone to the way you answer your conscience."

When you're not unfailingly conscientious, you create anger. Angry consumers fight back angrily now. You've probably heard it said that every dissatisfied customer tends to tell five or ten friends about his bad experience.

Brian Manasco, writing in the newsletter *Inside 1 to 1* (August 20, 1998), quotes author Gary Heil, who cites the case of one consumer who claims that Starbucks mistreated him. He "sought revenge by taking out a $10,000 full-page ad in the *Wall Street Journal* that slammed the company. The disgruntled individual incorporated an 800 number into the ad and requested a donation from callers. (Upon making his money back, he took out another negative ad.)"

The Web can compound the public relations problem with an interactive megaphone that can shout around the world: "Heil noted how a Sony engineer in Toronto got even with United Airlines by launching his own "Untied Airlines" Web site. Phone company Nynex has also become the subject of a spoof site. It's an increasingly common occurrence—one that has corporate lawyers working overtime. Under the circumstances, companies have no choice but to build stronger customer relationships and ensure that they are offering a high-quality service experience. The corporation's image is no longer its own."

I hasten to add that it's a lot more its own (and a lot less at the mercy of the eccentric) when it's covered by the insurance of a strong brand.

## WORD-OF-MOUSE

The millions of people going on the Internet magnify the eager gossip quotient that can help or hinder. Rather than word of mouth or word-of-reverse-mouth, *Fortune* magazine (1998) calls it word-of-mouse. Writers Gary Hamel and Jeff Sampler report, "Word of mouth has an upside and a downside for every company. Both the upside and the downside are magnified exponentially online, where opinions propagate like *E. coli* in room-temperature chicken."

One company (Hotmail) calls it viral marketing. "More modestly, the Web means that potential customers can always get some kind of opinion—delighted or scathing—from someone who has experience with your product or service. I may not know anyone who has taken the *QE2* across the Atlantic, but someone out there is dying to tell me . . . On the Web all customers have a megaphone, and most are willing to use it. Like eager combatants who will shout down a bumbling orator on Speaker's Corner in Hyde Park . . . customers will ultimately decide which messages get heard online."

## Monitor Your Brand

Meanwhile, you can keep track of what is being said about you. The American Association of Advertisers offers eWatch's custom-filtered Internet monitoring to help protect brand reputations in cyberspace. Six hundred companies have already signed up to keep the pulse of the buying public with www.ewatch.com.

The monitoring covers more than 50,000 public Internet discussion message boards, discussion forums on online services (including AOL, CompuServe, MMSN, and Prodigy), and Web site bulletin boards on Yahoo!, Motley Fool, and Silicon Investor. eWatch can also monitor your competitor's Web sites daily for additions or deletions.

The fact that eWatch exists, and has such extensive subscription, proves that a little paranoia is becoming to a vigilant brand.

Of course, some problems crop up that you don't have to click on to eWatch to find out about. One not-so-fine morning, you can wake up to find them plastered in big type all over the front page of your daily newspaper.

## 'Fess Up

I'm talking about brand catastrophes, such as the contaminated Coca-Cola that forced pulling 2.5 million bottles of the product off shelves in France and Belgium in the summer of 1999 (*Financial Post*, 1999). It's testimony to the power of the brand that the effects of the biggest recall in Coke's history are likely to be nothing more than the loss of about $60 million. But it was a PR nightmare that could have been made less severe had Coca-Cola been more immediately forthright about its responsibility. The company tried to minimize the problem, presumably in hopes that it would simply blow over. Fat chance.

Apart from the fact that dozens of people got sick, the Belgian government closed down plants in Antwerp and Ghent for ten days. Finally, when Coke got its act together, Chief Executive M. Douglas Ivester went to Belgium and said, "Quite honestly, we let the people of Belgium down."

At least this was candid. As part of the post-catastrophe marketing push, Ivester offered to buy everyone in Belgium a Coke. There were apparently quite a few non-takers.

Recent business history is full of such disasters, and the one lesson to learn from all of them is that complete transparency and immediate disclosure set the best course of action. The best example I can think of is the Tylenol product-tampering case referred to earlier in this book. It was never the company's fault, but swift action and complete transparency saved the day for the brand. Every brand can plan and rehearse catastrophe management. You can pray that you never have to use it, but as the Boy Scouts say, "Be prepared."

For those marketers who play at the truth, who do not deliver what they say they will, who fudge in the face of crises, I'm tempted to play with the chilling words Karl Marx wrote in the opening line of *The Communist Manifesto*. I would change, "There is a specter haunting Europe[;] the specter of communism" to, "There is a specter of conscience haunting marketing; the specter of consumerism."

CHAPTER 27

# Palliative Care: Managing Mature (and Deathbed) Brands

In 1935, Hollywood stars Gary Cooper and Clark Gable each bought an SSJ Duesenberg convertible coupe roadster. They might just as easily have bought car brands with names like Delahaye, Delage, Isotta-Franschini, Bugatti, Hispano Suiza. These were all well-known glamour marques in their day, and now—like the Hollywood studio star system—long gone.

German pioneers Daimler and Benz get credit for the first internal combustion engine and the birth of the automobile industry, but a French car called Dion Bouton is credited with being the first really affordable brand in the early 1900s that wasn't just a novelty for the rich (*Financial Post*, April 1999). Dion Bouton produced a huge number of cars and actually survived until 1950.

Closer to home is the demise of familiar American names like Stutz Bearcat, Packard, Studebaker, Nash, Hudson; to say nothing of the ancient Stanley Steamer, supposedly driven forever by the mythically cheapskate comedian Jack Benny, as he avoided spending to buy a new flivver.

Going beyond car brands: Of the twelve companies that first made up the Dow Jones industrial average a little over a hundred years ago, only General Electric is still alive and kicking.

Napoleon Bonaparte said, "All empires die of indigestion," but it isn't gastric distress that kills a gold-producing goose. New technologies come along to maim and murder entire industries (you've

## CONSPICUOUS CONSUMPTION REVISITED

Retired engineer Roy Gullickson of Phoenix, Arizona, has a dream to bring back the Packard marque that went belly-up in 1950 (*Financial Post,* 1999). The idea is to sell you an American car that betters the status feel of a Rolls or a high-end Mercedes V-12.

His voluptuously curved Packard 12 will cost you a cool $140,000, but this is a bargain compared to an old one that can cost up to $1.8 million. Mr. Gullickson needs $10 million to proceed from prototype to production, which he hopes will begin turning out limited quantities in 2002. It sounds entirely possible. As he says, "A pro athlete could buy a Packard 12 on a week's pay."

probably noticed we don't take the time to cross the country by train very often, and we rarely call for typewriter repair). Changing fashion can do the same (men no longer wear natty fedoras as a matter of course every day, and women don't wear hats that look like exotic bird nests and block your view in the theater the way they used to).

> The fact that brands die is not as surprising or important as how moribund brands can be revived.

### REVIVING BRANDS

Marketing mistakes can also take their toll. But the fact that brands die is not as surprising or important as how moribund brands can be revived.

During the seventies, Volkswagen had a 10 percent share of the U.S. market (*Business 2.0,* 1999). After the last of the old Volkswagen Beetles were sold in North America in 1979, Volkswagen's share slowly diminished to less than 1 percent.

Two decades later, the New Beetle returns with a rejuvenating facelift to popular acclaim and a million big smiles of nostalgic pleasure. Further armed with the acclaimed Golf, Jetta, and Passat, and a focused promise, the VW brand is winning back its former prominence.

It's interesting that the three cars aim at different economic segments, but all three make a unified promise of cool driving performance—something akin to the young person's BMW. This is good marketing. There's no doubt what VW stands for in its concise model lineup.

The once-popular, but dead-as-a-door-nail, Indian motorcycle (already discussed) is being brought back to life by enthusiast entrepreneurs. This shows the staying power that great brands possess.

A brand is indeed a collection of memories. When they make a comeback, we're often ready to welcome them with open-armed affection and willing wallets.

While Volkswagen and the Indian motorcycle appeared to be six-feet under, there are a vast number of still-living-but-faltering brands that can learn how to regain vigor.

The kind of sustained super-growth that has kept General Electric listed on the Dow for over a century is rare as snake's teeth. Growth takes constant nurturing, and can never be taken for granted as simply a byproduct of running a currently profitable brand. Most brands don't survive more than thirty years, and that's the analog time span.

## THE EMERGING BRANDS' FUTURES

About all the new digital brands emerging today, who knows? It's healthy that the zoom to fame of many hi-tech brands, such as Microsoft, Cisco, Intuit, Dell, Compaq, Amazon, and so on, is accompanied by extreme paranoia on the part of their leaders. The current ethic generated by that paranoia seems to be "get fast, or get out of the way."

As Cisco CEO John Chambers (*Business 2.0*, 1999) says, "Today, we are witnessing the emergence of an Internet economy in which the game is no longer about big companies or countries beating the smaller ones, but the fast versus the slow."

Like the New Beetle, we're all happy to see a brand, such as Macintosh, gain the ruddy glow of health again after what looked like a serious illness. Mac had lost its huge popularity as 'the computer for the rest of us,' but it still had avid fans rather than just customers.

As Senior Director of Worldwide Marketing Allen O'Livo (*New York Times*, 1997) said, "We had to make the Apple brand stand for something again. One of our strengths is that Apple users have an emotional attachment to our brand. To restore and rebuild meaning into the Apple brand, we first made an appeal to that attachment. Then we followed up with a rational appeal based on our products."

A $100 million ad campaign helped revitalize Apple's antiestablishment image. It featured creative geniuses, such as Albert Einstein, Miles Davis, and John Lennon, who "think different." This campaign reinforces the idea that Apple is a different kind of computer brand.

On the product front, this was reinforced with different-looking, new machines, including the iMac that comes in different colors other than the usual beige, gray, or black. It's a well-reviewed consumer machine for under $2,000. Apple sold 278,000 of them in six weeks, making iMac the hottest computer launch ever. Apple CEO Stephen Jobs said, "Innovation has nothing to do with how many R&D dollars you have. When Apple came up with the Mac, IBM was spending at least 100 times more on R&D. It's not about money. It's about the people you have, how you're led, and how much you get it."

## IN THE NICK OF TIME

David A. Hagerty got a bit of a shock when he took over the presidency of Dunlop Sports in 1994, and found his company losing $2 million on $12.4 million of its U.S. tennis-related sales (*New York Times*, 1997). Something had to be done fast, and a product innovation provided the way to go. The brand developed a longer, oversized, premium racquet called the Max Superlong.

Adding an inch of length apparently helps achieve the promise of a stronger serve. Getting a hard-serving pro, such as Mark Philipoussis, on board as an endorser helped prove the point. The innovation of a larger racquet and the emotional appeal of a big serve helped turn the loss around. Add a lot of staff sweat and in

1997 Dunlop earned about $5 million on $25.2 million in tennis equipment sales.

## A REVIVING JOLT

Maytag Appliances wasn't exactly dying when it got to be a hundred years old, but the brand's arteries were hardening, and it was stuck in a slow-growth industry. President William Beer performed a metamorphosis that now contributes over $2 billion of the corporation's total revenues of $3.4 billion. And as with all Lazarus brands, vastly improved numbers are the result of leadership, energizing staff with a vision of the possible.

It's a terrific story that starts with challenging the idea that people only buy a new appliance when the old ones wear out. Beer believed that was nonsense: If you offer people *really* new appliance ideas—ones that "wow" the customer—they will want them badly enough to chuck out the old ones.

The Gemini range with two ovens is a result of innovative consumer research I've already talked about. He calls it changing the purchase cycle from "wear out" to "want in."

This new direction involved many changes within the company, but what I find most fascinating about the Maytag story is how the brand culture changed to accommodate the risk of innovation with a new view of failure—a view that starts at the top. Says Maytag Corp executive Lloyd Ward, "You need to celebrate your failures as much as your successes. Said another way, you need to redefine failure as a learning experience. Everything you do is an opportunity to deepen focus and get better understanding, so you can do significantly better in your next try. No beheadings is not enough. I'm suggesting a proactive framework for people to feel the room to explore, take risks, and innovate."

Don't you just love that kind of thinking? It revives faith in corporate America. It's exactly what's needed for a troubled brand (or

> And as with all Lazarus brands, vastly improved numbers are the result of leadership, energizing staff with a vision of the possible.

## THE RETURN OF THE YO-YO

Kids first began to "walk the dog" and "skin the cat" in 1930, but somewhere along the road, the phenomenon of the yo-yo took a nap; until 1990, when it acquired the new technology of something called a transaxle, which allows mere mortals to perform a 15-second "sleeper" (Fortune 1999).

The yo-yo's popularity is now bigger than it ever was. Manufacturers like Duncan, Yomega, and Playmax can't keep up with the demand. *Playthings Magazine* says Yomega yo-yos are the No. 2-selling toy in the country, behind Beanie Babies. And just think: You can buy a nice, sterling silver yo-yo from Tiffany's for a mere $110.

any other brand, for that matter). Oscar Wilde said cynically that, "Experience is the name everyone gives to their mistakes," but I prefer the story of how Thomas Edison tried about 99 times to invent the electric light bulb before he succeeded. When asked if he worried about so much failure, he said, "Not at all. I learned 99 ways how not to make an electric light bulb."

If I may be allowed another quote, I like the thought from Bill Moyers that could easily apply to Maytag's innovative brand thinking: "Creativity is piercing the mundane to find the marvelous."

### LOSING PRESENT AND FUTURE FOCUS

Levi's recent sales troubles and consequent plant closings, as they move to overseas manufacturing (with the layoff of 5,900 workers in the United States), can be attributed to many things. But perhaps the most obvious is a falling out of fashion through a loss of focus on the present, let alone the future (*Financial Post*, February 1999).

The Levi's people got caught with their pants down because they aren't listening carefully enough to what the customer wants. It's easy to make puns about getting too big for their britches.

Kurt Barnard, a retail consultant in Montclair, New Jersey, says "They are dealing with a stodgy product that has basically not changed—it's not a fashion item . . . They have become, over the years, too arrogant in assuming the name Levi is going to be fashionable and a top-seller forever." The article that contains this quote says the Baby Boomer's children "are hunting for the flared leg, dark denim or baggy styles from the likes of Tommy Hilfiger, Gap Inc., and JNCO, and lower-priced jeans from retailers such as Sears Roebuck & Co and Wal-Mart Stores Inc. . . . Caught between hip labels and bargain brands, Levi was also slow to latch on to the khaki trend, which has created a turnaround for the Gap."

However, Levi's are said to be mounting a khakis counterattack by retailoring the image of Dockers and rebranding them as Dockers Khakis with a new, hip ad campaign, sponsorship of concerts and other promotions (*Financial Post*, March 1999).

At least one other commentator thinks, however, that the customization route could be the brand's salvation (*New York Times*, 1999). Kenneth Harris of Cannondale Associates says,

> Levi's has to get back to their core business, great products at a reasonable price, but at the same time move it to the next level, which is mass customization—ordering jeans made to fit and getting them fast.
>
> They've already started to do this[,] but they have to go much further, possibly with their own stores nationwide. That way they can take control of their own destiny. Levi's have to become "my jeans" once again.
>
> And they should never lose sight of the fact that, regardless of what happens domestically, they *are* blue jeans to the rest of the world. They invented them; they still have cachet. The world is theirs to lose.

As we now know, Levi's has dropped its plans for massive interactive customization over the Internet. And it strikes me that everything Levi's has been doing is reactive rather than proactive. It is important to react quickly to change, but it is better to create it. Staying ahead of the game is what powerful brands do, and they do it by listening.

> It is important to react quickly to change, but it is better to create it. Staying ahead of the game is what powerful brands do, and they do it by listening.

Remember, too, that when you sell $6 billion worth of pants every year, you might expect to sometimes encounter a few big hiccups along the way. As Guy Browning said in *The Guardian* recently, "People who have very little experience of office life, such as vicars and pet show organizers, sometimes say they want to be businesslike. Those of us who are actually in business know that 'businesslike' tends to mean a series of escalating calamities relieved only by miraculous, last-minute escapes and heart-stopping close shaves" (*Financial Post*, February 1999).

### FADE AND RISE

I don't know how true it is that old soldiers never die, but how does a fabulous brand name like Sears fade so badly as it did in the early '90s? And how does it rise like the mythic Phoenix in the mid-'90s? In retrospect, the answers are astonishingly simple: Sears didn't know that its core customers were females, not guys with dirty fingernails. And it appeared that it was going out of its way to annoy the life out of those females.

The stores were downright dowdy. Ladies underwear was displayed on the same kind of racks that were used to display paint cans. The stores felt empty, as though everybody had evacuated the place on a bomb scare. You have to ask why nobody could see these things before Arthur Martinez was hired from Saks Fifth Avenue in 1992. Or if they did see it, why nothing was done to save it from its near extinction. *Time* magazine (1996) quotes Jane Thompson, who heads the new home services venture, as she recalled a typical meeting in the brand's grim days: "We would just sit there and everyone would just stare at each other. We were not even able to get people to admit what the problems were."

You've heard of thinking out of the box, but this appears to be like trying to think while you're in one! If the people in a company can't talk among themselves with open minds, it's unlikely that they will be able to talk very convincingly to their fellow stakeholders. In the end, people simply stop caring. They drop even the rudimentary semblance of civility.

The demented Harry tells me that he once went into a Sears store in a mall to buy his wife some slippers. He stood around for what seemed an eternity, waiting for sales help. When it didn't come, he decided to try an experiment. He began crying out loud. He stood in the middle of the aisle, crying and sobbing louder and louder, "Please, please, please can somebody please help me," for several minutes.

Still nobody came to his aid. He finally left with dry eyes, but without a pair of slippers. I asked him if he left in the care of security personnel, but apparently even they ignored him.

How Sears got into trouble is actually just as simple as how it found redemption: It went to the place where the brand could be seen from the outside in. It is only from this vantage that the true story can be witnessed and understood, where you can oversee the twists and turns of the landscape, so you can plot a way out of what might appear to be a nightmare maze.

It developed a promise-centric focus that started with the customer, and worked its way back into the product and its supportive services.

Simple and obvious? Yes. Easy? No. There's nothing harder than seeing yourself as others see you. It gets even tougher when we're talking about the future, which is likely to be even wackier and more time-compressed than ever.

> The trick for leaders of a mature or troubled brand is not to try to manage change (which probably can't be done), but to stay at least a few steps ahead of it.

## LEADING CHANGE

Without the guidance of a crystal ball, the trick for leaders of a mature or troubled brand is not to try to manage change (which probably can't be done), but to stay at least a few steps ahead of it.

Peter Drucker (1999) says, ". . . unless it is seen as the task of the organization to *lead change*, the organization—whether business, university, hospital[,] and so on—will not survive. In a period of rapid structural change, the only ones who survive are the *Change Leaders.*"

The inestimable Mr. Drucker goes on to suggest that a change leader will adopt a policy of "Organized Abandonment"—that is, every process, market, channel, customer, and end-use is on trial for its life. Nothing is assumed.

"The question has to be asked—and asked seriously—'If we did not do this already, would we, knowing what we know now, go into it?' If the answer is 'no,' the reaction must not be 'Let's make another study.' The reaction must be 'What do we do now?' The enterprise is committed to change. It is committed to action" (ibid.).

Drucker gives an example of failed abandonment and change leadership when he quotes the case of GM trying desperately to hold on to declining brands like Buick and Oldsmobile, at the expense of a new brand such as Saturn. Buick and Oldsmobile continue to go downhill, while a lack of real, focused commitment to run with Saturn's success as a maker of small American cars has almost killed it. Killing off Oldsmobile and setting up Saturn with everything it needed to become an aggressive, independent competitor might have guaranteed its success (ibid.).

Drucker gives us a change-leader success example from publishing. The bulk of publishers' sales, and practically all of their profits, come from the "backlist"—the titles that have been out for more than a year or two—but resources and effort are only applied to marketing new titles. When one publisher asked, "Would we handle the backlist the way we do if we went into it now?," the answer turned up "no." And when asked, "What should we do now?," the firm reorganized itself into two separate units—one promoting new titles, the other promoting the backlist. "Within two years, backlist sales had almost tripled—and the firm's profits doubled" (ibid.).

## TOO FAR GONE

But while there are encouraging examples of brand resuscitation and salvation, there's often nothing left to do but pull the plug. Quoting an old medical proverb, Drucker says, "There is nothing as difficult or expensive, but also nothing as futile, as to try to keep a corpse from stinking."

A brand should be abandoned if you operate it under the understanding that it "still has a few good years left." These are the brands that tie up too much time, money, and talent. We talk about milking an old brand, but often, it is the old brand that is milking us. They are the old dogs that shunt time and attention away from the new pups—the services, products, and processes that signal the future and have a chance to prosper.

Seemingly sane companies spend millions to save old, infirm brands, but they begrudge spending pennies to birth new ones that could bring them new life. As Drucker says, "Change leaders have to *focus on opportunities. They have to starve problems and feed opportunities*" (ibid.).

## CHAPTER 28

# Constant Care: Managing Brand Equity

The key element in managing brand equity is being able to measure it, and that's something brands have never done well. It may be because something as emotional as reputation is always classified as "intangible." But I hope it is now clear that intangible doesn't mean invisible.

The real value of an intangible (such as reputational capital) becomes painfully clear when we see it going down the tubes. Look at IBM's reputation when it nose-dived in the late '80s. In the *Fortune* survey of most admired companies, Big Blue fell from number 7 in 1987 to number 32 in 1988 to number 354 in 1994 (Fombrun 1996). You don't need a long memory to recall the punishment suffered by IBM's stock price during its fall from grace. It lost more than 50 percent of its value.

When we read about Gillette's worth at $12 billion, Campbell's worth at $9 billion, Wrigley's worth at $4 billion, and Cisco's worth at more than $500 million, we're seeing a calculation of what the brand's reputation is worth. That worth is found by adding up the value of its shares and subtracting the liquidation value of its physical assets.

The ultimate job of a CEO is not only to keep this capital intact, but to understand that it rises and falls primarily on something as fragile (and often irrational) as the way people feel. But the problem is, a liquidation scenario is a really primitive way to measure a brand's financial value.

## THE QUESTIONS TO ASK

All CEOs know that one of the fundamental decisions they have to make is how much to spend on marketing to make a brand grow. It prompts a lot of questions, such as:

**How much will more spending increase sales?**
**Will the increased sales cover the extra spending?**
**If not, how much will it reduce profits?**
**Is this loss of profits now justifiable?**

Will the growth in sales or market share that this extra spending buys put my brand in a stronger position to earn higher profits in the future?

In the complex world of uncertain customer demand, sometimes-rapacious distributor practices, and ever-present competitive challenge, answers to these questions are never easy. They involve a fundamental strategic tradeoff: spending versus profits. Or spending for potential long-term sales/share/profits versus short-term profits.

The questions are critical. CEO heads roll when the wrong choice is made. Feelings inside and outside the brand are affected. Wall Street frowns. And worry about wrinkling the broker's brow is often why necessary spending is put aside to meet myopic, short-term considerations.

> All CEOs know that one of the fundamental decisions they have to make is how much to spend on marketing to make a brand grow.

The financial world is all about numbers: today's numbers. With the new breed of day trader, it's often this minute's numbers. In their fixation on current stock price, the gnomes of Lower Manhattan usually ignore business realities, such as the constant tradeoff between spending and profits.

## THE WEB MYSTIQUE

This is why we watch in wonder at the reinvestment ethic of brands like Amazon.com. We've never seen anything like it. These brands seem able to convince investors to bid up their skyscraper stock prices on future value only. Such is the mystique of the Web start-up.

Wall Street actually believes guys (like Amazon's Jeff Bezos) when they say it would be wrong to give up building the brand tomorrow for a profit today. Practitioners of the old investment paradigms on Wall Street scratch around in their wisdom for clues on how to evaluate this new-wave investment phenomenon, but there's nothing in the conventional vocabulary to help them figure it out.

## PUTTING THE DOLLARS INTO CONTEXT

Hi-tech start-ups may indeed confound the conventional evaluation of P/E ratios. But we still need a context in which to measure the results of brand-building spending, in terms that make brand sense—as well as financial sense—on an on-going basis.

It seems that the only time our accountants recognize intangible assets (brand value) is when a business is sold. They gratuitously call it "goodwill," as though it's a one-time phenomenon that will go away when the new owner takes over.

In the takeover mania of the 1980s, however, businesses were bought only because they could then be split into pieces for later sale at an overall higher price. Typically, such "asset stripping" was only possible because someone saw that the so-called "intangible" assets were much greater than the sum of the tangible assets. "Asset stripping" could only occur in a buy-sell situation because "goodwill" was the only acceptable method for accountants to measure "brand equity."

I hate to say this, but the American accounting profession has done nothing to rectify this failure. They use the simple measurement tools that were first laid down in the days of the quill pen. With the narrow mindset of assets and liabilities, debits and credits, there is no attempt to provide business with procedures that seek to measure one-half of the critical strategic tradeoff: how spending today will enhance tomorrow.

Profit seems to be all that matters, even if it means the pursuit of profit today destroys the business tomorrow. It's a little like a referee who ignores the purpose of the game but still insists on setting and enforcing the rules.

## An On-going Measure of Brand Value

Thankfully, there is one accounting body that gives us valuable new tools for a better process. The UK Accounting Standards Board has endorsed an *on-going* measure of brand value that can be reported on the *on-going* balance sheets of UK companies.

The method is called a Cash Flow Based Income Valuation. Without going into technicalities, it establishes a clear, quantifiable projection of the value of a company or brand. This measure is expressed in terms of the stream of money that the brand generates for its *current* owner, and it includes an estimate of the future value of the brand for the *current* owner.

This is a refreshing change from figuring value on what has always seemed like a worst-case, buy-sell scenario.

When the UK calculations are compared over time, the success or failure of brand-building spending can be clearly stated.

A CEO can now go to the financial world and say, "Yes, profits are down 20 percent this year because we decided that we had to spend 45 percent more on advertising to bolster our 15 percent brand share in a much more competitive environment. This increased spending has raised our share to 17 percent. Aggressiveness in defending our brand franchise has delivered a strong message to our competition that any new attempts to gain share at our expense will not be easy. We estimate that we can now hold a share of 16 percent, which will pay for the added spending in eight months; more importantly, future profit for the brand should now be 10 percent higher each year."

This better way to financially evaluate a brand could liberate the CEO from the pressure of short-term financial necessities. It makes it possible for the CEO to rationalize what is prudent, rather than what is merely expedient.

It even performs the difficult task of making the accountants happy!

# PART Eight

# BRANDING BEYOND

# THE OBVIOUS

# Branding Cities and Countries

It's astonishing how much better government and its agencies can be when they start to think like brands with you and me as customers. I call them Civic Brands. Some of our illustrious cities could take the hint that the word civic sounds a lot like the word civil.

New York City is universally famous for rough-and-ready rudeness. It even has its own form of charm, which is often reflected in the attitude of its police force. In contrast, the London bobby behaves as though he went to a charm school for diplomats. Both are public servants, but one often acts as though it is the public that is the servant.

Before I get an irate call from Mayor Rudolph W. Giuliani, it is not my intent to dub all NYC cops as ill-mannered, but I dislike being referred to as "Mac" (as in, "Move it, Mac") by a guy playfully swinging a night stick. This kind of attitude reminds me that I love New York, but I wonder if New York loves me. Add on a propensity for brutality, and it's an attitude that prompted His Honor to issue wallet-sized directives to his 38,000 cops, telling them to say "hello" and "thank you" when they talk to the public (*National Post*, 1999). He feels it necessary also to instruct his boys and girls in blue to address you and me as "Mr.," "Ms.," "Sir," and "Ma'am," but he tells them they can skip the formalities while making an arrest.

## VIEWED AS A BRAND

You wonder how much higher the civility bar could be raised if his police force really started to think of itself as a brand, and you and me as real customers. How about City Hall doing the same? Would the IRS change its fear-striking tune more readily if it were IRS Inc.? It has started to realize that you and I butter its bread, but calling us customers is a long way from treating us as customers.

If Congress became a brand, would it expand its collective mind beyond the boundary gossip and partisan thinking of the Beltway? What it would take is for Congress to *really* listen, but perhaps that's asking a lot.

## A PLEASANT CHANGE

The civility bar for public service can be raised, and we're astonished when we hear people, such as the enlightened Reuben Greenberg (*Fast Company*, May 1999), chief of police in Charleston, South Carolina, say, "We are a service organization. Our customers are the citizens of Charleston. In my 17 years as head of this organization, the question that I've always asked myself is, Are citizens happy with the job that we are doing?"

He gives a dozen reasons why I would think the answer has to be a resounding, Yes. Here's one that comes close to enchanting. He says, "Ultimately, we don't just want to fight crime—we want to make life better for people. So all of our officers can make on-the-spot decisions to help citizens. Say it's raining, and an officer drives by and sees a woman and two kids huddled under an umbrella, waiting for a bus. If that officer doesn't have a call, he'll put those people in his car and take them wherever they want to go. After all, people like these are the ones who pay our salaries—and who pay for the car that the officer is driving."

It seems that this sort of leadership and initiative is more effective than printing up cards with instructions on how police officers should address their constituency with Pleases and Thank Yous, as they do in New York. What's so strange about expecting common courtesy from a cop? Why does it feel strange when *any* civil servant is nice to us?

A politician who thinks like a brand manager is always refreshing. The popular mayor of Milwaukee, John Norquist, now in his third four-year term, has

> A politician who thinks like a brand manager is always refreshing.

made a career out of casting aside conventional political thinking (*Fast Company*, December 1998). For ten years, he's been forging a new way to run Milwaukee, including faster, cheaper, and better. He states, "The goal is the success of the people of Milwaukee, not the growth of government. The idea is for people to thrive. We organize our efforts to add value to people's lives."

He measures success by outcomes, such as reducing spending by 20 percent over the last eight years. The city's payroll is down by 10 percent. Milwaukee's unemployment rate has dropped to 4.5 percent. Property values, even in low-income neighborhoods, have increased by 7.5 percent.

Crime is down to its lowest levels since the 1980s. Workers wages have increased at a rate that is three times the national average. He has done all this without relying on the largess of the federal government. He sees citizens as customers, "as people you want to please."

How's that for a breath of fresh political air? If he keeps it up, Milwaukee will be known for more than beer and brats.

There are other examples, but these few offer us hope that government can simply become more human in the way it goes about our business. Humans dealing with humans in human ways is called branding.

The question is: Do these leaders signify a new and exciting proliferation of branding? It might just be a generational thing. New blood from the ranks of the Boomers bring a fresh point of view that remembers that government service really is about service first, and government second; in fact, we shouldn't call it government service; we should call it service government.

## THE ULTIMATE CHALLENGE

The ultimate challenge for branding would be to take on the branding of a country. Geoff Mulgan thinks it can be done. Working out of Prime Minister Tony Blair's office at 10 Downing Street, Mulgan believes Britain's image can be turned from an archaic Rule Britannia to a contemporary Cool Britannia, and that the economy will benefit beyond tourism.

Reflecting Mulgan's thoughts, Daniel H. Pink (*Financial Post*, 1999) writes, "What a country should do is devise a marketing strategy that builds an attractive brand. Several countries have already figured out the rules of this game. Spain has branded itself—in part by using Joan Miro's bright and lively 'Espana' painting as a national logo and as a symbol of the nation's post-Franco optimism. Ireland, long seen as a sleepy land of pastures and pubs, has recast itself as a 'Celtic Tiger.'"

## CLICHÉ FACTS AND PERCEPTIONS

I'm sorry, Mr. Pink. I'm glad that Ireland has entered a time of new and welcome prosperity and now sees immigration rather than emigration. I'm also glad to hear the food is better and that Irish gastronomy is no longer simply a measure of how well the spuds are done. But just because the Irish have learned how to make a good living from computer chips doesn't mean such a dramatic change in reputation as you suggest. Old perceptions die hard. I still feel that Ireland is damp and green and rural and populated by loquacious drinkers of Guinness. I like to think of it populated with leprechauns in cloth caps and pretty red-haired colleens with names like Maureen O'Sullivan.

I don't want to give up these images, even in the name of economic progress and Dublin's soaring house prices. Even if the prosperity dries up and the European Union no longer has the billions to spend on shoring up the country's infrastructure, Ireland will still give us a powerful bank of colorful perceptions to draw on.

The cliché feelings we have for countries have to be based on something, and I think that something is often the facts.

I hate to disillusion Mr. Mulgan and Prime Minister Blair, but the rest of the world doesn't want to relinquish its perception of England as royal and regal and reserved and old and full of pomp and circumstance. We like it being a land of hope and glory, a sceptered isle set in a silver sea. We don't want them for ourselves, but we get a kick out of such anachronisms as lords and ladies of the realm, and a royal family that seems

> The rest of the world doesn't want to relinquish its perception of England as royal and regal and reserved and old and full of pomp and circumstance.

to rule not much more than a succession of stately flower shows and afternoon teas in grand surroundings. We don't even mind the satisfying surprise that royals can be just as naughty as the rest of us.

We know these things are cliché "facts," and that England can also make computers or jet planes or motor cars for export as well as they created the kings and queens and others of great distinction buried beneath the inscribed floor slabs of Westminster Abbey. (As ad man Clifford Field once wrote of the abbey, "Tread softly past the long, long sleep of kings.")

One side of the equation need not be sacrificed for the other, as long as we don't try to destroy the side that matters in the right brain. The cliché facts will always dominate our feelings, and they can help us find the essential meaning of a country (the way a state like Florida essentially means sunshine).

England could guide its industries toward categories that match its perceptions—such as fine crystal and silver and linens, well-crafted furniture, elegant cars, bespoke fashion, ocean liners and airplanes and hotels that deliver the attentive service of yesterday, earthy pop culture (like Carnaby Street and the Beatles and the Rolling Stones).

I suppose we have to work technology in there somehow, so why not technology served up with exceptional service manners that separates it from all other technology?

The point is that you can change the perception of a country very slightly, as long as you don't think you can rid the rest of us of our treasured feelings and perceptions. If you try, you will either fail or simply confuse people.

I would advise England to forget about an anachronism like Rule Britannia and a vulgarity like Cool Brittania, and capitalize on the feelings we have for it: of tradition and self-deprecating wit. I would perhaps try to brand it as a gem of good manners and gentle service, which would serve both tourism and industry. This suggests that it could be "Jewel Britannia!" This could give the country transcendence over a relic of empire like Rule Britannia, while staying within the boundaries of its entrenched identity.

## ENTRENCHED NEGATIVE FEELINGS

Entrenched memories that generate negative feelings are too bad for countries like Germany and Japan. More than half a century after

WWII, we might be starting to give up on our feelings about Hitler and Tojo, but they still linger in the deep recesses of our right brains where long-term memory resides.

We know both countries make fine brands, and produce great minds and fine people, but the old feelings linger on. It may be unfair, but we probably remember Germany more for Goering and Goebbels than we do for Bach, Beethoven, Brahms, or Goethe. Germany seems more penitent about its past than Japan, but it may be that the polite and formal Japanese don't express emotion very well and find it too embarrassing to say "sorry."

If Germany can pull anything out of its modern mythology, I think it can mean something along the lines of "meticulous," which I think has all kinds of potential for branding. If Japan means anything, it means "careful"—at least to me, who goes on about these things without the slightest benefit of formal research.

---

## IRELAND'S NEW LOVE OF GREEN

Despite my sentimental view of all things Irish, I must note that its economic progress is nothing less than stunning (*Business 2.0* 2000). It shows what a country can do to turn itself around. Ireland's Industrial Development Agency has coaxed over 1,200 multinationals to its emerald shores. These include Dell Computer, Hewlett-Packard, Netscape Communications, and Sun Microsystems. The country is now the world's second-largest exporter of software. One way to explain the attraction is a 10 percent corporate tax rate, which makes a nice welcome. Another is that 40 percent of the 3.7 million population is younger than 25 and forms a well-educated workforce—a workforce now willing to stay home, rather than seek opportunity overseas. Remarkably, an estimated 25,000 emigrants have returned to reap the benefits. I would like to think that the quality of the Guinness also has something to do with it.

As Bill Gates has been known to say, "Often you just have to rely on your intuition."

## COUNTRIES' REALISTIC AND IDEAL BRANDS

Let me stick my neck out with some other branding suggestions boiled down to one or two words, which I think answer the question of how countries can realistically and ideally make us feel. France: pleasure. Italy: style. Spain: exotic. Greece: classic. Canada: honest. USA: daring. Scotland: hardy. England: traditional. Ireland: social. Wales: gentle. Entire cultures can revolve around such words in the way they organize and project themselves.

Russia is rougher. Its present pain was predictable. When the Soviet Union crashed, Russia no longer meant anything. It lost its identity. It not only lost what it stood for, it lost also what it was against. In a person, we would call it an identity crisis, and we know it can cause an emotional breakdown. Russia's breakdown is similarly emotional. The entire country appears to be a madhouse, with consequences we continue to feel daily.

> R ussia will not recover until it gets a grip on an identity— either one from its past (which seems unlikely), or one that signifies its future.

Russia will not recover until it gets a grip on an identity—either one from its past (which seems unlikely), or one that signifies its future. It seems glib to suggest that branding could come to the rescue, but countries are like brands, in that they both live by meaning. They are the product of dominant, intrinsic myth.

My stab at stamping Russia emerges from a word I think they, and the rest of us, could accept: passionate.

Smaller countries with names that aren't daily on the lips of the larger world stand an ideal chance of influencing our feelings for the sake of their economies. Size is not the point of identity.

Look at how we feel about Switzerland. Tiny Britain wasn't joking when it called itself Great. Monte Carlo is about the size of New York's Central Park, but it throws a bigger shadow on western consciousness than Egypt. Indonesia's East Timor is more like a community than a country, but as shown by recent events, it appears as willing to fight for independence as much larger states. After the basic necessities of survival, the quest for identity is among the most powerful and atavistic of human concerns. It's possible, for example, that the French Canadian concern for a distinct identity could be powerful enough to actually break up our neighbor to the immediate north.

I hope it doesn't make me hopelessly provincial, but I think of Greenland, Iceland, Finland, Norway, and Denmark as countries I know are strong, but of which I have no firm perceptual grasp beyond vague cliché. There are countries in Africa beyond the wartorn that most of us have never heard of.

And who outside of South America knows much about Chile or Paraguay, or even a behemoth like Argentina? They could all be taking the best of their cultures and marketing them to the rest of us with a vengeance. If South America is a mystery behind a somewhat see-through curtain, it's time the curtain was parted.

The United States probably doesn't need any more publicity than it already gets, but the Voice of America could become more than an instrument of sinister propaganda if we decided to broadcast our own version of our identity to the rest of the world.

It shocks us when we discover that a lot of the world's peoples don't like America or Americans. We think we're the good guys, but a lot of people see us as black hats. They fear our size and clout. They see us as doctrinal bullies. They see us as interested only in the opportunistic buck. That we pursue life, liberty, and the pursuit of happiness, and became home for many of history's most wretched peoples, is often lost in harmful stereotype.

If we truly are all part of a global economy, these could be the branding opportunities of the future. It might not be as difficult as it appears. After all, mate, look what Paul Hogan's Crocodile Dundee did for the continent of Australia!

CHAPTER **30**

# Should You Be a Brand?

The first time I saw an article about how individuals should think of themselves as brands, I felt a little repulsed (*Fast Company* 1997). I didn't like the idea of thinking of myself, or anybody else, as a package of attributes to be marketed, or to be dialed up and down like public sentiment in a political poll. But the article was by Tom Peters, and I felt compelled to read it. Since then, I've seen the idea in several other publications, and I've tried it on for size.

## BRAND YOU

Brand You is an idea that works for people who don't need to be reminded that life can come with a nonrefundable sense of humor. As long as you understand that a brand contains all the trust of a handshake, you're fine. If you—as a real, live brand—want to communicate that you are the person who will do what you say you will do when you say you will do it, *being* a brand can help you maintain that focus. But to keep Brand You from becoming too grim and taking yourself too seriously, Brand You must resolve to *enjoy* doing what you say you will do when you say you will do it.

The idea is to become the CEO of Brand You. If you have a job, your boss is your customer and Brand You is the supplier of services. Your wages become your sales, and it's easy to see how it puts a new perspective on how you perform and conduct yourself. It puts a new perspective on your present and, certainly, on your future, which is probably one of your vital interests; one that Brand You might try not to leave to the blowing of the wind.

Branding yourself will help you resolve to sharpen and re-sharpen your skills, and to always acquire new ones. You will think beyond the financial transaction of your job. You will work at creat-

ing value in your relationships with others—from the person at the reception
desk to the person in the back room
who prepares your paycheck. In other
words, you will be the kind of person
you would like to hire, or the kind of
boss you would like to work for. And if
Brand You can engender fanatical loyalty, so much the better.

## LOYALTY BETWEEN COMPANY
## AND EMPLOYEE

There used to be more loyalty between
companies and their employees in the
days before the adoption of the euphe-

> Branding yourself will help you resolve to sharpen and resharpen your skills, and to always acquire new ones.

mism we know as downsizing. In the days when people actually
pursued a one-company career, there was a premium placed on
"climbing the ladder." You found something you were good at and
exploited it in one place.

Nowadays, as Tom Peters (ibid.) says, you might think of yourself differently. You're not an employee or a staffer. "You don't
'belong to' any company for life, and your chief affiliation isn't to
any particular 'function.' You're not defined by your job title[,] and
you're not confined by your job description." Rather, says Peters,
loyalty is still alive and well, but it is loyalty to your project, your
team, your customers—and yourself. "We are the CEOs of our own
companies: Me Inc. To be in business today, our most important job
is to be head marketer for the brand called You."

He goes on: " . . . the main chance is becoming a free agent in an
economy of free agents, looking to have the best season you can
imagine in your field, looking to do your best work and chalk up a
remarkable track record, and looking to establish your own micro
equivalent of the Nike swoosh."

## LOYALTY TO YOURSELF IN TODAY'S MARKET

Considering the fraying of the bond between workers and employees, it's not bad advice. Since 1989, major corporations have issued
more than 3 million pink slips annually. Considering that a job
search usually lasts a month for every $10,000 of a person's salary,

you're looking at a lot of sorely missed paydays. Rosy employment statistics point to a growing shortage of good available help, but it doesn't seem to quell the canning of huge numbers of people.

What's surprising is that Wall Street interprets downsizing not as a source of potential trouble for a company in the market place, but as a sign of greater efficiency. Companies that feel compelled to fire thousands are often rewarded with a higher stock price for their supposed prudence in getting rid of bloat. You would think allowing bloat to occur in the first place would be a sign of poor management, or of irresponsible management not paying attention to the preservation of the brand's assets.

## FORMING BRAND YOU

In forming Brand You, Peters suggests intense self-examination and the writing of a statement that starts with answering the question: What is it that my product or service does that makes it different?— in 15 words or less. The answer should light up the eyes of a prospective employer.

Once, I playfully wrote what I thought would be Harry's mission statement: "Nobody enjoys working as hard as I do to deliver consistently effective creative work." When I showed these fourteen words to him, he crossed them out and wrote: "My work will never fail to make you happy."

Harry then wrote what he thought would be my mission statement. He wrote, "Leadership from ingrained integrity; results from great expectations." I told him flattery would get him everywhere, except in line for a bonus. I also told him that he could have profited by thinking of himself as a brand rather than a part-time playboy who has been known to faint at the sight of a well-turned ankle. His answer: "But that's the Brand Me that everybody knows and loves!"

You can create visibility for Brand You by writing articles for magazines that are devoured by other people in your field. You can start an online, idea-sharing club to extend your network influence. You can take on freelance projects to enhance your repertoire of skills and make new contacts. You can offer to speak (as long as you have a good speech that will either illuminate our minds or leave us weak-kneed with laughter) at a trade show or the Chamber of Commerce.

And of course, you can conduct yourself in every one of your dealings as a person who will stand up to be counted with great gusto and good cheer every day of your life. The latter is probably as good a way to succeed as any. As an employer, I can tell you that skilled, positive, decent people with high emotional intelligence are worth their weight in gold, whether they think of themselves as brands or not. As Albert Einstein said, "Try not to become a man of success but a man of value." As I say, "Work to become, not to beget."

In another issue of *Fast Company*, (1999), Tom Peters says that in the new economy, all work is project work, and you can make them all go Wow! You can use projects to show your value, to leave a legacy, or to make yourself a star. "Project work is the vehicle by which the powerless gain power . . . Somewhere, in the belly of every company, someone is working away in obscurity on the project that 10 years from now everyone will acknowledge as the company's proudest moment."

> **S**killed, positive, decent people with high emotional intelligence are worth their weight in gold, whether they think of themselves as brands or not.

He suggests that you "volunteer for every lousy project that comes along: Organize the office Christmas party. (Turn that dreadful holiday party into an event that says 'Thanks for a terrific year' to all employees.)"

Never let a project go dreary on you. Use the project to create surprising new ways of looking at old problems. No project is too mundane to become a Wow! project if you attack it with passion and recruit Wow! people to help you with it. Everything is a golden learning opportunity if you keep your eyes and ears open. Five criteria for judging each project are Wow! Beautiful! Revolutionary! Impact! Raving Fans!

Peters gives an example of turning a dull chore assignment— such as cleaning up the warehouse—into a Wow! project: You see quickly that what looks like a messy warehouse is really a poorly organized warehouse. This involves necessarily both incoming parts from suppliers and outgoing parts to customers, which in turn, makes the case for a new distribution system that would feed flaw-lessly into a newly reorganized warehouse—a warehouse that will now stay neat because of newly designed processes that fit the new distribution system perfectly.

In *The 7 Habits of Highly Effective People* (1990) and *Principle-Centered Leadership* (1992), Stephen Covey puts forward the idea that leadership is not equated with any kind of position. We have bought into this top-down control model, but we can ignore it if we choose. He says you can become your own pilot program for leadership from the position you now occupy.

> If you want to be the boss, start today by assuming that you already are.

Assume responsibility. Be proactive. Flex your boss muscle. Exceed your authority. As Harry says, "It is better to ask for forgiveness than for permission." If you want to be the boss, start today by assuming that you already are. If the barriers are too great for your future development, think about your alternatives. Covey says, "Never let your professional development be governed by your company. People without options are running scared. They tend to become reactive. When you have alternatives of employment, you don't have to be angry, whine, or moan, you just go somewhere else."

This advice is particularly sage if your boss is a control freak, or who thinks of you as nothing more than a profit center and contrib-utor to his personal pension fund.

## What's in a Name?

One author even suggests that you should take a good look at your name and change it if it represents a negative image. And it's there that I draw the line. A rose wouldn't smell as sweet by any other name, and neither would you. If your name is Eddie Schmuck (we know one), I think you should wear it proudly. Let the rabble with ordinary names snigger at your moniker as you leave them in the dust with your competence and good cheer. Would Faith Popcorn be as successful in the trend-analysis business if her name were Mary Smith? Faith Popcorn is a gold-mine kind of name (Faith is the one

## BRAND YOU AS A BOSS

If you want to be a better brand of boss, create a leadership paradigm that encourages personal responsibility (*Financial Post*, 1999).
Develop a common purpose and a common value system that everybody in the organization can follow with a sense of mission. Never supervise a person's methods; say instead, "That's your job. How you do it is up to you."

When an employee asks for help, offer how you would approach the project. Remember that the leader is a kind of servant who asks the employee, "What are you learning? What are your goals? How can I help you?" Don't do performance appraisals. They insult people. Let your employees judge themselves; usually they will judge themselves more harshly.

None of this means giving up direction. It's simply empowering people within agreed-upon guidelines.

who came up with the word "cocooning" to describe the aging Baby Boomers' habit of staying home).

Remember it was an Englishman named Crapper who invented the flush toilet (thus, the nickname for the commode). It's a guy named Schwab who practically invented the online brokerage business, without any concern for a Germanic name that doesn't exactly tinkle in the ear like angels' bells.

If your name is Ronald Bumstead or Louie Pecker, remember that all good brands make an effort to stand out with a stand-out name. If your name is out of the ordinary, you're lucky; in fact, it's the guy called Smith who should change his name to Schmuck.

Who in their right mind would call a company Yahoo!? The guys who want to stand out, who want to say we're way beyond ordinary, who want to announce a new kind of iconoclastic force—that's who!

It's a lot more interesting and involving than the Generals of the nineteenth and early twentieth century—like General Electric, General Dynamics, General Motors, General Telephone and Electronics, and so on. Come to think of it, a funnier name would be General Yahoo! I wonder if this was the intended humor behind the name of the high-tech General Magic?

As Harry says, however, "You might want to rethink a name like Hitler. Having the name Hitler is like chewing tobacco and the amazing amount of spitting that goes along with it. There's nothing funny about it. It has no socially redeemable qualities. It lacks any form of grace on a first date. And it's obviously bad for the state of your longevity. If my name were Hitler, I'd change it to Montana. I love the name Montana; in fact I'd change both names. There's something not quite right about Adolph Montana."

Harry might also have changed his name if he wanted to go into the fashion business, and he was called Ralph Lifshitz. He would have changed it to Ralph Lauren.

## MANAGING ONESELF

In *Management Challenges for the 21st Century* (1999), Peter F. Drucker takes the hype out of making yourself a brand by simply calling it, "Managing Oneself." With the rise of the "knowledge worker," he says it's more and more crucial for career longevity. Drucker says you don't plan careers. You prepare for them, and you do so by searching out the answers to three critical questions:

**What are my strengths?**
**How do I perform?**
**What are my values?**

> **D**rucker says you don't plan careers. You prepare for them.

All three are important, but I find "How do I perform?" to be the most illuminating.

Drucker gives us an extraordinary insight when he says most people perform by either reading or listening, and it is imperative that you know which of these you primarily use. During WWII,

Allied commander General Dwight Eisenhower was always sharp as a tack at press briefings. All questions were answered thoroughly and in beautifully polished sentences. When he became president, however, he was terrible in front of the press and with its questions. He rambled, often incoherently, and was a laughingstock for bumbling speech.

The difference between the two situations can be found in the fact that Eisenhower was a reader, not a listener. During the war, he insisted that all questions be submitted to him in writing prior to a press briefing. This allowed him to read everything before he prepared his response (which he probably wrote). In Washington, however, he had no such luxury. He had to respond on the spot after simply listening to press questions, and he found it very difficult.

By contrast, President Lyndon Johnson was primarily a listener. Drucker says one of the reasons Johnson destroyed his presidency is that he didn't know he was a listener. He thought he had to do the same as his predecessor, John Kennedy, who was a reader. Johnson thought he had to absorb everything from written reports. We're talking here about reports from brilliant writers, like Arthur Schlesinger and Bill Moyers. But he apparently never got one word of what they wrote, simply because he didn't know he learned by listening, not reading.

## A SENSE OF MISSION IS A SENSE OF "BEING SENT"

The word "mission" reminds me of the story of the guy who looks up to heaven and says angrily, "God, how come the world is in such a mess? All this hunger and poverty and war and disaster? It's terrible! Why don't you send somebody down to fix it?"

Suddenly the guy hears a whisper in his ear. He realizes it's the voice of God. It says softly, "Ah, my friend, but I did send somebody. I sent you."

You've heard the expression, "He's good on his feet." When I hear that, I know the subject is somebody who is a listener (and probably a talker), not primarily a reader or a writer.

## THE DIFFERENT TYPES OF LEARNERS

Most writers perform and learn by writing rather than reading or listening. Harry says he can't go to the bathroom without a pen in his hand. He says, "I write; therefore, I think." Writers often don't do well in school and find it torture (like Winston Churchill) because they are required to learn by listening and reading rather than writing. This insight leads one to wonder about an entire educational system that imparts knowledge by teachers talking to a class full of students, regardless of their learning predilection. It certainly favors the listeners.

> **W**riters often don't do well in school and find it torture (like Winston Churchill) because they are required to learn by listening and reading rather than writing.

Many people actually learn by talking. You can almost hear their brainframes processing as they verbalize what's going on in their noggins. A lot of college professors say they learn what they want to write for publication from talking out a subject in the classroom.

Still others learn by doing. You can see how important it is to know how you learn and perform, so you don't make the mistake of putting a value on one method over the other.

It's not only important how you perform, but you have to know how the people around you perform. If your boss learns by listening, don't make her life difficult by writing everything. A listener-boss might say, "I want that report on my desk by Monday morning." But don't make the mistake of just writing it. Make sure you get the chance to tell it. Of course, if the boss is a reader, don't waste her time, or incur her wrath, by doing everything verbally.

## MIND YOUR MANNERS

As Drucker says, in all your dealings, you have to assume relationship responsibility *as a duty*. This includes the simple but effective idea that good manners go a long way to helping you get good results. Drucker adds, "Bright people—especially bright young people—often do not understand that manners are the 'lubricating oil' of an organization."

With more than manners in mind, you are bound to meet people you have to struggle to get along with. This is hardly a very good reason for Brand You to deprecate their intelligence.

You might think somebody is dumb because they don't agree with your point of view, but the state of another's intellect is often not the issue. For example, the dumb one is unlikely to see himself in an unfavorable light, but the degree of his dumbness probably goes up with the degree of your frustration. If you really think he is dumb, the natural conclusion is that you are the smart one. If you are indeed the superior intellect, you presumably have the brainy wherewithal to persuade him to your point of view!

Years ago, I took Harry through this logic when he was having a dispute with a valued client. He gave me a baleful look and mumbled, "Now that really is dumb!"

You have to take responsibility for figuring out how the people you deal with perform and learn and communicate, so that you can adjust how you can best work with them. Ask them to tell you their preferences, and they will appreciate it.

You don't have to like all the people you will meet in your working life, but it is helpful to respect, and hopefully, trust them. They will feel it if you do. Nine times out of ten, they will respond in kind. As you take responsibility for your relationships, it's amazing how simple manners can pave the way. Perhaps lessons in branding should start with the reading of Emily Post.

## WRITE YOUR OWN STORY

In the end, you have to write your own story. George Bernard Shaw said, "This is the true joy in life, the being used for a purpose recognized by yourself as a mighty one . . . being a force of nature instead of a feverish, selfish little clod of ailments and grievances complaining that the world will not devote itself to making you happy."

PART Nine

SUMMARY

CHAPTER 31

# Get Branding!

The problem with a book like this is that it can motivate a boss or an owner to *do* something. It can make you feel as though the way you muddle through running your career or your business is hardly good enough, and the time has come for some big moves. It can generate a deep desire to become a broom of sweeping change.

If the book is as powerful as I would like it to be, you may feel something akin to an epiphany. You're going to march into the office tomorrow morning with every intention of shaking the tree to its very roots. You're going to demand *initiative*.

Well, hold your horses.

This is not a motivational diet book that promises a new and radiantly skinny you in ten short days. It's not a serendipitous idea you pick up from *Reader's Digest* that will transform your life with a new vision of God. It's a business book, intended to offer you some ideas that could help you do a better, more profitable, more satisfying job for yourself and all your stakeholders. But please go slowly.

The Information Age may travel at the speed of light, but you can approach your new, improved brand at a more human pace. While it's good to feel motivated, it's also good to stop once in a while to ask of your progress, "But how does it make you feel?"

Start with you. What obvious personal strengths do you feel as a result of reading this book? Just as importantly, what obvious weaknesses? And most important of all, what can you do to change *in small ways*?

Simply ask yourself what changes you might make in yourself that would help your business. If you want to be really gutsy, ask your employees to evaluate you and to suggest three changes they would like to see you make in yourself. Ask some trusted customers and suppliers to evaluate your performance—both yours and that of your company. After absorbing it all, make one small change a week.

If you have a few employees, get them all in a room, or take them all to lunch, or away for a weekend of chat and games and good food, and use Commander D. Michael Abrashoff as a leadership role model. He didn't make the changes on his ship. He was merely the catalyst. The changes were made by his crew. He knows that people tend to resist change, but they embrace it when they instigate it. Asking them for their opinions, questions, and answers will motivate them mightily. Giving them the power to do what they see has to be done is immeasurably effective. It says volumes about you and your style of leadership, and how you want your company and its brands to be perceived.

> While it's good to feel motivated, it's also good to stop once in a while to ask of your progress, "But how does it make you feel?"

In his book, *Direct from Dell* (1999), Michael Dell says, "It's easy to fall in love with how far you've come and how much you've done. It's definitely harder to see the cracks in a structure you've built yourself, but that's all the more reason to look hard and look often. Even if something seems to be working, it can be improved."

Talk *with* your staff. And get them talking to each other. If you have departments, start with one of them and share questions about a few little things that might lead to improvements in the way you do business.

For example, ask each member of the department for three suggestions that will improve how they do business with customers. Get them to share the suggestions. Stimulate them with the idea that you believe it's much more important to develop relationships than just transactions. Instill the attitude that getting credit doesn't matter as much as getting results, that it's *their* company and *their* future that's at stake.

Get them all talking. Thomas Petzinger wrote a chapter in his brilliant *The New Pioneers* (1999), titled "Nobody's as Smart as Everybody." In it, he writes about groups of minds:

> Will they explore a wider, more creative space through social interaction or through outside command? Though the answer should be obvious, consider the case of the heart surgeons from five hospitals in New England who spent 1996 observing each other's practices and talking about their work. The result was a stunning 24 percent decline in mortality rates in bypass surgery, the equivalent of seventy-four saved lives, a result they could never have obtained through the traditional continuing educational regimen of listening to lectures, reading articles, or even logging into artificial "knowledge management" systems . . . as one biologist quips, "I link, therefore I am."

If you think only professionals can get results through the simple, human process of comparing notes, go back and read about Commander Abrashoff's accomplishments with young, wet-behind-the-ears, high school graduates. I bet he doesn't have many Ph.D.'s on his payroll.

Start a dialogue on the broader discussion of mission and how to develop one. Don't just do this with your top people. Start at the grass roots. You might be surprised at how interested your people might be in getting beyond just working for wages. Read other books on the subject of branding and creative leadership, but remember the advice of Peter Senge (*Fast Company*, 1999)—that your company isn't a machine that can be "fixed" by a mechanic; it's a living organism that needs "gardeners" to keep it healthy and growing. Don't just change it; cultivate it, and remember that everything in a garden starts by being small.

Senge's garden analogy reminds me of the Buddhist expression that when

> **D**on't just change it; cultivate it, and remember that everything in a garden starts by being small.

you want a tree to grow, you don't water the leaves; you water the roots.

Long ago, Peter Drucker said, "Success does not require special gifts, special aptitude, or special training. Effectiveness as an executive demands doing certain—and fairly simple—things. It consists of a small number of practices."

Small steps can obviously come from inside your organization, but they can include forming alliances with other companies as a way to learn. You can also make a small acquisition or form a joint venture for modest expansion before you bet the farm on big changes.

Pilot everything of importance. Piloting helps you to learn the positives and negatives from making small changes so you can be a lot smarter about making big ones.

## THE BASICS

A lot of this stuff is basic. Senge (*Fast Company*, 1999) says,

> Most people would rather work with a group of people who trust one another. Most people would rather walk out of a meeting with the belief that they've just solved an important problem. Most people would rather have fun at work. It may be obvious[,] but we've observed again and again that personal enthusiasm is the initial energizer of any change process. And that enthusiasm feeds on itself. People don't necessarily want to "have a vision" at work or to "conduct a dialogue." They want to be part of a team that's fun to work with and that produces results they are proud of."

These are all conditions you can lead and manage. The point here is that we shouldn't get caught up in the jargon of corporate change; that change is useless until it helps people do their jobs better for their own and their customers' satisfaction. People feel (and are) truly important when they get a sense of how important their contribution can be.

> **P**eople feel (and are) truly important when they get a sense of how important their contribution can be.

That's the secret of Commander Abrashoff having the best ship with the best crew in the whole Pacific fleet. It's why Richard Branson has such a huge following of both employees and customers for his Virgin brands. It could be the secret to you having the best brands in the best company in the market you want to dominate best!

But while change may be necessary and worthwhile, it's axiomatic that all change is disruptive. Good change and bad change take a similar emotional toll on a person's system. It's the same for brands.

It might be necessary to make friends for a while with ambiguity and paradox. They are the best pals of creativity. And just be sure that you get the intended result when you initiate change. Don't let change bite the hand that feeds it.

Alexander Rose (*Financial Post*, 1999) writes,

> In the time of Socrates, the Delphic Oracle was considered the center [*sic*] of the Earth. Greeks would travel to the Oracle to ask questions of the gods and receive a reply, which unfortunately took the form of an amphiboly (a statement whose meaning is indeterminate in a peculiar way). Thus, in 559 BC, the fabulously wealthy King Croesus of Lydia asked the Oracle whether he should wage war against Persia and was told that if he did so[,] he would destroy a great kingdom. Taking this as a yes, King Croesus attacked the Persians under Cyrus the Great, but lost the war and destroyed his own kingdom.

The moral is that change is fine, as long as you keep an eye out for those darned amphibolies!

After all is said and done, we should remember the root of the word "company." Peter Senge (*Financial Post*, 1999) tells us that it goes back long before the Industrial Age; in fact, the word "company" has the same root as the word "companion." It means, "the sharing of bread."

# Developing Your Own Personal Unity of Knowledge

If you got through this book without too much trouble, it's highly likely that you can get through a few others that I would like to recommend to you. Not many of them are directly connected to branding, but I've never considered the subject of branding to be composed from one note. You get a feel for it from the consilience of your own knowledge; how everything from disparate disciplines can "jump together" in your own noggin in your own time.

As CEO of Brandtrust, I consider wide reading a necessary (and enjoyable) part of my job. I read dozens of books in a year. There's never a time when I don't have more than one on the go in an effort to continue learning, as I keep away the boredom of flying and keep up with the chess pieces as they move across the branding board. Here are a few books I highly recommend:

You get a very thorough treatment of integrated marketing from *Driving Brand Value* by Tom Duncan and Sandra Moriarty. I think of it a little like a brand bible. The style tends to be a little academic, but at least you won't have to put up with the antics of my friend Harry, as you have in this book!

For the subject of one-to-one marketing, consultants Don Peppers and Martha Rogers give you two books. Which one you read depends on how you intend to put the knowledge gleaned to use. In their words, "It is not necessary for you to have read *The One to One Future* in order to get the full benefit of *Enterprise One to One*. We wrote the first book as a 'why-to' book. *Enterprise One to One*, by way of contrast, is a how-to book—a tool kit chock-full of practical, experience-based advice." The authors also put out a newsletter called *INSIDE 1to1,* to which I subscribe (for a free subscription, e-mail subscribe@1to1.com). Martha Rogers, by the way, works with us at Brandtrust as a Brandtrustee.

> Leadership may have come to you as a natural, God-given trait, but I see no reason on earth why it also cannot be an acquired one.

Harry Beckwith's extraordinary commonsense and experience come shining through in *Selling the Invisible*, which he subtitles *A Field Guide to Modern Marketing.* I've said it several times already, but Harry Beckwith is not the same person as the just-plain Harry who appears in this book. Some people, by the way, think I made up our Harry. This is not true. He made up himself.

Al Ries writes with great passion about the need for focus and the dangers of losing it with such things as line extensions and other temptations. In his to-the-point fashion, his book is called *Focus.* There's great profit in reading it.

Leadership may have come to you as a natural, God-given trait, but I see no reason on earth why it also cannot be an acquired one. In either event, reading can only help you understand and improve your personal brand of it. Read *The Effective Executive* and *Management Challenges for the 21st Century* by my favorite teacher and business writer, Peter F. Drucker (in fact, read any of his dozen management books).

Read *Principle-Centered Leadership* by Stephen Covey.

And by all means, read Thomas Petzinger Jr.'s *The New Pioneers*. I couldn't put the latter down, and Harry raves about it. Here, you see and feel the way of the new leaders, and you discover that there are thousands of them working busily without the benefit of the big headlines out of Silicon Valley. Petzinger teaches us that trade and technology are fundamentally human. His book reflects this with its refreshing human scale.

For a feel of what's happening in technology—what it means and where it's taking us in the broad-stroke sense—there are lots of books I could recommend, but five of my favorites are: *Real Time* by Regis McKenna, *Being Digital* by Nicholas Negroponte, *Blur* by Stan Davis and Christopher Meyer, and *Road Warriors* by Daniel Burstein and David Kline.

Your life is changing; you should know about it. These are all well-written books that I found totally engrossing, as well as edifying. I have not listed them here in order of preference; rather, this is the way they sit on my messy bookcase.

One last suggestion is *The Roaring 2000s*, by Harry S. Dent Jr. I suggest it because brands need people with money to buy them, and Dent says there will be a lot of them around until 2008. He explains why the big Boomer cohort will then be past its prime spending years and how the North American economy could be in for a lean spell. It's good information for a long view of the economy, including an insightful explanation for the lack of inflation and other economic phenomena. He happens also to give what I believe is good investment advice, as well as millennial trends in real estate and other matters of personal finance.

Francis Bacon said nearly four hundred years ago: "Some books are to be tasted, others to be swallowed, and some few to be chewed and digested." My reading suggestions belong on the latter plate, and I wish you *bon appétit*.

Now, for how *Emotional Branding* came about:

I've worked in the branding business for twenty-five years, but for most of that time, I didn't know it. The years were happily spent in advertising agencies—some as an employee and one (Arian, Lowe & Travis) owned by my partners and me. While branding was a good part of the work we were really doing on behalf of our clients, we didn't think to call it that.

We called it 'positioning' or 'searching,' for what the Ted Bates agency called the USP (Unique Selling Proposition). We proselytized giving a brand a distinct personality to establish a strong brand character. We talked about advertising as a dialogue between clients and their customers. We saw ourselves as the representative of the consumer in our client's offices. But we didn't associate any of this with branding.

It was only when we refined the process of discovering the dominant emotions that drive brands that we realized we were helping our clients to create brands, not just effective advertising. This was more than a decade ago, and I like to think that Arian, Lowe & Travis was one of the first ad agencies to grasp the importance of the brand perspective.

Our process takes a prismatic view of a company's employee relations, products, services, suppliers, and customer beliefs, and then distills the discoveries into critical insights that lead to specific action. It's a customized, collaborative process that turns up a lot more than traditional strategy. It provides a path that a company can follow, inside and out, in the quest for customers willing to come back with the regularity of boomerangs. The deep-dive insights gleaned from this work helped put a lot of meat on this book's bones.

After more than fifty successful applications of the process, I decided that it was time to found Brandtrust—an organization devoted to raising the brand-building process to its rightful position, as the most important ingredient in business success. Its mission: to provide clients with *the* preeminent consulting resource for the analysis and strategic planning synthesis that will build their brands.

Why form a separate entity rather than continue working through Arian, Lowe & Travis? For some of the reasons I talk about earlier, brand building is too important to have as an adjunct activity. Brand building and advertising aren't the same.

Clients should feel free to come to us for brand work, regardless of where they choose to buy any advertising that might be necessary. And of course, separating the two functions eliminates a potential conflict of interest. I preach the need for focus and must, therefore, be prepared to practice it.

For me, good ideas are simply warm and fuzzy notions until they are written down to be scrutinized, scrapped, praised, damned, or fought over before action gets taken. Writing your thoughts clearly is demanding work, particularly if you perform by talking your way to lucidity, but I felt I must write them down to avoid any slips between the mind and the lip.

You can sometimes escape logic and good sense in speech, but it's difficult to do so when it's staring back at you in black type from a white piece of paper. I want to make sure my words are where my mouth is. It took a book to get it done.

I do massive amounts of reading, but I couldn't find a single book on branding that satisfied my two criteria: One, to cover the subject with reasonable depth; two, to be easy to digest. Some very good academic books are perhaps more complete, but a bit ponderous. Some more popular books give you easy reading, but don't cover the subject thoroughly enough.

> **G**ood ideas are simply warm and fuzzy notions until they are written down to be scrutinized, scrapped, praised, damned, or fought over before action gets taken.

So this book was born to clarify my own thoughts, to get my own head straight, and to avoid what the prison warden said in the movie *Cool Hand Luke*, "What we got here is a failure to communicate."

I got a lot of help with the writing from Harry. Harry has a last name, but prefers to maintain his own brand mystique. Harry's a cloak-and-dagger kind of guy (all cloak, no dagger).

My Brandtrust colleague John Summers helped enormously with the book's organization and with Chapter 27, on managing the money side of brand equity. And he read an early version of the manuscript with great care before he ripped it without mercy into more readable shreds.

I had in my mind a mythical reader who has real doubts about branding as *the* essential business tool. I imagined him as a crusty, no-nonsense executive, needing something to read besides the *Wall Street Journal* on the twice-daily commute between Scarsdale and New York City. My reasoning was: If I can make a compelling case to a skeptical, hard-nosed business man, maybe I can make it entertaining and illuminating to converted brand builders looking for more grist for their mill in a think book.

It's up to you how well the book succeeds in these aims, but I hope that I have at least communicated the passion I feel for the subject and the conviction with which I hold it dear. Most of all, I hope I've avoided writing's most critical sin: I hope I haven't bored you.

# REFERENCES

## CHAPTER 1

Beckwith, Harry. 1997. *Selling the Invisible*. New York: Warner Books.

*Fast Company*. August/September 1998.

*Financial Post*. April 12, 1999.

Fombrun, Charles J. 1996. *Reputation: Realizing Value from the Corporate Image*. Boston: Harvard Business Press. p. 89.

*New York Times Magazine*. September 13, 1998. "The Swoon of the Swoosh" by Timothy Egan. p. 66.

*New York Times Magazine*. September, 1999.

## CHAPTER 3

Aaker, David A. 1991. *Managing Brand Equity*. New York: The Free Press.

Advertisers, 1996. I borrow this phrase from the booklet: *Your Brand Is Your Future*, American Association of Advertisers.

*Fast Company*. August/September 1997.

*Financial Post*. April 9, 1999.

*National Post*. January 29, 2000.

## CHAPTER 4

Aaker, David A. 1991. *Managing Brand Equity*. New York: The Free Press. p. 8.

Beckwith, Harry. 1997. *Selling The Invisible*. New York: Warner Books. pp. 152–153.

*Fast Company*. August/September 1997. p. 98.

*Fast Company*. December 1998. p. 120.

*Financial Post*. April 23, 1999.

*Forbes*. November 1, 1999. p. 230.

Petzinger, Thomas, Jr. 1999. *The New Pioneers*. New York: Simon & Schuster. p. 44.

**CHAPTER 5**

Aaker, David A. 1991. *Managing Brand Equity: Capitalizing on the Value of a Brand Name.* New York: The Free Press. p. ix.

Duncan, Tom and Sandra Moriarty. 1997. *Driving Brand Value: Using Integrated Marketing to Manage Profitable Brand Relationships.* New York: McGraw Hill. p. 56.

*Financial Post.* March 31, 1999.

*INSIDE 1to1.* October 29, 1998.

Light, Larry with Richard Morgan. 1994. *The Fourth Wave: Brand Loyalty Marketing.* New York: Coalition for Brand Equity. Most of the numerical facts in this chapter come from this fine little booklet. You can get a copy for a small charge from AAAA Publications Department at 212-850-0777 or fax 212-682-8136.

Light, Larry and Jim Mullen. 1996. *Your Brand is Your Future.* New York: AAAA Publications.

*National Post.* May 1, 1999.

**CHAPTER 6**

*National Post.* October 20, 1999.

**CHAPTER 7**

Beckwith, Harry. 1997. *Selling The Invisible: A Field Guide to Marketing.* New York: Warner Books.

*Delaney Report.* February 15, 1999.

*Harvard Business Review.* July/August 1989.

*Fast Company.* August/September 1997.

*Fast Company.* April 1998.

*Financial Post.* March 31, 1999.

McKenna, Regis. 1997. *Real Time: Preparing For The Age Of The Never Satisfied Customer.* Boston: Harvard Business School Press.

*National Post.* October 30, 1998.

*Wall Street Journal.* May 3, 1999.

**CHAPTER 8**

*Business 2.0.* April 1999.

Drucker, Peter F. 1999. *The Frontiers of Management: Where Tomorrow's Decisions Are Being Shaped Today.* New York: Plume (The Penguin Group).

Duncan, Tom and Sandra Moriarty. 1997. *Driving Brand Value: Using Integrated Marketing to Manage Profitable Stakeholder Relationships.* New York: McGraw-Hill. p. 8.

*Fast Company.* December 1988. p. 120.

   Ibid. p. 175.

*Inc.* June 1999.

McKenna, Regis. 1997. *Real Time: Preparing For The Age Of The Never Satisfied Customer*. Boston: Harvard Business School Press. pp. 53–55.

*Montreal Gazette*. May 3, 1999.

## CHAPTER 9

*Business 2.0*. April 1999.

Dell, Michael with Catherine Fredman. 1999. *Direct from Dell: Strategies That Revolutionized an Industry*. New York: Harper Collins. p. 22.

Duncan, Tom and Sandra Moriarty. 1997. *Driving Brand Value: Using Integrated Marketing to Manage Profitable Stakeholder Relationships*. New York: McGraw-Hill. p. 32.

*Fast Company*. November 1996. pp. 177–186.

*Financial Post*. January 15, 1999.

*Fortune*. December 7, 1988. p. 100.

*New York Times Magazine*. November 15, 1998.

## CHAPTER 10

Aaker, David A. 1996. *Building Strong Brands*. New York: The Free Press. p. 138.

Ibid. p. 140.

*Fast Company*. April 1999.

The *Financial Post Magazine*. March 1999.

*Harvard Business Review*. January/February 1999.

*Marketing*. October 16, 1999.

*National Post Business*. September 1999. p. 76.

*New York Times Magazine*. March 21, 1999.

Pine II, B. Joseph. 1999. *The Experience Economy: Work Is Theater and Every Business a Stage*. Boston: Harvard Business School.

## CHAPTER 11

Burstein, Daniel and David Kline. 1995. *Road Warriors: Dreams and Nightmares Along the Information Highway*. New York: Dutton. p. 3.

Covey, Stephen. 1990. *Principle-Centered Leadership*. New York: Fireside. pp. 95–97.

*Delaney Report*. February 15, 1999.

Dent, Harry S. 1998. *The Roaring 2000s: Building The Wealth And Lifestyle You Desire In The Greatest Boom In History*. New York: Simon & Schuster. pp. 203–204.

Drucker, Peter F. 1999. *The Frontiers of Management: Where Tomorrow's Decisions Are Being Shaped Today*. New York: Plume (The Penguin Group).

*Fast Company*. October 1998.

Fombrun, Charles. 1996. *Reputation: Realizing Value From The Corporate Image.* Boston: Harvard Business School Press. p. 9.

Petzinger, Thomas, Jr. 1999. *The New Pioneers: The Men and Women Who Are Transforming the Workplace and Marketplace.* New York: Simon & Schuster. p. 25.

## CHAPTER 12

*American Way.* June 15, 1999. p. 75.

Beckwith, Harry. 1997. *Selling The Invisible: A Field Guide to Modern Marketing.* New York: Warner Books. pp. 212–213.

Drucker, Peter F. 1999. *The Frontiers of Management: Where Tomorrow's Decisions Are Being Shaped Today.* New York: Plume (The Penguin Group).

Duncan, Tom and Sandra Moriarty. 1997. *Driving Brand Value: Using Integrated Marketing to Manage Profitable Stakeholder Relationships.* New York: McGraw-Hill. p. 135.

*Fast Company.* April 2000.

*Forbes.* February 8, 1999.

*Harvard Business Review.* July/August 1989.

   Ibid.

   Ibid.

## CHAPTER 13

Drucker, Peter F. 1999. *Management Challenges for the 21st Century.* New York: Harper Collins. p. 149.

*Fast Company.* April 1999.

*Fast Company.* May 1999.

*Fast Company.* June 1999.

*Financial Post.* April 21, 1999.

*Financial Post Business.* September 1999. p. 71.

*Fortune.* May 24, 1999.

*Harvard Business Review.* January/February 2000.

*Inc.* October 1999.

   Ibid.

*National Post Business.* September 1999. "What Makes Antoine Run." p. 71.

Petzinger, Thomas, Jr. 1999. *The New Pioneers: The Men and Women Who Are Transforming The Workplace And Marketplace.* New York: Simon & Schuster, 1999. p. 75.

## CHAPTER 14

*Business 2.0.* March 1999.

*The Economist.* June 26, 1999.

*Fast Company.* February/March 1999.

*Financial Post.* February 18, 1999.
  Ibid.
  Ibid.
*Financial Post.* May 29, 1999.
*Fortune.* December 7, 1998.
*Harvard Business Review.* January/February 2000.
*Marketing.* July 19, 1999.
Peppers, Don and Martha Rogers. 1997. *Enterprise One To One: Tools for Competing in the Interactive Age.* New York: Currency Doubleday. pp. vii-xxi.
  Ibid. p. 10.

## CHAPTER 15

Burstein, Daniel and David Kline. 1995. *Road Warriors: Dreams and Nightmares Along the Information Highway.* New York: Dutton, 1995. p. 34.
*Business 2.0.* December 1998.
*Business Week.* July 26, 1999. p. 61.
*Fast Company.* September 1999. p. 212.
  Ibid. p. 210.
*Financial Post.* February 15, 1999.
*Financial Post.* June 29, 1999.
*Financial Post.* August 13, 1999.
Riordan, Stacey. *INSIDE 1to1.*

## CHAPTER 16

*Advertising Age.* November 2, 1998.
  Ibid.
*Business Week.* July 26, 1999.
*Business Week.* August 23–30, 1999. p. 26.
  Ibid.
Fombrun, Charles J. 1996. *Reputation: Realizing Value From The Corporate Image.* Boston: Harvard Business School Press. p. 60.

## CHAPTER 17

Aaker, David A. 1991. *Managing Brand Equity.* New York: The Free Press. pp. 1–6.
Beckwith, Harry. 1997. *Selling the Invisible.* New York: Warner Books. pp. 143–149.
*Financial Post.* February 17, 1999.
*Financial Post.* December 10, 1999.
*New York Times Magazine.* March 14, 1999.
*Montreal Gazette.* February 2, 1999.

Ries, Al and Laura Ries. 1998. *The 22 Immutable Laws of Branding: How to Build a Product or Service into a World-Class Brand*. New York: Harper Collins. p. 74.

**CHAPTER 19**

*Business Week*. October 11, 1999.
*Fast Company*. September 1999. p. 94.
Ibid.
Ries, Al. 1996. *Focus: The Future Of Your Company Depends On It*. New York: Harperbusiness.

**CHAPTER 20**

Drucker, Peter F. 1999. *Management Challenges for the 21st Century*. New York: Harper Collins. p. 131.
Duncan, Tom and Sandra Moriarty. 1997. *Driving Brand Value: Using Integrated Marketing to Manage Profitable Stakeholder Relationships*. New York: McGraw-Hill. p. 10.
Ibid. p. 56.

**CHAPTER 21**

Duncan, Tom and Sandra Moriarty. 1997. *Driving Brand Value: Using Integrated Marketing to Manage Profitable Stakeholder Relationships*. New York: McGraw-Hill. p. 85.
Ibid. p. 9.
Ibid. pp. 6–7.
Ibid. pp. 41–42.
Ibid. pp. 151.
*Fast Company*. November 1999. p. 288.
*Harvard Business Review*. July/August 1999.
Petzinger, Thomas, Jr. 1999. *The New Pioneers: The Men And Women Who Are Transforming The Workplace and Marketplace*. New York: Simon & Schuster. p. 33.

**CHAPTER 23**

Ries, Al and Laura Ries. 1998. *The 22 Immutable Laws of Branding: How to Build a Product or Service into a World-Class Brand*. New York: Harperbusiness. p. 78.
Ibid. pp. 8-9.
Ibid. p. 121.
Ibid. p. 162.

**CHAPTER 24**

Branson, Richard. 1998. *Losing My Virginity: The Autobiography*. London: Virgin Publishing.
Ibid. p. 45.
Ibid. pp. 163–164.

**CHAPTER 25**

Dent, Harry S. 1998. *The Roaring 2000s: Building the Wealth and Lifestyle You Desire in the Greatest Boom in History.* New York: Simon & Schuster. p. 200.

Drucker, Peter F. 1999. *The Frontiers of Management: Where Tomorrow's Decisions Are Being Shaped Today.* New York: Plume (The Penguin Group). p. 224.

*Fast Company.* October 1998. p. 64.
   Ibid. p. 149.

*Fast Company.* January 1999.

*Financial Post.* May 13, 1999.

*Montreal Gazette.* November 9, 1998.

*National Post.* November 10, 1998.

*National Post.* January 13, 1999.

Petzinger, Thomas, Jr. 1999. *The New Pioneers: The Men and Women Who Are Transforming the Workplace and Marketplace.* New York: Simon & Schuster. pp. 18–23.
   Ibid. pp. 165–167.
   Ibid. p. 180.

**CHAPTER 26**

*Financial Post.* June 26, 1999.

*Fortune.* December 7, 1998. pp. 81–92.

*Hour.* Sept. 3–9, 1998.

*INSIDE 1to1.* August 20, 1998. Brian Manasco.

Petzinger, Thomas, Jr. 1999. *The New Pioneers: The Men and Women Who Are Transforming the Workplace and Marketplace.* New York: Simon & Schuster. p 93.

**CHAPTER 27**

*Business 2.0.* May 1999.

Drucker, Peter F. 1999. *Management Challenges for the 21st Century.* New York: Harperbusiness. p. 72.
   Ibid. p. 73.
   Ibid. p. 77.
   Ibid. p. 82.

*Financial Post.* February 23, 1999.

*Financial Post.* March 16, 1999.

*Financial Post.* April 16, 1999.

*New York Times.* March 15, 1997.

*New York Times.* February 28, 1999.

*Time.* December 23, 1996.

**CHAPTER 28**

Fombrun, Charles J. 1996. *Reputation: Realizing Value from the Corporate Image.* Boston: Harvard Business School Press. p. 8.

## CHAPTER 29

*Business 2.0.* January 2000.
*Fast Company.* December 1998.
*Fast Company.* May 1999.
*Financial Post.* February 4, 1999.
*National Post.* April 8, 1999.

## CHAPTER 30

Covey, Stephen R. 1990. *The 7 Habits of Highly Effective People.* New York: Fireside.
Covey, Stephen R. 1992. *Principle-Centered Leadership.* New York: Fireside.
Drucker, Peter F. 1999. *Management Challenges for the 21st Century.* New York: Harperbusiness.
*Fast Company.* August/September 1997. pp. 84–94.
  Ibid.
*Fast Company.* May 1999.
*Financial Post.* 1999.

## CHAPTER 31

Dell, Michael. 1999. *Direct from Dell.* New York: Harperbusiness.
*Fast Company.* May 1999.
*Financial Post.* March 24, 1999.
  Ibid.
Petzinger, Thomas, Jr. 1999. *The New Pioneers: The Men nd Women Who Are Transforming the Workplace and Marketplace.* New York: Simon & Schuster. p. 152.

# INDEX